19 MAY 2012

11 MAR 2013

8 JAN 2020

Essex Works.

For a better quality of life

LTN

Please return this book on or before the date shown above. To renew go to www.essex.gov.uk/libraries, ring 0845 603 7628 or go to any Essex library.

Essex County Council

I'm Not Really Here

I'm Not Really Here

Paul Lake

Century · London

Published by Century 2011

10 9

Copyright © Paul and Joanne Lake

Paul and Joanne Lake have asserted their right under the Copyright,
Designs and Patents Act 1988 to be identified as the authors of this work

First published in Great Britain in 2011 by
Century
Random House, 20 Vauxhall Bridge Road,
London SW1V 2SA

www.randomhouse.co.uk

Addresses for companies within The Random House Group Limited can be found at:
www.randomhouse.co.uk

The Random House Group Limited Reg. No. 954009

A CIP catalogue record for this book
is available from the British Library

ISBN 9781846058240

The Random House Group Limited supports The Forest Stewardship Council
(FSC®), the leading international forest certification organisation. Our books
carrying the FSC label are printed on FSC® certified paper. FSC is the only forest
certification scheme endorsed by the leading environmental organisations,
including Greenpeace. Our paper procurement policy can be found at:
www.randomhouse.co.uk/environment

Printed and bound in Great Britain by
Clays Ltd, St Ives Plc

This book is dedicated to my father, Ted Lake and to my mentors, Ken Barnes, Tony Book, John Mercer and Glyn Pardoe

Acknowledgements

I'm grateful to so many people for their help in getting *I'm Not Really Here* off the ground. It was my good friend, the photographer Kevin Cummins, who started the ball rolling by introducing me to his literary agent before a City v Arsenal game. Kevin Conroy Scott, from the Tibor Jones agency, lent me his ear, read some draft chapters and gave me the impetus and confidence to tell my story. He also helped me to find a top-drawer publisher in Century, whose Director of Publishing, Ben Dunn, has been nothing short of fantastic, as have his colleagues Charlotte Bush and Briony Nelder.

I've received equally invaluable support from other quarters. Alison Vaughan, a great friend and former City workmate, wielded her red pen and critiqued the chapters, author and historian Gary James cast his statistical and analytical eye over the detail, and Fred Eyre – writer and pundit extraordinaire – kindly offered his wise words and expert advice. Other pals that have helped with read-throughs, photographs and memory jogs include Jason Beckford, Tony Wood, Billy Duffy, Ian Brightwell, Tudor Thomas, John Mercer, Kevin Cowap, Geoff Durbin, David Clayton, Chris Bailey, Ian Cheeseman, John Clarkson, Dominic Warwood, Neil Davies, Adam Roland, Eric Mullender, Sharon Latham, Roland Cooke, Arthur Reid and Neil Smith. Numerous staff at Manchester City Football Club have lent their backing to this book, but I'd like to offer my sincere gratitude to Garry Cook, Sarah Lynch and Vicky Kloss.

I would, of course, like to extend my heartfelt thanks to the wonderful Lake family – Mum, Susan, David, Michael and Tracey, and all my nieces and nephews – who have supported me through thick and thin. I must also give a mention to my in-laws – the Parker/Radcliffe/Atherton clan – particularly Eric The Blue and Pauline. And not forgetting my three beautiful children – Zac, Edward and Hannah – who make me feel like the proudest dad in the world, all day, every day.

But my highest praise is reserved for Jo: my co-writer, my best friend, my wife. She's the Sybil to my Basil, the Mildred to my George, the Marge to my Homer, and I simply couldn't have done this without her.

Manchester, August 2011

Contents

There are lessons to learn
When you've waited your turn
And things didn't turn out
Quite the way that you dreamt about

Badly Drawn Boy, 'Life Turned Upside Down'

We are not, we're not really here
We are not, we're not really here
Just like the fan of the invisible man
We're not really here

Traditional Manchester City chant

Prologue

25 August 1990: The Crest Hotel, Buckinghamshire
Game On

It's the opening day of the new season, and we're just hours away from our match against Spurs. The manager, Howard Kendall, is announcing the team line-up at lunchtime and the players and staff are having a stroll around the hotel grounds. There's none of the usual laughs and larks this morning, though, as the lads nervously await the final selection. We're all desperate to see our names up on that team sheet, and having to hang around for this 11th-hour reveal is nothing short of agonising.

Go on, Gaffer, pick me, I say to myself as I walk alongside my shell-suited colleagues. *You saw what I could do in pre-season. Let me pull on that blue shirt today. Don't leave me on the bench.*

I'm chatting with my team-mates David White and Ian Brightwell when the manager, who's been pacing ahead with the physio, solemnly beckons me over. My heart sinks. Here we go. Here's where I get dropped. And here comes Howard to let me down gently. Three of us (Colin Hendry, Steve Redmond and I) are vying for two places, and no doubt it's yours truly who's drawn the short straw. Col and Reddo are highly experienced centre-halves and I'm a play-anywhere utility man – if someone's going to be disappointed, it's probably going to be me.

'We need to talk,' he says, gesturing for me to take a seat at a nearby bench. I sit down and fear the worst.

'The thing is, Lakey, I've been having a good chat with the coaches, and . . .'

. . . *and I'm not playing you today*, says a little voice in my head.

'. . . and I want to make you captain.'

My jaw drops. I can't believe what I'm hearing.

'Bit of a surprise, eh?'

'Just a bit, Gaffer . . .'

'You've really impressed me in pre-season, son. You've grown up, you've matured, and I reckon the time's right for you to step up a gear.'

'Yeah, but—'

'You'll be fine, don't worry,' says Howard, sensing my shock. 'I wouldn't have asked you if I didn't think you could hack it. I know it's in you, I just want to bring it out.'

Though I barely hear him he goes on to explain that the

captaincy might be the springboard for my career as a skipper, not just for my club, but for my country too. Christ. And there was me thinking I was going to be keeping the subs' bench warm.

'I know we've got other leaders in the camp already, but don't let that bother you,' he adds. 'They'll see exactly why I've plumped for you, and they'll back you. And if you need to give somebody a bollocking – yeah, even Peter Reid – just do it. You'll get more respect from the lads if you boss them around a bit, believe me.'

'I won't let you down,' I say.

'I'm sure you won't,' replies Howard, patting me on the back. 'This could be the making of you, Lakey.'

And with that he ambles off to rejoin the coaching staff, leaving me sitting on the park bench, shaking my head in disbelief.

After a post-lunch phone call to my parents ('you can't get a better accolade than that, Paul,' says my choked-up dad) I retreat to my hotel room to steal half an hour's solitude. I need some time to come to terms with this. The fact that I've edged my good mate Reddo out of the team is shocking enough, but to have leapfrogged seasoned professionals like Reidy and Adrian Heath to the captaincy is unbelievable. But I'm determined to do myself justice and to do everyone proud. My parents, my team-mates, the boss, the fans; I'm desperate not to disappoint the most important people in my life.

The captain's armband is pride of place when I run out onto

the White Hart Lane pitch later that afternoon. Outwardly I'm focusing on my new duties and responsibilities, yet inside I'm doing cartwheels as the City faithful greet me with a raucous chorus of 'there's only one Paul Lake . . .'

They're probably as surprised as me that I'm leading out the team today, but as fellow Blues I'm sure they understand how much this honour means to a native Mancunian. Like them, I've also watched from the stands as local-born City captains like Mike Doyle and Paul Power have marshalled the troops. Now it's *my* turn to skipper the team that I've adored since childhood, and it feels incredible.

Buzzing with excitement, I trot to the centre circle, nodding as I pass Gary Lineker and Paul Gascoigne, both fresh from their Italia '90 exploits, before shaking hands with my Spurs counterpart, Gary Mabbutt. And, as the referee blows his whistle on that sunny August day, I enter a new phase in my life.

This is it. Let the good times roll.

12th January 1996: The Beaumont Hospital, Bolton
Game Over

A week has passed since I reluctantly announced my retirement from football. I'm laid up in a private hospital, recovering from major surgery to straighten a right leg that has started to warp badly after the trauma of 15 operations.

Despite feeling dreadful – my knee's throbbing, my head's

thumping – I attempt to manoeuvre myself out of bed to fetch a newspaper from across the room. Staggering towards the table, I lose my footing and accidentally rip the plastic cannula out of my leg. Shit. *Shit.* A thick jet of blood suddenly torpedoes from my knee, splattering the magnolia walls like a blast from a paintball gun. A fumbling attempt to re-insert the tube fails dismally; I'm panicking, I'm shaking and the blood spurts relentlessly.

I drag myself over to the emergency cord and give it a weak tug. Within seconds a nurse sprints into the room. The poor woman flinches; she's probably never seen so much blood.

'Oh my God . . . uh, okay . . . just stay put, Mr Lake; we'll get this sorted,' she stammers. As she frantically tries to stem the flow, I just stand there helpless, watching my lifeblood drain away and form a crimson puddle on the carpet.

It's at this precise moment that the stark reality of my predicament hits home, the truth smashing into me like a set of studs to the solar plexus. *Just look at the state of you,* sneers a voice in my head. *You're a joke. You're a mess. You're f***ed.*

I start to sob uncontrollably, the hot tears streaming down my face and dripping onto my green hospital gown. I've done lots of crying lately, but this is uncharted territory. I'm howling like a wild animal in distress, as the deep-rooted pain that I've tried to suppress for years finally rises to the surface.

To her credit, the nurse goes about her business, eventually patching up the wound and reconnecting the tubes. Soon there's a knock at the door and the hospital physio, Philippa – ignorant of the drama within – breezes in to tell me that a pair of former City team-mates, Niall Quinn and Tony Coton, have come to visit. She stops in her tracks at the sight of a blood-soaked, tear-stained 27-year-old and glances over to the tall shadows hovering beyond the door.

'Don't worry, Paul, I'll have a word with them,' she whispers. 'They can come back another day, can't they?'

I nod and try to thank her, but the huge lump in my throat prevents any speech; I can't even lift my head up to look her straight in the eye. But my loyal physio, who's been my rock over the past few months, is well aware of the dark place that I'm inhabiting. She gives my hand a squeeze, tells me that everything will be all right and helps me back to bed. After they've cleaned me up, Philippa and the nurse edge out of the room, closing the door gently behind them.

I need to be alone. I don't want anyone else – not my team-mates, my best friends or even my beloved family – to witness the depths of my pain and self-pity. After five miserable years of dashed hopes and false dawns, I need this privacy to finally get to grips with the fact that my career as a professional footballer is over, and that the sport I was put on this earth to play is no longer part of my life.

I lie there and stare out of the window towards the bleak Pennine moors. My right knee throbs relentlessly, a reminder of the succession of failed operations that saw me go from Manchester City captain and England hopeful to a useless bastard with a leg that's so wrecked that I'd struggle to jog round the park, never mind kick a ball around for 90 minutes.

I start to feel dazed and light-headed – losing a pint of blood is probably taking its toll – and as I sense myself drifting away, scenes of a former career begin to flicker before me like an old Pathé newsreel. A grainy montage of goals and passes, of headers and tackles, of team-mates and managers, of stadiums and crowds, all accompanied by muffled commentators' voices.

'He's a player beyond his years, is Paul Lake . . .'

'Lake stayed on his feet, and that was the key . . .'

'And there goes Lake, City's jewel in the crown . . .'

Accompanying this kaleidoscope of nostalgia is the stomach-churning knowledge that I'll never experience those footballing heights again.

I'm finished. It's over.

1

Sheila Take a Bow

October 1968. Don Revie's Leeds United were topping Division One, Bob Beamon was leaping to new heights at the Mexico Olympics, and Sheila Lake's baby bump was as big as a space-hopper.

Barely a fortnight before the birth of their fourth child, my parents were summoned to St Mary's Hospital to be given the bombshell that Mum was expecting twins. There was none of that ultrasound scan stuff in those days; apparently some doctor had just happened to hear not one, but two faint heartbeats through his stethoscope. Dad's immediate reaction was to smack his palm against his forehead, whine 'just my bleedin' luck', and storm out of the maternity ward, leaving my poor mum alone with a Lucozade and a *Woman's Realm*.

He spent the next couple of hours careering around the back streets of Manchester in his beige Austin Maxi, chain-smoking roll-ups and trying to digest this shock news. You could understand him freaking out, I suppose; there were already three kids under the age of six in the Lake household and the unexpected arrival of double trouble was going to stretch his wages even further.

Dad soon came around to the idea, however, and became the Proudest Father in Manchester™ when Mum gave birth by caesarean section on Monday 28 October 1968. I arrived first, a writhing tangle of knees and elbows, with my twin, Tracey, making a far daintier appearance five minutes later. After a week in St Mary's, we were driven home in our carrycots to be introduced to our three older siblings, and for the next couple of years our house was brimful with the usual baby bumph of bottles, bibs and terry-towelling nappies.

The family home was a red-brick semi on Bowker Avenue in Haughton Green, a suburb on the east side of Manchester, about six miles from the city centre. It was a predominantly working-class area with plenty of shops, parks and street corners to keep the average youngster happy; happy enough for the Lake kids to regularly sing 'we all live in a house in Haughton Green' at the top of our voices to the tune of 'Yellow Submarine'.

My mum and dad both hailed from Ardwick, an inner-city district that was home to many second- and third-generation Irish families. Sheila McGinty and Ted Lake met as teenagers and sealed their courtship with a low-key wedding at St Aloysius' Roman Catholic church in 1955, not long after Dad had completed his national service. The newlyweds bought a small terraced house in Abbey Hey, just a mile or so down the road from Ardwick, and in 1962 their first child, Susan, was born. David arrived two years later, by which time my parents had saved enough money to make the upwardly mobile move to 'the Green' where the houses had driveways, front porches and back gardens. Child number three, Michael, appeared on the scene in 1966, followed finally by me and Tracey.

Producing enough offspring for a five-a-side team might have fazed some women, but Mum took it all in her stride. She was a dedicated and devoted mother who lived and breathed the family, and could never do enough for her children. Mum had a remarkable life force, always rising ridiculously early in the morning to get her brood ready for school and frequently burning the midnight oil in order to Flash the lino or conquer the Mount Kilimanjaro of ironing that a quintet of kids produced.

My father was a quiet and unpretentious man. He grafted for Britain – he was an asphalt technician – and had the sandpaper hands and the weather-beaten complexion to show for it. A proper homebody, he was never happier than when he was relaxing in the lounge watching *Rising Damp* with a fag in one hand and one of Mum's brews in the other. Whilst not a noted sportsman (he'd played football during his army days, but that was the extent of it) he was a keen armchair fan who could often be found glued to the boxing from Madison Square Garden or the darts from Frimley Green.

Dad was a very practical and proactive kind of bloke, one of those dependable handymen who could fix anything from a snapped fan belt to a faulty washing machine. He was an electrician, carpenter, builder and plumber all rolled into one; the archetypal jack-of-all-trades. I remember him building a shed from scratch one weekend – sawing, then hammering, then creosoting – and can still picture him standing in the garden when he'd finished, admiring his handiwork as he wiped the sweat from his brow.

Not every chore gave him so much pleasure, though. I recall him once having to remove a used condom that a teenage Romeo had ceremonially draped on our front hedge.

'Sheila, there's a bloomin' sheath on the bush,' he'd hissed when Tracey and I had innocently pointed it out before school one morning. Dad promptly stomped into the garden armed with a bamboo cane in one hand and a bucket in the other to perform an elaborate hook-a-duck routine, while a bemused Tracey and I watched from the front room.

'What's a sheath, Dad?' I asked him as he marched past us, fuming.

'Ask your mother,' came the reply.

My twin Tracey and I were joined at the hip when we were kids. Our high spot of the week was the Saturday-morning trip to a local general-store-cum-newsagents, otherwise known as the Happy Shop. Not because it was sweetie heaven (which it was) but because the owner was a right miserable sod. Mr Happy was a dead ringer for the comedian Alan Carr but was certainly no fan of laughter. His hatred for children was palpable, and he would glower at us as we dithered in front of his sweet counter making the life-or-death choice between a pink shrimp or a flying saucer. Clutching our white paper bags – and a bar of Old Jamaica for Dad – Tracey and I would then scamper back to catch the last half of *Tiswas*.

As I grew older, I used to adore watching the early evening wrestling on *World of Sport*. I'd hurry home from my Saturday afternoon football game, bursting into the lounge just as Kent Walton opened the show with his customary 'greetings, grapple fans'. Broadcast live to the nation from some godforsaken provincial leisure centre, it featured a cast of middle-aged blokes with huge pot bellies prancing around in clammy body stockings. Kendo Nagasaki, Catweazle and Jim Breaks were my heroes – I perfected the latter's famous submission technique after months spent pummelling Dad on the Axminster – but I also loved the tag match spectacles that pitched heavyweights like Big Daddy and Dynamite Kid against Giant Haystacks and Pat Roach. The wrestling itself was pure pantomime, of course. The fact that the bouts were so obviously rehearsed, and were no more a credible and competitive sporting event than *It's a Knockout*, never detracted from my enjoyment.

I'm sure I wasn't the only working-class 1970s kid whose life seemed to revolve around watching telly and eating sweets. It wasn't long, though, before something else came along to totally rule my world.

My football fuse was lit at about 7 a.m. on Christmas Day 1974. The whole of Bowker Avenue probably heard my yelps of delight as I tore through the layers of wrapping paper to reveal – *yessssss!* – a beautiful, snow-white Mitre match ball. You could keep your Stretch Armstrongs and your Evel Knievel Stunt Bikes, because this precious ball, with its porcelain-smooth skin and brand-new leathery smell, was the best present I could have ever hoped for. It didn't leave my side all day; I sat it on my knee during the morning Mass and the afternoon turkey-fest, and then spent an hour whacking it against the garage door while the family watched *Billy Smart's Christmas Special*. I even took it to bed with me that night, hugging it tightly under the eiderdown so that my brothers couldn't get their sweaty mitts on it.

From that Christmas onwards, every spare minute was spent playing football in the park, usually with Mike and a dozen of his friends. At weekends and school holidays all the lads would meet up after breakfast at Simon Whelan's house, heading over to Haughton Green Park armed with scuffed footballs, jumpers for goalposts and a few old Ben Shaw's lemonade bottles filled with tap water. There we'd re-enact our own City versus United games, the goalies pretending to be Joe Corrigan and Alex Stepney and the outfield players masquerading as Colin Bell and Stuart Pearson. We'd have international matches too; staging England versus Brazil showdowns and rattling off our own John Motson-esque commentaries as we darted round the pitch ('and it's Zico to Falcao, Falcao to Socrates, Socrates checks inside and drives an unstoppable shot into the top corner . . . goooooaaaal!'). By midday we'd be ravenous, and would break off for a whistle-stop lunch at our respective houses – Mum rustling up some ham butties, a bag of salt 'n' vinegar Chipsticks and a mug of tea – before returning to the park for the second half.

Mike and I would invariably be the last ones standing. As dusk set in we'd still be practising aiming the ball at the crossbar, alternating between our left and right feet, since Dad had always told us that only the best footballers could kick with both. Playing in the twilight also helped to increase our concentration levels, forcing us to focus more on the ball's flight, its touch, its bounce, even its noise (we could decipher whether a ball had been clipped, parried, driven or headed just by listening to the different sounds it made). Honing these night-vision skills definitely improved our reading of the game, and made our daytime football seem floodlit in comparison.

We often found ourselves in hot water for staying out too late, particularly if we had school the next day, and Tracey was regularly dispatched by Mum to drag us home.

'Michael, Paul, get back *now* – Mum's going spare,' she'd say, scowling at us because she'd had to miss the last five minutes of *Fame* to come and haul us back. More often than not Mike and I would arrive home with patties of mustard-coloured dog dirt stuck to the soles of our boots, and Dad would spend the next half-hour gouging out the muck with the aid of a kitchen knife and a squirt of Stardrops.

I was never happier than when I was on a football pitch. Whereas other kids got their kicks by solving an equation in maths class, or doing the Rubik's Cube in 20 flicks of the wrist, the only place I could truly express and value myself was on a football pitch. It gradually began to dawn on me that I might have a talent for the game, too. I was aware that I had decent speed, skills and stamina – I could run for hours without breaking sweat – and the pleasure that I felt as I passed, dribbled, tackled and scored was intense.

Mike and his mates were two years my senior yet I'd often find myself streaking past them, their curses hanging in the air as I nutmegged them and sprinted towards goal. They'd often try to take revenge with a swift whack to the shins, but I had this knack of anticipating and avoiding their tackles and would further infuriate them by skipping over them or swerving past their outstretched legs.

Having a ball at my feet seemed like the most natural thing on earth. My ability to control it, read it and pass it was wholly instinctive, and my innate sense of awareness – of my environment, of the ball, of my team-mates – stemmed from pure intuition. I didn't quite know how, or why, I found football so easy; I just did, and that was that.

'You've got a gift, son,' Dad would often tell me.

At the age of eight I was picked for the Denton Youth FC under-12 side, playing alongside lads a couple of years older than me, including my brother Mike. Our manager was a straight-talking disciplinarian by the name of Ernie Jones, and I was thrilled when he doled out my first proper football kit, an eye-catching strip comprising black shorts and a black and yellow striped shirt with a felt number 8 on the back.

That, together with my new shin pads and tape (a surprise present from Mum and Dad) made me feel like a bona fide footballer, as did the prospect of playing on a massive pitch with – get this – real nets, mown grass and proper white lines. That sense of belonging, that feeling of being a small cog in a big wheel, was incomparable to anything I'd ever felt before.

I played in the position of an old-fashioned inside-forward and found myself thriving on the bigger stage, enjoying the opportunity to show people what I could do, putting in decent performances week-in-week-out and scoring goals for fun. I remember once bagging a wonder strike, controlling the ball in mid-air and volleying it over the keeper's head.

'I've never seen anything like it from someone so young, and on a pitch so heavy,' a spectator said to Dad after the game. 'He's so exciting to watch, your lad. Always looks like he's going to score . . .'

In the summer of 1978, Denton Youth FC embarked on a football tour to Garden City in Long Island, New York State. As we had never been abroad before, it was an exciting prospect for the Lake brothers. On the day of our departure the team had its picture taken for the local newspaper, posing on the steps of the Town Hall with our long hair, pointy collars and draughty bell-bottoms, looking like the Denton branch of the Brotherhood of Man fan club.

Each squad member was placed with a host family in the States, and Mike and I were both dispatched to the Middletons, a lovely all-American, baseball-cap-wearing family whose 13-year-old son, Chris, played for the local side, the Garden City Colts. The neighbourhood consisted of wide tree-lined avenues, flanked by pastel-coloured, timber-clad houses with verandas at the front and swimming pools at the back. Pleasant though it was, the place reminded me of the town in those spooky Hallowe'en films.

'Check that flippin' window's locked, Mike . . .' I'd whisper at bedtime, fearful of a machete-wielding Michael Myers paying us an early-hours visit.

The majority of our tour games were played against older and bigger sides comprising teenage beefcakes with Burt Reynolds chests and Lee Marvin voices. Whilst it was often a case of men against boys, us Brits generally held our own and managed to beat the Garden City Colts on the three occasions we played them. I bagged two hat-tricks during the tour, including one against a side called Huntington. We'd been trailing 3–1 at half-time, and I came on, played out of my skin and helped Denton Youth to an unlikely 4–3 victory.

'Damn, who *is* that kid?' I recall hearing one fella drawl from the sidelines.

'He's staying with me,' replied a proud Mr Middleton.

On our last night we were invited to watch New York Cosmos play Seattle Sounders at the Giants Stadium with Franz Beckenbauer, Carlos Alberto and ex-City star Dennis Tueart gracing a starry Cosmos line-up. As if those names weren't illustrious enough, my team-mates and I found ourselves being shepherded onto the pitch prior to the game to meet Pelé, who'd ended his career with Cosmos the previous year. As I was introduced to him I couldn't stop grinning, imagining what Mum and Dad would say when I told them that I'd shaken hands with the greatest footballer of all time.

A week later we returned to earth with a bump, swapping the splendour of the Giants Stadium for Stockport Road playing fields, the venue for the annual Catholic Schools' Cup. My school team, St Mary's RC Primary in Denton, was fortunate enough to be managed by the most inspirational teacher I've ever met. John Mercer ran the side with great passion and gusto, encouraging us to play to our best ability without ever compromising our enjoyment.

'Look lads, we've got probably the most balanced team in Tameside,' he told us before our match against local rivals St Ann's. 'Let the ball do the work, don't worry about making a mistake, and always remember that there's plenty of goals in our side.'

He wasn't wrong. We scored 14 that day, and I notched up so many that I was made to go in nets for the last ten minutes to spare our opponents any further embarrassment. Getting my name on the score sheet became a bit of a habit for me, and I went on to slot in over 100 goals for St Mary's that season.

The high point of my fledgling career was winning the 1980 Smiths Crisps Six-a-Side Championship. It was a nationwide under-11s tournament with an initial entry of over 5,000 schools, and the final was to be staged at Wembley, no less, prior to an England v Scotland international. Almost as thrilling as a trip to London was the fact that, in recognition of our achievement, each member of the St Mary's team received a brand-new football kit as well as a big box of Smith's Football Crazy crisps. A 1970s lunchbox staple, Football Crazy were fluorescent yellow potato puffballs with a powerful smoky bacon flavour that repeated on you for ages. Not that it bothered me, though. I used to get great satisfaction from belching out Football Crazy-flavoured burps a full two days after I'd eaten the things.

On the eve of our Wembley showdown, the St Mary's team – together with Mr Mercer and the head teacher, Mr Chapman – caught the train down to the capital. As we all loitered on the platform at Euston station, laden with enormous kitbags, Mr Mercer suddenly spotted a familiar figure climbing out of a carriage.

'Lads, lads, look over there,' he hissed, pointing at a stocky, balding fella in his 60s wearing a tweed suit. 'It's Bob Paisley.'

We stared in awe at the Liverpool boss, who just a month earlier had steered the Reds to yet another League Championship. A totally unfazed Mr Mercer sidled up to him and, after exchanging a few words, beckoned us over. We bounded across like puppies and lined up to shake hands with Paisley, a very kindly man who happily chatted to us and wished us good luck. Even Mr Mercer, who was a diehard Manchester United fan, realised that we were in the presence of greatness.

'You'll never meet a better manager than Mr Paisley, lads,' he said as we walked out of the station. 'Best in the business, that fella.'

At midday on Saturday 10 June, togged up in our new stripy black and blue kits, we trotted onto the hallowed Wembley turf. Prior to kick-off we were introduced to the guest of honour, Chelsea and Arsenal star John Hollins, who told us to expect a crowd of 70,000 that day.

'Enjoy every moment, boys,' he said with a friendly smile, 'cause you may never get the chance to play at Wembley again.'

The grand final had pitched us against the much-fancied St Cuthbert's School from Sunderland, who were such hot favourites that Tyne Tees TV had sent a film crew all the way down to London to cover the game. Granada TV obviously couldn't be arsed. The Mancs weren't fazed by the Mackems, however, and put in a masterful performance to beat them 2–1 and seize the honours. It just happened to be me who scored the winner, too, a powerful left-foot strike that I smashed into the far corner. It wasn't long before the final whistle went and, after a team hug with a proud Mr Mercer, seven sweaty little lads – me, John Clarkson, Wayne Jefferies, Dave Ringland, Paul Kirkham, Peter Murphy and Chris O'Brien – climbed the famous steps to the royal box to be presented with the trophy.

Flippin' 'eck, I remember thinking. I've scored the winner at Wembley. What'll Dad think of that?

*

By the time I'd started secondary school, I found myself playing up to four competitive matches each weekend. Dad would come and watch at least one, always standing a couple of yards behind the touchline wearing his beige Harrington jacket, sporting his Eric Morecambe glasses and puffing on an Embassy No. 6. He usually stood alone, away from the main group of parents, preferring to keep his thoughts and opinions to himself.

Dad would often raise his eyebrows at a few of the other fathers who, thinking they were Denton's answer to Brian Clough, would give stern warnings to their offspring before a game.

'Pick yer man up, close him down, switch the play . . .' one particular father would bellow as he crouched down and gripped his son by the shoulders. During the game this bloke would scamper up and down the touchline, swearing and gesticulating, and berating his kid if he put a foot wrong. Dad loathed this – 'empty vessels make the most noise' was his pet proverb – and his pre-match pep-talk comprised a simple 'do your best, son,' followed by an affectionate ruffle of my hair. Not being put under pressure undoubtedly helped my performances, allowing me to relax and play my own game, safe in the knowledge that, win or lose, there wouldn't be any cold shoulders or Spanish inquisitions.

Sometimes Mum would join Dad on the sidelines. One such occasion produced my most embarrassing football moment of all-time. I was about 12 years old, playing for the school team, when an opposing defender unintentionally smashed the ball straight into my face. It stung like hell, and I squatted on my haunches for a few moments in order to compose myself. As I came to, I glanced up to see my mum galloping towards me clutching her handbag, her sheepskin moonboots dodging the divots. Barging past the players and the referee, she then proceeded to smother my nose with a large white handkerchief before loudly instructing me to 'have a good blow, son . . .'

Sniggers abounded as I, cringing with embarrassment, prayed for the turf to open up and swallow me.

'What d'you go and do that for?' I whined after the match, still smarting with shame.

'You were hurt, and I'm your mum,' was her succinct reply.

In addition to my regular weekend games, I also made sporadic appearances for Denton Boys under-13s, a side that comprised the most promising young players in the area and staged three or four fixtures per season. It was towards the end of one of these particular matches that my dad, watching from pitch-side, felt a tap on his shoulder.

'Can I have a word, Mr Lake?'

Dad turned round to see a burly, ruddy-faced Alf Roberts lookalike wearing a black trench coat and clutching a notebook.

'The name's Ted Davies. I do a bit of scouting work for Manchester City. I've been hearing some good things about your boy, so I thought I'd better come and take a look for myself.'

The scout told Dad that he'd been watching me for the last hour and, from what he'd seen, was keen for me to come down and train with one of City's junior teams. He scrawled his telephone number on a piece of paper, pressed it into Dad's palm and told him to give him a call the next day should I be interested.

When I emerged from the changing rooms Dad was standing by the car, his arm raised aloft to catch my attention. I jogged over, threw my kitbag into the boot, clambered into the passenger seat and waited for Dad to kick-start the ignition. It usually took at least three wheezy attempts for the engine to splutter into action.

'All right, Dad. What d'you reckon of the game, then?' (I always looked forward to our little post-mortems.)

'Good match. You played well. You just need to use your left foot more.'

Then he turned to face me, and spoke the words that would change my life for ever.

'Manchester City are interested in you, son.'

I paused, not entirely sure that I'd heard him correctly.

'What was that, Dad?'

'Manchester City. They've been watching you. One of their scouts was here this afternoon. He collared me after the game.'

'*The* Manchester City?'

'Yes, you daft ha'porth, *the* Manchester City. This fella, wants to know whether you want to go down and train with one of their kids' teams, Blue something . . .'

'Blue Star . . .'

'That's the one. I said I'd ask you, so . . .'

'Tell him yes, Dad. Tell him *yes*,' I said, my heart thumping with excitement.

When we got home, Dad carefully pinned the telephone number to our cork notice board, in readiness to dial the next morning. I couldn't take my eyes off it, memorising every digit just in case a freak gust of wind blew it out of the kitchen window.

*

Within a week I'd joined the ranks of Cheadle-based Blue Star, one of the many Manchester City feeder teams operating in the area. I turned up for my first evening training session with mixed feelings of excitement and apprehension. While buoyed by the thumbs-up from City's scouting team, and delighted to have been given such an opportunity, I was acutely aware that I'd now have to move up a gear, perhaps way above my comfort zone. I'd now be vying for attention with some of the most talented players in the region, and I knew that I'd have to play consistently to the best of my ability if I was going to convince people of my potential. I was so desperate to impress it hurt. Ray Hinett, the Blue Star manager, made me feel at ease and took time to introduce me to my new team-mates.

'Lads, this is Lakey. It's his first night tonight, so let's make him feel at home?'

As I shook their hands in the changing room and said a timid hello, little did I know how deep these friendships would become.

One player that I couldn't help but notice that night was a boy called Steve Redmond. A loud and lively Scouser, he was a fantastic player with great presence and attitude. He oozed confidence and cockiness, but commanded everyone's respect because he had the footballing talent to justify the swagger.

Completely opposite to Reddo was a shy and thoughtful lad from Sale by the name of Andy Hinchcliffe. He and I were the babes of the side – we were a year younger than the rest – but like me, Andy punched above his weight. Even at that relatively tender age he had great natural ability, possessing a sweet left foot that could have rewired the back of a television.

Dad would usually ferry me to Blue Star's Sunday morning matches in his tan Hillman van, a vehicle so corroded with rust that, if you moved the car mats, you could see white lines and cats' eyes whizzing beneath you. Judging by the other parents' motors, it was clear that many of my team-mates hailed from the wealthier side of the tracks. Indeed, on the occasions when Dad was either working or watching my brothers play, it would be my team-mate Gary Yates and his dad who'd collect me, Mr Yates rolling up in his gleaming bronze Ford Cortina with its newfangled electric windows and snazzy Motorola stereo.

It didn't take me long to realise that my football boots weren't quite as upmarket as my contemporaries', either. I'd always thought that my black and white Gola World Cups (paid for in instalments from Mum's mail order catalogue) were nifty enough, but when I joined the Blue Star squad it became clear that Adidas and Puma footwear were all the rage. I happened to mention this to my friend John Clarkson's dad, who observed that it wasn't the bloody boots that bloody mattered but the bloody player wearing them. From then on, Mr C's wise words would always be in the back of my mind each time I polished my Golas.

Confusingly, though, the name of this satellite team would often get changed for no apparent reason, with Blue Star evolving into Midas, and Midas becoming Pegasus (someone at City obviously had the *I-Spy* Book of Greek Mythology). Joining the Midas set-up was Ian Brightwell, a talented young player with an impressive Olympic pedigree. Both his parents had been medallists at the 1964 Tokyo Games, his mother, Ann Packer, winning gold in the 800 metres and his father, Robbie, bagging silver in the 400 metres relay. Ian had clearly inherited their sporting prowess and was a supreme athlete who could play effortlessly in any right-hand-side position. A Rottweiler on the pitch, Ian (or Bob, as everyone called him) was pretty mild-mannered off it, and we soon became firm friends. I got to know the Brightwell family very well, particularly Ian's dad Robbie who would play a large part in my career further down the line.

Bob, Reddo, Andy and I were the backbone of the Midas-cum-Pegasus team, buttressed by a conveyor belt of young hopefuls. Why some lads managed to make the grade and others didn't was something that never failed to intrigue me. Whilst I came across plenty of players who clearly hadn't either the ability or commitment for a football career (and had ended up pursuing the route signposted Beers, Birds, Fags and Fry-ups), there was a significant minority of teenage cast-offs who were desperately unlucky not to pass muster. Fellow team-mates such as Anthony Gore, Matt McNair and Neil Smith were seriously talented, and I remember being mystified when they were released by the club.

What bothered me was not just the fact that these players were let go by City, but that they seemed to drift out of professional football altogether. I presumed that Anthony, Neil and Matt would go on to ply their trade at lower league teams, and for many years afterwards I habitually pored over the *Manchester Evening News' Pink Final*, hoping to read that they'd made it elsewhere. But that never appeared to be the case, and they seemed to completely drop off the football radar.

I bumped into Neil fairly recently, and over a beer he explained his feelings of devastation after being rejected by City, and how he'd never really recovered from it. In his eyes he'd reached the pinnacle with Blue Star, and any other team was always going to be a pale imitation. Thoroughly disillusioned, he abandoned any hopes and ambitions of becoming a professional footballer and became one of the many starry-eyed youngsters to fall by the wayside. Sad, really.

With such fierce competition for places, I felt unbelievably fortunate to be taken on by City as an associated schoolboy in July 1983. Youth team coach Tony Book was with me as I signed the official forms in the head teacher's office at St Thomas More High School, with a journalist and a snapper from the *Denton Reporter* in attendance.

In those days, you sometimes heard rumours of certain clubs plying families with an array of gifts and household appliances in order to secure their son's signature. That certainly wasn't the case with City, though. I think the most Mum and Dad received was a couple of match tickets and half a Double Diamond in the bar afterwards. But, while Mum could have done with a brand-new Hotpoint washing machine, and Dad wouldn't have said no to the latest Black and Decker Workmate, both of them were nonetheless delighted at how things were panning out for their youngest son. But, being the sensible and level-headed parents that they were, they made great efforts to keep my feet on the ground. No favouritism, no privileges and no preferential treatment. In fact, the first thing I was asked to do when I returned home that historic day was to put the bins out.

However, pledging my immediate future to City saw me almost immediately take my foot off the gas when it came to my schoolwork. Unlike the rest of my classmates, I felt I didn't have to rely on a great set of academic results to determine my career path, and my studies were effectively relegated from Division One to the Conference. I still had to attend compulsory sessions with a careers adviser who, along with many of my teachers, thought I was deluded to assume that my future employment lay in football and was daft not to have another profession to fall back on.

'You can't put all your eggs in one basket, Paul. You'll need a Plan B if City let you go, you know,' she said, wagging her finger reprovingly. 'I see from these notes that you're good at English and History. Ever thought about becoming a librarian?'

I still came out of secondary school with eight moderately graded 'O' levels, but would have no doubt performed better had I focused more on Henry VIII's six wives than lunchtime five-a-sides. I was, of course, totally naïve to assume that my academic life would come to a complete halt at the age of 16. As far as I was concerned I was going to be a footballer, full stop, end of story. I wouldn't entertain any thoughts of alternative jobs and, thinking that I'd never have to sit another exam in my life, gleefully binned all my school books.

In common with millions of schoolkids around the UK, *Top of the Pops* was my main TV highlight of the week. Every Thursday night, my siblings and I would jostle for position in front of the box while Mum and Dad sat at the back of the lounge, tutting and shaking their heads.

'Is that a bleedin' man or a woman?' Dad would ask as Boy George or Pete Burns preened before the cameras, lip-glossed to within an inch of their lives.

The show's presenting duties would be given to Radio 1 DJ duos like Simon Bates and Steve Wright, or Gary Davies and Peter Powell, who, with their Farah slacks, tinted specs and inane chat, were cheesier than Switzerland. I used to love it when John Peel did a stint; I always got the impression that he'd rather have cleaned the BBC toilets with his tongue than have had to witness Dave Lee Travis doing the twist to 'Teenage Kicks'.

It was with a slight twinge of sadness, then, that I'd had to forsake my weekly music fix in 1983. Once I'd signed schoolboy forms my Thursday night ritual had to make way for practice sessions at Platt Lane, Manchester City's training ground located around the corner from Maine Road. The sacrifice was entirely worth it though, as these footballing masterclasses were led by Tony Book.

Known affectionately as 'Skip' by everyone at the club, Book had captained the side during its most successful era, a purple patch spanning the late 1960s and early 70s which embraced the League Championship, the FA Cup, the League Cup and the European Cup Winners' Cup. He'd also managed City for six years, the pinnacle being a memorable League Cup victory over Newcastle in 1976. Dennis Tueart's match-winning goal, an extraordinary bicycle kick, became the stuff of legend. It also became the root cause of hundreds of head injuries as City fans across Manchester recklessly attempted to recreate their hero's acrobatics.

Skip was sacked as manager in 1980 by City chairman Peter Swales. However, he was so highly regarded that he continued working at the club in a coaching capacity for almost two decades. He became something of an institution at Maine Road, and I recall a member of staff comparing him to the much-photographed postbox on Manchester's

Corporation Street that famously survived the IRA bomb blast of 1996. Despite the chaos that City experienced throughout his tenure, Skip would invariably be the last man standing, keeping his head down, his mouth shut and getting on with the job with dignity while everything else disintegrated around him.

I relished the opportunity to learn from someone who'd been there, done that and worn the sky-blue T-shirt, but I'd heard rumours that Skip was incredibly tough, and didn't suffer fools, fakes or, as the footballing jargon goes, fanny merchants. I spent four years under his wing, the latter two as an apprentice, and could fully understand why some people found him hard to warm to. The product of an army upbringing, Skip was a committed authoritarian whose brusque manner could be pretty intimidating. However, beneath the gruff demeanour lay a quick wit and a sense of humour drier than happy hour at the Priory.

It was widely acknowledged that Skip was one of the best coaches in the business, with a knack for spotting slackers and shirkers a mile off. And there was none of that cringe-making over-familiarity that can exist between coaches and their charges; he just got on with the serious task of making us better players. But what I most admired about him was his transparency and candour. Football is a hotbed of back-stabbers and bullshitters, but Skip was neither.

His ethos was straightforward. By doing the simple things well and nailing the fundamentals, you created a solid basis upon which to showcase your skill and flair. He advocated a brand of pared-down football in which a simple ten-yard pass dispatched at the right moment could be more effective and efficient than a flamboyant nutmeg or a showboating step-over.

Those who ignored Skip's doctrine, those played lazily, casually or just downright badly, would be in danger of being fast-tracked to the top of his football scrap heap.

'If you don't buck your ideas up, you'll be joining the queue at Aytoun Street job centre,' was his tactful way of putting it.

I reckon the majority of City's youngsters benefited from Skip's autocratic approach, but it didn't suit everyone. Chris Coleman was a prime example. A great lad and a very talented left-back, Chris didn't cope well with Skip's ruthlessness and took many of his criticisms to heart. He became desperately unhappy at Maine Road – the fact that he was deeply homesick for his native Wales compounded his misery – and it was agreed by all that City probably wasn't the right club for him, and that he should be allowed to leave on compassionate grounds.

In hindsight it was probably one of the best moves that Chris ever made, as he returned to Wales and went on to have a long and distinguished career with successful spells at Swansea City, Crystal Palace and Fulham as well as his national team. He's since made a creditable leap from player to manager, although I'm sure his coaching style is slightly mellower than that of his old City mentor.

As Chris and I found out to our cost, it was horrendous to

be at the rough end of one of Skip's volcanic eruptions. One September morning, a fellow apprentice received one of the most legendary tongue-lashings of all time. A good finisher with decent pace, this lad wasn't the most tenacious of players, however, and would infuriate the coaching staff by shying away from tackles and going missing-in-action during matches.

Prior to an 'A' team game, Skip had ordered us all to wear studs, since the Platt Lane pitch had been left greasy after a heavy downpour. So, as instructed, we all donned the correct footwear. Apart from this one player, that is, who strode into the changing room wearing his usual rubbers, causing Skip to stop dead in his tracks.

'Hey, you. What did I say about wearing f***in' rubbers today?' he barked, jabbing his forefinger accusingly. This was met by a casual shrug of the shoulders.

'But these are a lot more comfy, Skip, and . . .'

His voice trailed off as he suddenly realised the grave implications of his insubordination. The rest of us winced and waited for the inevitable explosion. Skip didn't disappoint.

'Comfort? Comfort? F***in' comfort?' he shrieked, his face turning puce with rage.

'But Skip, I . . .'

'Well if it's f**kin' comfort you want, f*** off home on your f***in' comfy bus, go and sit in front of the TV on your f***in' comfy couch with your f***in' comfy slippers and watch f***in' Saint and Greavsie. Now f*** off.'

'But Skip . . .'

'I said f*** off.'

So he did. Back home he went, trudging dejectedly towards the bus stop with the offending boots in his kitbag. Skip was unrepentant; the boy's attitude had been disrespectful and unprofessional and he needed to be told.

It was a very sheepish lad who turned up for training the following Monday, though I think the damage had already been done as far as our coach was concerned. Suffice to say that it wasn't a huge surprise when he wasn't offered another contract.

However, for every also-ran there were plenty of Skip's protégés who achieved great success, and it was testament to him that most of his charges went on to play first team football in some capacity. Lads like me, David White and Andy Hinchcliffe stayed at City, while others went on to forge fruitful careers elsewhere, in John Beresford, Earl Barrett and Neil Lennon's case at Newcastle United, Aston Villa and Celtic respectively.

One of the major perks of being at City was the allocation of a couple of tickets for each home game, as well as a pair of passes for one of the post-match hospitality lounges. I always took my dad, who loved being behind-the-scenes on a Saturday afternoon.

After the final whistle we'd head out of the stands towards the inconspicuous door that led to Maine Road's inner sanctum, treading on sky blue carpets and passing through oak-panelled corridors until we reached the busy hospitality area. Sometimes Dad and I would be invited over to Chief Scout Ken Barnes's room, a cosy bolthole facing the club kitchens. Once dubbed 'the best wing-half never to have played for England', Ken was a former Manchester City star who had a pivotal role in his team's 1956 FA Cup Final victory. Extremely down to earth and incredibly funny, he also happened to be the father of one of my all-time heroes, the celebrated City and England winger Peter.

During the week his room was used as an administration office but on a match day it was his social club. The liquor ran freely, the cigarette smoke was thick enough to chew on and the banter among the hubbub of ex-players and backroom staff was always lively. Ken was a friendly host who made the fathers and sons feel ten feet tall, addressing the dads by their first names (mine could never quite get over being called 'Ted' by the great Ken Barnes), and memorising everything about the youngsters, from which school we attended to which pop groups we liked.

As I sipped my glass of Coke and dipped into some Big D nuts, he'd often quiz me about the game we'd just witnessed.

'So, who d'you think played well for us today, Paul,' he'd ask in his broad Brummie accent, 'and who's not worth paying in Smarties?'

My response would be typically on the nervous side – my mild stammer didn't help, coupled with the fact that people like Denis Law and Bobby Johnstone were often sitting within earshot – but Ken would diplomatically find some-thing to agree with even if my observations were a bit feeble. He'd then offer his own outspoken critique to everyone in the room, panning or praising the Blues depending on that day's performance. He was refreshingly frank and was usually bang on the mark.

Ken was just one of the many genial people who made those match days so special for Dad and I. As we walked to and from his room we'd be met with a sea of friendly faces, handshakes and kind comments ('I watched you play for Blue Star this morning, Paul – you did great, son . . .'; 'Good to see you again, Ted, I hear your Mike's doing the business at Curzon Ashton . . .'). And, while Maine Road in the mid-1980s may have struggled to compete with Anfield's trophy cabinet or Old Trafford's perceived glamour, the club's homely and unpretentious atmosphere really appealed to me. For a quite ordinary, straightforward kind of kid without, I hope, any airs or graces, City seemed the right place to be. I don't think that any of the flashier clubs would have been on a similar wavelength, and deep down I knew I'd found my spiritual home.

I was chuffed to bits when the club offered me a coveted YTS traineeship in July 1985.

'How you are off the pitch is how you are on the pitch, son,' was Skip's nugget of advice as I kicked off a thrilling new chapter in my life. For the next two years I received the princely sum of £26.50 per week, so there was no chance of me enticing Miss World with a king-sized bed strewn with banknotes, George Best-style. My wages wouldn't have covered even the pillowcase. Because I was still living at home, Mum and Dad were entitled to a weekly payment of £65, which paid for the big shop at the Co-op.

The average day in the life of a Maine Road trainee would comprise a morning training session at Platt Lane, after which we'd perform traditional boot-boy duties for City's senior players. I was tasked with scrubbing the studs belonging to goalies Alex Williams and Eric Nixon, as well as the outfield trio of David Phillips, Gordon Davies and Sammy McIlroy. All five treated me pretty well, unlike some of the first-team pranksters, who revelled in sending other trainees to the club secretary to ask for a long stand, or to the kitchens to ask for a flask of hot steam, or to the chairman to ask for a Guinness allowance. Tee-bloody-hee.

Our afternoon chores would range from mopping floors and scrubbing walls to scouring baths or cleaning toilets. Plunging my arm down a slimy Maine Road u-bend was never a barrel of laughs – especially if the first team had been for a vindaloo at the Punjab Palace the night before.

Woe betide any apprentice who dodged his duties, however.

'Hey, Glyn, have you seen the f***in' dust on that?' Skip would screech at his trusty sidekick, brandishing a slightly blackened fingertip that he'd run across a skirting board that we had supposedly cleaned.

'Whitey, Lakey, Brighty – get your f***in' spikes on. Twelve laps of the pitch – *now*.'

'You lads'll never learn,' Glyn would always say, suppressing a grin and shaking his head as he led us back out through the tunnel for our latest dose of punishment.

Glyn Pardoe was a celebrated former City full-back (the club's youngest ever debutant, in fact) and was still skilful enough to be first pick in our Friday morning five-a-sides. He also happened to be a gem of a bloke, possessing a gentle nature which counteracted the prickliness of his fellow coach. If I was ever at the wrong end of one of Skip's ear-bashings, Glyn would sidle over, put his arm around my shoulder and say something soothing like, 'Y'see, Lakey, what doesn't kill you makes you stronger, pal.' He had a tendency to speak in clichés, did Glyn, but his carefully chosen words usually got through to us.

After training (and prior to passing my driving test) I'd catch the number 53 bus from Moss Side to Belle Vue. I'd then wait for the connecting 204, 216 or 226 back home to Haughton Green and, as it approached, I would always lean back, craning my neck to see if Dad was sitting on the top deck. Whenever his car conked out – as was often the case – he'd have to get the bus back from his workplace at Manchester Building College. Occasionally we'd time it just right and were able to travel home together. Catching the

216 was always an added bonus because it took a longer route through suburban east Manchester, giving us extra talk-time.

It was probably the only chance Dad and I got to speak at length to each other away from the hurly burly of family life – our Saturday afternoon trips to Maine Road petered out when I became a full-time trainee – and I'd really look forward to our homeward-bound catch-ups. Our conversation would inevitably turn to football, and I would always listen intently to his tips and observations, his fag ash sprinkling onto my knee as he animatedly sketched team formations in the air.

'If you're playing centre-half, always hit your full-backs first, son. They've got more time to pass because it's not as tight, and your wide midfield players can sit off and keep their shape, can't they?'

'Yeah, you're right, Dad.'

'And here's another thing. Why try to dribble past two and put the ball in the box if there's an easier pass to make earlier on? Let the ball do the work.'

Occasionally, though, the enormity of my City potential would hit home, and Dad's emotions would get the better of him.

'Always do your best, son,' he'd say, looking me straight in the eye. 'Sometimes it'll work, sometimes it won't, sometimes you'll fall flat on your arse, but don't ever stop trying, will you, eh?'

'As if, Dad . . .' I'd groan.

'It's just that you've got the opportunity for such a good life, Paul. I mean, who knows where all this could end?'

And then he'd quickly turn his face towards the window so that I couldn't see his eyes misting up.

'Grab your kitbag, son, it's nearly our stop,' he'd say hurriedly. 'We'll bloody well miss it one day, all this bleedin' nattering . . .'

2

Destiny Calling

For most of my childhood, Dad was something of a football neutral. He was quite happy for both Manchester teams to do well and, until I joined forces with City, never really nailed his colours to any particular mast.

It was actually our milkman, Albert Gains, who turned me into a City fan. Mr Gains was a partisan Blue and the proud owner of two season tickets and, well aware that the Lake kids on Bowker Avenue loved kicking a ball about, asked Mum one morning whether Mike or I fancied accompanying him to the occasional match. She knew damned well what our response would be.

My first taste of Maine Road was a midweek game in September 1975, a floodlit 1–0 victory over Stoke City in which Rodney Marsh prodded in the winner. After the final whistle I couldn't get home fast enough to tell Mum and Dad about all the amazing sights and sounds – the sea of sky blue scarves and the chants from the Kippax just blew me away – and within a few days I'd plastered my side of the bedroom with City posters nicked from Mike's *Shoot!* magazines. It didn't take long for my school books to become defaced with MCFC doodles and squad lists, and I'd regularly find myself drifting away in the classroom, my concentration waning as I replayed a variety of goals and moves in my head while Mrs Hampson droned on in the background.

I'd love to say that Albert and I travelled to the match in a milk float bearing clanking crates of gold tops, but we didn't. We actually went in an orange Datsun Cherry, our journey taking us to Moss Side along the busy Manchester Road. Being a creature of habit, Albert would always park up in the same cul-de-sac just off Claremont Road, where he'd be accosted by a gang of teenage skinheads demanding 50p to 'mind your car please, mister' (a euphemism for 'you'll find a brick on your back seat if you don't cough up, Grandad'). Handing over the small change, Albert would smile weakly and ask the lads to take good care of the car, knowing full well that, come kick-off, they'd probably be feeding his coins into a fag machine or exchanging them for a can of Kestrel.

Our short walk to the ground would take us through a maze of mossy alleyways (we often had to slalom around the overflowing bins and old mattresses) and along roads fringed with red-brick terraces. Some front gates were guarded by forbidding-looking Moss Side matriarchs who, with arms folded and brows furrowed, would attempt to ward off fans from littering their yards with cans and chip trays. We'd pass blokes sporting Paul Calf mullets loitering on street corners, flogging knock-off City souvenirs while nervously looking over their shoulders for any looming policemen. I always knew when the Old Bill was in the vicinity because these lads would suddenly stuff their dodgy wares into a holdall before vaulting over a wall and crouching in a backyard until the coast was clear. I revelled in all these cops 'n' robbers capers.

As Albert and I approached the stadium, we'd be hit by the familiar Maine Road whiff of sweaty hot dogs and steaming horse dung. My excitement would really start to mount when we joined the throng of City fans that congregated on the forecourt. With my cherished blue-white-and-maroon-striped scarf knotted round my wrist, I'd watch wide-eyed as thousands of supporters poured in from the passageways and alleyways, converging in that communal hum of anticipation that always prevailed before a home game. Some fans would head straight to the turnstiles leading to the Kippax, Platt Lane, Main or North Stands, and others would join the queue snaking towards the souvenir shop. A couple of hundred more would amass in front of the main entrance, trying to catch a glimpse of a player or a VIP supporter like Bernard Manning or Eddie Large being ushered through the security cordon. You had to tell jokes and dodge salads to qualify as a celebrity City fan in those days.

The presence of a huge BBC or Granada outside broadcast lorry parked on the forecourt would always create a buzz of excitement, too.

'Looks like we're on telly tonight, Paul,' Albert would

observe. 'All the more reason for not making fools of ourselves, eh?'

He and I would then proceed to weave our way to the Main Stand entrance – me gripping on to his coat-tails so I didn't get lost in the crowd – before presenting our season ticket books to the fella at the turnstile who tore out the stubs and let us through. We'd then make a beeline for our seats in H Block, parking ourselves on the plump velour cushions that Albert always brought along. As I grazed on a bag of Sports Mixtures I'd pore over the City programme, trying my luck with the football quiz, guessing the time of the 'Golden Goal' and predicting the scores from the Division One fixtures listed alphabetically on the back page. My heart would race when the tinny tannoy blared out the opening bars of 'The Boys in Blue', the rousing anthem (penned by 10cc's Godley and Crème) that heralded the City lads' entrance.

> *City . . . Manchester City*
> *We are the lads who are playing to win,*
> *City . . . the Boys in Blue will never give in*

It was cheesy as hell, but I loved it.

As both teams stretched and limbered up on the pitch I scrutinised their kits, studying the material and design with the critical eye of a Savile Row tailor. My favourite all-time City strip was the classic sky blue Umbro shirt with the pointy white collar, coupled with second-skin white shorts. It was modelled to great effect by one of my big heroes, Dennis

Tueart, as he bombed down the right flank, leaving defenders flailing in his wake. Tueart also wore white tie-ups with a number 7 motif and v-shapes cut out of them which to me were a real fashion statement at the time. I once attempted to make my own pair of Tueart-style tie-ups at home, mutilating a couple of Dad's handkerchiefs with a pair of blunt nail scissors, and getting a rap on the knuckles when I got found out.

I can still visualise Dennis the menace sporting that fantastic kit when he deftly head-butted George Potter during an ill-tempered FA Cup tie against Hartlepool in January 1976. When the inevitable red card was brandished, us Blues' fans – already full of the joys of a 6–0 triumph – applauded our star winger off the pitch. Potter was red-carded too, becoming one of the first players in history to have been sent off while unconscious. I seem to recall reading the back pages of Dad's *Daily Mirror* the next day, featuring a contrite Dennis visiting a dazed-looking George in hospital.

Maine Road was a people-watcher's paradise for a youngster, especially one like me with a limited concentration span. If the game ever entered a drab spell there'd always be plenty of distractions to keep me occupied, like counting the cigarette lighters sparking up in the Platt Lane end or watching the pigeons roost beneath the Kippax Stand roof. I was also fascinated by Peter Swales's head. Our seats weren't far from the directors' box and I'd often find myself gawping at the City chairman's black, matted hairdo, trying to fathom out whether or not it was a wig.

'Paul, will you stop flamin' staring?' Albert would hiss, poking me in the ribs. 'It's rude.' I could never help myself, though.

Helen the Bell was always a great diversion. A sturdy blonde bombshell in her 60s, with a gravity-defying beehive, Helen Turner was a Maine Road icon. She'd sit directly behind the goal in the front row of the North Stand decked out in sky blue and brandishing a huge town-crier's bell which she'd clang incessantly during lulls in play, often rousing an occasionally jaded crowd into a chant of 'c'mon City, c'mon City . . .'

I went through much of my childhood thinking she was Joe Corrigan's mum, only because he always used to hop over the hoardings and give her a big kiss before kick-off, as she presented him with his match day sprig of heather.

'Ah, Big Joe's dead kind to his mum, isn't he?' I once blurted out, only for Albert to put me straight and shatter my illusions.

'She's not his mum, Paul, just his biggest fan,' he smiled.

The resident City goalies, Corrigan and Keith McRae, were well accustomed to Helen's bell, but witnessing the opposing keeper's reaction to her deafening ding-dongs was a great source of delight to me, especially if it was their first visit to Maine Road. Some of these goalies would almost leap out of their shorts when she let rip, and I'm sure she must have helped the Blues' cause on many an occasion by unnerving a keeper or two. Helen the Bell is sadly no longer with us, and for that the club is an emptier place. If slightly quieter.

Another Maine Road 'attraction' was the allegedly state-of-the-art electronic scoreboard that spanned the underside of the North Stand roof. It was perceived as really hi-tech when it was first unveiled in the early 1970s, but when all the fuss had died down it was quite obvious that it was, well, a bit crap really. Half of its bulbs blew within a month, and it could accommodate only one meagre row of flickering text. It was so woefully slow that I always imagined it being operated behind the scenes by some doddery old pensioner with jam-jar glasses and a rug on his knee, typing one-fingered on a word processor.

Even the most basic scoreboard announcement or advertisement would have to be broken up into four or five stuttering screenings: *'Come to . . .* (long pause) *Ashfords Furniture . . .* (very long pause) *for all your . . .* (extremely long pause) *home requirements.'* Or *'Could Gary Smith . . .* (pause) *please phone home . . .* (pause) *because your wife has gone . . .* (scoreboard freezes for five minutes) *into labour.'* Baby Smith would have probably been born and signed up to the Junior Blues by the time Daddy had got the message.

During the interval, we'd extract the other half-time scores from the bloke in front of us who spent the entire match with a transistor radio glued to his ear. He seemed more bothered about relaying goal flashes to the rest of H Block than any on-pitch action ('Latchford's just got another one . . . Everton 2–0 up now . . .'). I often used to wonder to myself why, come three o'clock, he didn't just stay at home, watch Frank Bough's *Grandstand* teleprinter, yell out the latest scores to his missus and save himself a tenner each Saturday. But the results service he provided was about 50 times faster than our slothful scoreboard and allowed me to pencil the scores in neatly in the match programme.

Like many fans of a certain age, Albert liked to leave ten minutes before the end of the match to 'beat the traffic'. I used to find this really infuriating, but it wasn't my place to argue with my kindly benefactor as he packed his cushions and his flask into his holdall before briskly ushering me up the stone steps and out of the stadium. I'd trudge back down Claremont Road, my heart sinking if I heard one of those uproarious cheers that signified a late City goal, something that was especially hard to bear if I'd just had to sit through a tedious 0–0 for 80 minutes.

Often it was a collective groan that would emanate from the ground as City conceded a soft goal in the game's dying moments. Before long, hordes of pissed-off fans would swarm past us, shaking their heads and muttering stuff about never paying to watch that shower of shite ever again. Sensing the possibility of supporter road rage, Albert would be ever more eager to get the hell out of Moss Side and would start doing one of those Peter Kay-style Dad-jogs until we reached the Datsun. And, after checking that various car parts were still intact, he'd yank out the choke and start the journey back to Denton, always in good time for the comforting *da-da-da-dah, da-da-da-dah, da daddly da da daaah* of Radio 2's *Sports Report*.

*

Fast-forward eight years, and my match-day vantage point got even better. Me and the other YTS trainees would assemble in front of the Maine Road tunnel five minutes before kick-off, standing proud in our nylon tracksuits and listening out for the padding of studs on Astroturf that signalled the emergence of the first team. After customarily applauding out the lads – back-slapping and well-wishing senior players like Neil McNab and Paul Simpson as they ran out to salute the City faithful – we'd clamber up to our plum position behind the coaching staff. I'd give Albert in H Block a quick wave before spending a few moments to take in the stadium panorama, the four tall stands and the multicoloured advertising hoardings framing a moving collage of home and away shirts.

As I sat and watched the game unfold I'd often feel like a puppy straining at the leash, dying to scamper onto the pitch for a piece of the action. Seeing lads who I trained with every day facing players such as Kevin Keegan and Glenn Hoddle served only to whet my appetite, making me more determined than ever to keep working my arse off so that I could play my own part on this magnificent stage.

The apprentices would usually turn up at Maine Road at about two o'clock on a match day, giving us just enough time for a hasty shower and shave following our morning fixtures. We relished being allowed to use the VIP entrance because the waiting City fans would often thrust their autograph books into our hands, giving us the chance to scribble the ridiculously showy signatures that we'd spent years practising in our bedrooms.

Our pre-match tasks included doling out players' complimentary tickets, getting shirts signed and sorting out last-minute stud adjustments. True to form, Skip and Glyn would act as chief whip-crackers but, on match days, would be joined in their mission by the stadium caretaker, a little silver-haired bloke called Jimmy Rouse. Jimmy was a much-loved Mr Fix-it who'd been at City since time immemorial, although by the mid-1980s his advancing age was starting to hamper his faculties. He had his own little den next to the boiler room and, despite being a cantankerous old goat, was always treated like a king by Skip and Glyn. The late, great Brian Clough loved listening to Jimmy's gripes and grumbles and used to slip him a £20 note each time Nottingham Forest came to play.

Jimmy was a bit absent-minded, though, and had a habit of casually leaving his false teeth lying around the caretaker's room. This would often prove much too tempting for us mischievous trainees who would sneak in, nick his gnashers and balance them on top of an unsuspecting youth team player's corned beef sandwich. Before long Jimmy would be on the warpath, all gums blazing.

'There's too much f***ing about in this place,' he'd lisp before angrily reclaiming his teeth and stomping back to his broom cupboard.

Sometimes, on the way back from a match day errand, I'd tiptoe into a hospitality lounge known as the Blue Room to gaze in awe at the polished wooden plaque that adorned the wall. Listing all the players who'd gained international honours while at the club – idols of mine like Kaziu Deyna, Asa Hartford and Dave Watson – this roll-call served both as a reminder to me of City's auspicious past and as an incentive for my own career and the honours that I hoped it would bring. Only a distant shout of 'where the f***'s Lakey?' would interrupt my trance-like state, prompting me to scamper back down to the dressing-room area to face the inevitable rollicking.

As it turned out I didn't have to wait long to gain my first honours with City. The 1985–86 season brought with it a hat-trick of medals. Winning the Pontins League Championship with the reserves and the Lancashire League title with the 'A' team was fantastic, but nothing that year quite compared with the sweet victory over Manchester United on Tuesday 29 April which brought the FA Youth Cup trophy to Maine Road for the first time in its history.

As the cup campaign loomed, our teenage team was starting to create quite a buzz in football circles, with many pundits tipping the 1986 crop of players for future stardom. Underlining the tremendous potential of the side was the fact that two of the lads, Paul Moulden and Steve Redmond, had already been blooded in the first team and had acquitted themselves brilliantly, playing with a maturity that belied their youth and inexperience.

In addition to Reddo and Mouldy, there was a glut of home-grown players waiting in the wings for their own share of the spotlight and – if the Piccadilly Radio phone-ins and the *Manchester Evening News* letters' page were anything to go by – this was generating much excitement among our supporters. City's top brass were also pleased with our progress, largely because the club didn't have a pot to piss in. Empty coffers meant that they were unable to flash any cash in the transfer market; they were quite literally banking on the youth team to make the successful transition to the senior squad and, in so doing, save them some dosh.

If you can't buy 'em, rear 'em appeared to be the motto of a club ever more reliant on its large scouting network and its conveyor belt of young hopefuls.

Funnily enough, there was never an ounce of envy or enmity between my team-mates and I. A healthy rivalry existed among us, as you'd expect, but we genuinely enjoyed sharing in each other's success and were pleased, not peeved, when any of us made his debut. None of us had a clue (and didn't much care) how our wage packets compared; all that concerned us was getting picked in the morning, and bagging three points in the afternoon.

Our on-pitch telepathy – half of it drummed into us by Tony Book, half of it spontaneous – was awe-inspiring. During a match we'd find ourselves linking up effortlessly and instinctively, complementing each other's strengths and covering for each other's flaws. The rapport between David White and I was a case in point. Playing right-back, I'd often overlap him on the wing before getting to the by-line and crossing the ball, only for the goalkeeper to come and pluck it out of the air and throw it out to his left side. I'd never have to worry about being exposed, though, because I could guarantee that Whitey would have automatically dropped back into the right-back position in order to pick up my man.

Conversely, if things were tight on the wing, and if Dave's heels were hugging the touchline, he'd knock the ball back to me, knowing intuitively that the resultant pass would be looped over the full-back's head for him to run onto. Safeguarding each other became second nature.

Our team spirit always reached a peak at Christmas-time and, despite our punishing schedule of games, we made the most of the festive period. I remember us running amok through the streets of Moss Side one snowy winter's morning, our daily jog from Maine Road to Platt Lane turning into a roving snowball fight as we yelped and hooted like a bunch of naughty schoolboys. Sometimes our missiles went astray, however, and the following day old Mrs Miggins on Lloyd Street would receive a cheque for a replacement window stapled to a sincere letter of apology from the club secretary, Bernard Halford.

An annual tradition at Maine Road was the trainees' Twelve Days of Christmas performance. The apprentices were tasked with adapting the carol's lyrics to name-check all the first-teamers ('one Nixon flapping, two Reidys punching, three Powers pointing . . .' and so on) and it would all be accompanied by appropriately daft actions. The players and coaching staff used to await this mini-pantomime keenly with its in-jokes and innuendo, and on the day of the show would gather in the away dressing room, eager to see what mischief the kids were going to get up to.

Some of our ditties ended up being more slanderous than others, depending on how we rated the player in question. The lads we liked and respected would get a relatively easy ride, but those who were deemed aloof, ignorant or obnoxious – especially those who 'forgot' to give their boot boys a Christmas bonus – would get seriously slated. I remember a trio of senior players going ballistic when we laid into them one Christmas. The training-ground battering we got next day was painful (and the bruises lasted into the New Year), but it was well worth it.

A self-confessed admirer of our youth team set-up was Alex Ferguson who, having replaced Ron Atkinson as Manchester United's manager in 1986, would often come to watch our games. Openly admitting that City's youth development system far outshone its Old Trafford counterpart, he swiftly set about the task of overhauling United's own School of Excellence. He continued to keep tabs on his rivals' stable of talent, though, which at that time included a certain Ryan Wilson, a nippy young winger who'd already captained England Schoolboys.

Rumour has it that, tipped off that the Blues had been slow to offer Wilson a contract, Ferguson opportunistically turned up on young Ryan's doorstep on his 14th birthday and promptly signed him on the spot. The lad changed his surname to Giggs, scored the derby winner against City in his full senior debut (bah!) and went on to become one of the game's greatest ever professionals.

The midway point of the 1985–86 season saw our youth team cruising through the early rounds of the FA Youth Cup, banging in seven apiece against Tranmere and Blackburn and beating Fulham 3–0 in the quarter-final at Craven Cottage. Our semi-final opponents were a much harder nut to crack, though. Arsenal were the red-hot favourites to lift the trophy, boasting a talented team which contained a couple of bright young things by the names of Michael Thomas and Paul Merson. We proved to be more than a match for them, though, narrowly losing by one goal at Highbury, winning the second leg at Maine Road 2–1 and earning our place in the final following a nerve-shredding penalty shoot-out. After that, the only obstacle between us and the trophy was the old enemy from Old Trafford.

At that time City and United's senior sides weren't exactly setting the league alight. City were festering in mid-table mediocrity and United weren't posing much of a threat to the Merseyside monopoly, so for a few days the local media gladly switched focus and gave an enormous amount of coverage to the forthcoming mini-derby. The *Manchester Evening News* even ran a four-page supplement on the impending clash, which Mum carefully folded up and saved for posterity.

We knew we were the stronger team, having outsmarted United twice in previous 'A' team fixtures, yet Tony Book was keen to dampen any overconfidence. We couldn't afford to take anything for granted, insisted Skip. We had to keep our composure, play our normal game, and not let the occasion get the better of us.

'Because this isn't just any old final,' he added. 'This is a chance for us to beat United and enter the history books.'

'F***in' bring 'em on,' yelled Reddo.

The first leg at Old Trafford finished all square at 1–1, but we had plenty of decent opportunities and were unlucky not to take a lead back home with us. I scored the equaliser with a penalty rebound – United's goalie, Gary Walsh, made an amazing save and got a hand to my initial spot-kick – but the honours remained even, despite the fact that we pretty much bossed the game.

The decider was staged at Maine Road the following week, and proved to be one of the most unforgettable experiences of my life. As we made our entrance onto the pitch that night, I remember feeling the full force of the noise, and crucially the warmth and affection that radiated from our supporters. The Kippax and Main Stands were packed to the rafters – among them the entire Lake clan and most of City's senior squad – and the North Stand turnstiles had to be hurriedly opened to accommodate thousands more diehards thronging into the ground (there were 18,000 there according to our state-of-the-art scoreboard, although it looked more like 25,000 to me). The terraces swayed to a medley of City anthems – as well as a few choice chants aimed at the cluster of away fans – and beneath the party atmosphere ran an undercurrent of hope and anticipation.

Our team couldn't have been more fired up, particularly David White and I. As native Mancunians, with sky blue blood coursing through our veins, just the mere mention of United got us wound up like coils. We were desperate to get one over on our cross-town rivals and the prospect of losing to them was inconceivable. There was no way we were going to let those Red whatsits ruin the party in our own backyard. No way.

The match was 90 minutes of one-way traffic, as we proceeded to tear United apart. Our opponents paid the price for failing to gain a first-leg advantage; being mentally and physically tougher, we simply bullied them out of the game. The performance of the night came courtesy of Paul Moulden. He ran United's defence ragged and scored our second goal in the 87th minute (David Boyd had nodded in the first), boosting his already phenomenal tally of career strikes.

Mouldy had already entered football folklore by scoring 289 goals in one season for Bolton Lads' Football Club, a magnificent achievement that was recognised in the *Guinness Book of Records*. He was one of the sharpest shooters that I'd ever seen, combining drive and aggression with a dazzling eye for goal. Being incredibly strong for his size – he was nicknamed Tattoo after the dwarf in *Fantasy Island* – meant that Mouldy was virtually impossible to mark. Not only that, he had this wonderful knack of knowing exactly when to push and shove his marker and remain undetected by the referee. Other teams no doubt saw him as a dirty little bastard, but I admired him for all his Artful Dodger-like craftiness.

Mouldy's late goal was the hammer blow to a United side that had been totally outplayed and not allowed to get a foothold in the game. The scoreline remained 2–0, and the FA Youth Cup was ours.

The post-match dressing room was awash with cheers and tears as we celebrated our win, the lads singing tunelessly and bouncing up and down with our arms around each other's shoulders. But what pleased me most that night was the look of sheer delight on Skip's face. I was so chuffed for him, Ken and Glyn, as their commitment and dedication had finally paid off. After all, there's nothing like a bit of silverware to show for your troubles, something tangible to make it all worthwhile.

Also basking in the glory of victory were chairman Peter Swales and his merry band of directors who, having been deprived of any honours for the best part of a decade, were delighted to acquire a shiny new cup to fill a gap in the trophy cabinet (no Shergar or Lord Lucan jokes, please). But not delighted enough, it seems, to put their hands in their pockets, judging by a faded copy of my YTS contract that I came across recently. All I can say is that it's a good job that the Class of '86 were motivated by football, not finances. Here's a little taster of that season's mouth-watering 'bonus scheme':

1985–86 YOUTH CUP BONUSES:

1st round:	£2 win, £1 draw
2nd round:	£2 win, £1 draw
3rd round:	£3 win, £1.50 draw
4th round:	£4 win, £2 draw
5th round:	£5 win, £2.50 draw
Semi-final:	£15 win, £7.50 draw
Final:	£25 win, £12.50 lose

So, totting it all up, I was £56 better off by the end of our cup run. I celebrated this bonanza by catching the 204 bus to the Manchester Arndale Centre, where I splashed out on a new pair of Arthur Ashe trainers from Allsports, a *Now That's What I Call Music 8* album, and a Terry's Chocolate Orange for my parents. But I wasn't complaining, I truly wasn't. All the money in the world couldn't have bought that cup-winning feeling.

Nevertheless, my bank balance became slightly healthier when I signed my professional forms around the time of my 18th birthday, in the autumn of 1986. Towards the end of their two-year contract all the YTS players were routinely summoned to a meeting with the chairman to discuss their future with Manchester City and, as my own day of reckoning approached, I was as nervous as the rest of them. A few weeks earlier a couple of well-regarded youth team regulars, Steve Mills and Steve Macauley, had been released by the club without a pro contract, so I wasn't assuming anything.

I was particularly gutted to see Millsy leave Maine Road because he and I had become great pals ever since he'd moved to digs around the corner from me in Denton. On the pitch he was solid and dependable (it was probably his lack of pace that hampered his top-flight chances, sadly), yet away from football the Sheffield Stallion was a party animal extraordinaire. Highlights of our escapades included a sun, sea and sangria holiday in Ibiza with Reddo and Whitey in tow, as well as a scary night spent sleeping rough at Derby station when we missed the last train home to Manchester following a U2 gig at Wembley. Millsy and I were also obsessed with the *Young Ones* (the comedy with Rik Mayall, not the movie with Cliff Richard) and often performed entire episodes for our team-mates in the dressing room.

I waited for Mr Swales for what seemed like ages on that fateful day, perched nervously on a hard wooden seat in the boardroom, biting my nails and glancing anxiously at my Swatch. It was a pretty daunting scenario for a wet-behind-the-ears teenager, bearing in mind that in those days we didn't have the luxury of football agents to advise or negotiate on our behalf (or at the very least sit next to us on the hard wooden seat).

The chairman eventually breezed in, firmly shaking my hand before settling himself into a gigantic velvet armchair which enabled him to peer imposingly down at me. He then folded his arms behind his head and nonchalantly rested his black Cuban-heeled boots upon the table, like Wyatt Earp in *Tombstone*. No doubt he was attempting to relax me with his

Daddy Cool demeanour, but it actually had the opposite effect of totally freaking me out.

Swales was quite an intimidating presence to us young players. Whilst he could often be quite pally-pally, he also had a hard-hearted side to his personality, which I'd witness to my cost later on in my career. On this occasion, however, the chairman was charm personified, showering me with compliments and sliding the hallowed forms across the table for me to sign. My signature almost veered off the page when I read that my new contract would incorporate a wage increase of nearly £300 a week. I was so chuffed I could have kissed his feet – now there's an image you may not want to dwell on – and I walked out of Maine Road feeling chipper about the future, relieved that I still had a job to go to, and grateful that my career remained on track.

Though I'd signed a new contract, it would take a few months before I made a mark on the senior squad. However, I soon found myself making another kind of 'mark' – of the skid variety, I'm ashamed to say – before a youth team game against Coventry City. It was prior to this game, you see, that I had the dubious honour of cacking my pants five minutes before kick-off (WARNING: anyone reading this over their morning muesli might be wise to skip the next few paragraphs).

It was in the Maine Road dressing room, during one of Skip's motivational pep-talks, that this highly embarrassing episode took place. I'd been suffering from a bad case of food poisoning – I hadn't been able to train all week – and had mistakenly thought that a bumper packet of Imodium had cleared it up. Obviously not, because as we all shouted a collective 'come on, lads', the accompanying clap must have loosened something in my nether regions, and I immediately felt a dreadful warmth oozing from my bowels to my undies.

Kick-off was a matter of minutes away, so I had to do something, and quick. I managed to sidle away from my team-mates, my bum cheeks clenched so tightly I could have trapped my FA Youth Cup bonus in there, and minced John Inman-like towards the toilets. I miraculously reached the cubicle without any significant seepage and removed the offending pants, wrapping them in an entire roll of toilet paper. But what the hell was I going to do with them? There's no way I could flush them down the loo, I certainly didn't want them fermenting in my kitbag and I couldn't exactly jog onto the pitch with them stuffed under my shirt. So, with time running out, I crept into Roy Bailey's deserted physio room and dropped the revolting bundle into his waste bin. It'd get emptied first thing in the morning, I reckoned, so Roy would be none the wiser.

'You okay?' asked Glyn Pardoe, as I rejoined my team-mates in the tunnel. 'You're looking a bit pale.'

'I'm fine, Glyn,' I said, adjusting my shorts and making a mental note not to attempt any scissor-kicks that night.

I arrived at the ground early the next day. As I entered the dressing room, the colour drained from my face when I caught sight of the un-emptied bin in the physio area. An indignant Roy Bailey was mid-phone call.

'Will you send Jimmy the caretaker over to sort these bleedin' drains out?' he angrily demanded. 'They're f***ing humming this morning . . .'

I eventually made my first team debut for Manchester City in January 1987. The manager at the time, Jimmy Frizzell, took me aside after training one wintry Thursday afternoon and told me that I was going to be replacing the injured David White for the Wimbledon game. Chuffed to bits at my inclusion, I floated out of Platt Lane into the path of Ken Barnes, who gave me a congratulatory pat on the back and offered me his two penn'orth. He told me to use my opportunity wisely and to look at the game as the perfect chance to gain some much-needed experience.

'Try and enjoy the fact that you won't be under any pressure out there,' said Ken sagely, 'because that won't be the case soon, I can bloody assure you.'

As I was about to thank him for his words of wisdom, he suddenly gripped my forearm.

'One more thing, Paul, son,' he whispered guardedly, surveying the car park for eavesdroppers. 'There are a few f***ing gobshites in that first team who aren't the players they think they are, and reckon that the world f***ing owes them a living. Just make sure that you let your football do the talking and those bastards will be looking over their shoulders, mark my words.'

As word of my good news spread, the piss-taking from the other young City players went into overdrive. This included a flurry of bets being placed as to what the post-Wimbledon headlines might be, with LAKE DIVES IN, LAKE MAKES A SPLASH, and LAKE SUPERIOR being peddled in a dressing-room sweepstake. My selection for the first team had also pricked up the ears of the local media. A photo session on the Maine Road pitch was followed by my first ever broadcast interview, given to Piccadilly Radio's Brian Clarke. I happened to catch his sports bulletin as I drove home that afternoon, wincing as I heard myself stuttering through a full house of clichés that included 'Over the moon', 'Take each game as it comes', and 'At the end of the day'.

My first senior appearance wasn't one of those fairy-tale dream debuts, alas; not by a long stretch. We managed to scrape a goalless draw at a bitterly cold Plough Lane, which actually wasn't that bad a result, considering we'd been bombarded by the usual Crazy Gang tactics of long balls, set pieces, elbows to the ribs and knees to the spuds. As it was I performed pretty steadily in central midfield, and whilst I didn't set the game alight, neither did I let the side down. On the coach back to Manchester it all felt a bit anti-climactic, but I tried to console myself with the fact that it could have been much worse. I could have gone in late on Vinnie Jones and had a proper baptism of fire.

Thankfully, the manager seemed happy enough with my efforts. Jimmy (or Frizz, as he was known to all of the staff) hadn't long replaced Billy McNeill as manager, but their Scottish heritage was virtually the only thing they had in common. Two more different personalities you couldn't find; a proper case of chalk and cheese. During his brief stewardship at Maine Road, McNeill had acquired a reputation as a no-nonsense, straight-talking type of guy. My own opinion of him blew hot and cold, our relationship hitting a particularly Arctic patch after an episode involving my elder brother.

In 1986 Mike was 19 years old and, rated by many as a quality attacking midfielder, still harboured ambitions of making it as a professional footballer. After receiving some rave reviews whilst playing for a local semi-pro side, Curzon Ashton, he was invited to join City on a non-contract, expenses-only basis and made six appearances for the reserves, netting three goals and even earning two Man of the Match awards. These achievements were made all the more remarkable by the fact that, to make ends meet, he was also working nights for British Rail as an apprentice driver, often coming straight to training after having clocked off his shift at dawn.

Things appeared to be going really well for Mike. He was relishing the whole City experience, and many people were sitting up and taking notice of the senior Lake lad. Despite the fact that he was knackered most of the time, his attitude and application were second to none, and everyone at the club seemed really impressed by him, including the manager. I personally loved having my brother around the place, and I shared in his excitement when he told me that Billy McNeill had asked to see him one morning before training. Could it be the offer of a contract, maybe? Could there soon be another Lake on City's books? We were both cautiously optimistic, since Mike had been playing really well.

I waited for him outside the manager's office, crossing my fingers for some good news. Ten minutes later, however, it was a glum-looking Mike that emerged. McNeill had decided to release him from the club ('I'm sorry, Michael son, this old ship hasn't got as many coats of paint as it'd like,' had been his cryptic way of pleading poverty) and my brother's hopes were dashed in an instant.

To his credit, however, he picked himself up, dusted himself down and went on to sign for Macclesfield Town before being snapped up by Sheffield United. Ironically enough, he scored a great goal for the Blades against City in 1992, a looping volley from a ridiculous angle that soared over Tony Coton's right arm. I didn't feature in that particular game but I remember feeling so pleased for my big bro', despite the fact that he'd put one past my own team. His strike was a contender for Goal of the Month, although he still says he'd have preferred to have scored it wearing a sky blue shirt.

An ankle fracture sustained whilst playing for Sheffield United, as well as a serious knee injury at Wrexham, put paid to Mike's football career a few years later. I remain convinced, however, that he was good enough to have played for City. And while my brother's experience had somewhat tarnished my relationship with Billy McNeill, no harsh words or dirty looks were ever exchanged. I wasn't deluded – I knew that football could be a cruel and callous business – but it wasn't very pleasant to see my big brother suffering such heartbreak.

In contrast to his predecessor, Frizz was a fun-loving, wise-cracking bloke whose acerbic comments would often render us helpless with laughter. One particular Thursday, during the latter part of the 1986–87 season, City left-back Clive Wilson had been touted in that morning's tabloids as a future transfer target for Chelsea. Not a massive surprise, since Clive was a quality defender who was probably due a money-spinning move, but we still gave him some stick for getting all high-and-mighty on us (which, being a lovely, unassuming lad, he was anything but). That same morning, however, Frizz had decided to organise a practice match between a first team XI and a reserve XI, the former comprising lads like Clive and Andy May, and the latter featuring youngsters such as myself and Jason Beckford. Against all odds we won it 2–1, with Clive having an absolute stinker of a game, comically falling on his backside after being skinned by Jason. The manager was less than enamoured at this sight, and let rip accordingly.

'Chelsea f***in' Football Club?' he bellowed. 'More like Chelsea f***in' Flower Show, you ****.' Clive, to his great credit, saw the funny side. He went on to have the last laugh, too, bagging a £250,000 move to Stamford Bridge in March 1987, claiming a fat signing-on fee in the process.

Frizz's stint as City manager was short-lived, however, and he was replaced by Norwich City's coach, Mel Machin, in the summer. This wasn't exactly a shock development, since the club had been giving out enough vibes that Frizz was merely keeping the hot seat warm for someone else (as someone said at the time, his coat was on a wobbly peg). Luckily, though, Frizz stayed on at Maine Road as its general manager, and latterly stadium manager. He struck up a great friendship with Ken Barnes – they shared similar opinions and characteristics – and they'd often put the football world to rights in the chief scout's office on weekday mornings, turning the air blue as they did so. Prior to training I'd always pop my head in to say hello, before being beaten back by a mushroom cloud of nicotine.

I was ridiculously nervous before my home league debut against Luton Town. I can sympathise with those West End actors who get first-night nerves, because I was worried sick on the eve of my own première performance. Although I was familiar with Maine Road, having already played there in the FA Youth Cup Final, a Full Members' Cup tie and countless reserve games, this was a completely different proposition.

On 21st February 1987, a throng of family and friends piled down to Maine Road to lend their support on my big day. Stupidly, I let the occasion get the better of me and was as jittery as hell for the first 20 minutes, so much so that a bloke in the stands was heard to sneer sarcastically, 'Here we go, yet another brilliant find from our illustrious football academy.' He was entitled to his opinion of course, but had the misfortune of sitting behind my mate Millsy's dad, who turned round, told him to shut the f*** up and punched him in the face.

Despite my colly-wobbles, I somehow managed to score my first ever senior goal a minute before the interval, latching onto a half-chance that had sped across the box and steering it into the far corner. The game ended all square after Luton's Brian Stein neutralised my strike in the 62nd minute. My post-match emotions were pretty mixed. I was delighted to open my goal account, but not massively impressed by my shaky performance. I think the burden of pressure that Ken Barnes had spoken of had definitely reared its head that day.

With the advent of my first team appearances came another kind of pressure, namely my new-found 'celebrity' status. As I made inroads into the senior squad, complete strangers started to let on to me as I went about my daily business, some even asking me to scribble autographs or pose for photographs.

As I was quite a shy lad, all this would sometimes make me feel pretty uncomfortable, and I had to pluck up courage to attend the various cheque presentations, school visits and press interviews that I was now obliged to undertake. Though I realised that public appearances were part and parcel of being a professional, I just didn't feel that I merited the attention because in my mind I was still your average, everyday, run-of-the-mill YTS kid. Doubtless I'd have benefited from some media training to boost my confidence, but City, like most clubs, had yet to embrace that concept. In fact, I got most of my tips from Granada TV on a Friday night, watching Elton Welsby interviewing old hands like Frank Worthington and Graeme Souness on *Kick Off.*

I don't think it was a huge coincidence that I also started to attract more attention from the opposite sex. This state of affairs, while welcome, was reminiscent of TV's Mrs Merton infamously asking Debbie McGee what she saw in the millionaire Paul Daniels, because I wasn't exactly the Brad Pitt of the squad. *Shoot!* magazine, the cheeky bastards, once even compared me to The Pogues' front man Shane McGowan, who had ears like FA Cup handles and teeth like tombstones. And being asked if I was Ivan Lendl's brother by a snotty-nosed kid at a Junior Blues meeting didn't exactly do wonders for my self-esteem, either. (In my defence, I feel I must point out that in 2008 I was nominated as a 'Blue Hunk' in City's match-day programme – don't laugh – by a female fan from Chorley who reckoned that I possessed 'film star looks'. 'Run, Forrest, run', remarked my wife when I told her.)

When out on the town in the mid-1980s, I'd often find myself giving a girl the glad eye, only for her to either tut disdainfully or blatantly blank me. Then I'd lip-read a bloke in her group telling her that she'd just snubbed Paul Lake, the Manchester City player, after which she'd miraculously change her tune. The lad in the corner with the purple paisley shirt and the mousey crew-cut would suddenly be trans-formed into an irresistible hunk, and before long Little Miss Fickle would be all over me like a rash, batting her eyelashes as she seductively sipped her Malibu and pineapple. It was all as shallow as hell, but it didn't make me look a gift horse in the mouth when one presented itself.

After a few short-lived dates and dalliances, I met the girl who'd become my first serious girlfriend. Karen was a pretty brunette who lived on Audenshaw Road in Denton and had attended the same secondary school as me. Her dad, Brian, was a massive City fan; not surprisingly we got on like a house on fire.

It was Karen who had the honour of being the inaugural passenger in my cherished first car, a used sky blue Ford Escort Ghia (its registration plate – OJA 154W – is seared on to my memory) that I bought on the never-never from Reddish Motors. Mike offered to touch up the bodywork a bit – there were a few scuffs and dents here and there – but I politely told him to piss right off, remembering the time in the early 1980s that he'd painted my Uncle Jim's Rover 3800 with maroon Dulux matt emulsion, Jim being of the belief that it would be cheaper than a garage respray. The end result was predictably hideous and the car became the laughing stock of Haughton Green, with guffawing locals pointing in amusement as it was driven around town with a circular bald patch on the roof where my brother had forgotten to remove the paint tin.

I couldn't wait to drive onto the Maine Road forecourt for the first time. I spent the night before visualising how I'd show off my pride and joy to my best buddies, Jason and Millsy, picturing myself casually propping up the bonnet to display the engine or highlighting the roominess of the boot and all those other things you're supposed to do with a new motor. I imagined taking them for a lunchtime spin near the ground, slotting 'Pump Up The Volume' into the cassette player and cruising the mean streets of Moss Side.

'Hey, that Paul Lake's going places,' the boyz-in-the-'hood would say as they enviously watched me drive past with my left hand cradling the steering wheel and my right elbow hanging out of the window. Playing for City's first team; face in the papers; nice sporty Escort; thumping tunes: now there goes one cool dude.

Sadly, though, it didn't actually happen that way. In my childlike excitement that morning I managed to flood the engine and had to abandon my sky blue dream machine on the drive. I legged it to the bus stop, leapt onto the number 53, arrived late for training and got fined £20 for my troubles. Cool dude my arse.

3

Lucky Man

I never lost sight of how lucky I was to play football for a living. You've got a job in a million, Paul . . . I remember thinking as I jogged towards our pre-season training pitch on a blazing hot day in July 1987, carrying a bottle of water in one hand and a pair of flip-flops in the other. You're being paid to kick a ball about with your pals in the sun. You're playing for the team that you've adored since you were a kid. Go on, pinch yourself . . .

I'd not long returned from a much-needed holiday in Ibiza which, to be honest, couldn't have come at a better time. Manchester City had been relegated to the Second Division a couple of months earlier – a horrendous experience for everyone involved with the club – and I'd badly needed some downtime (and some sunshine) to recover from such a body blow. While our demotion had been half-expected – an appalling set of results had effectively sealed City's fate in April – nothing could have prepared me for the emotional scenes that had followed our final game in the top flight, against West Ham. Witnessing grown men in blue shirts shedding tears on the terraces, and the abject despondence in our changing room, had been pretty hard to bear for an 18-year-old rookie who, being on the fringes of the squad, had merely gone down to Upton Park for the experience.

By the time July arrived, though, the lads had had six long weeks in which to unwind and, as I reported for my first day of training at Manchester University playing fields, it was a relief to enter an upbeat dressing room buzzing with plenty of high-fives and 'how-you-doin'?' It was great to take part in the catch-up chatter, too, listening to big-hitters such as Imre Varadi and Paul Stewart banging on about exotic trips abroad and new top-of-the-range golf clubs, and singletons like Steve Redmond and Ian Scott regaling us with tales of summer lovin' conquests and nights on the lash.

The first day of pre-season was always full of little rituals, the ceremonial unwrapping of our new training kit being a case in point. The arrival of our 'uniform' was a very big deal to us players, and we'd spend ages scrutinising the individually numbered shirts, shorts and shell-suits, double-checking that the quality and design met our exacting standards. There'd invariably be something for us to moan about; one particular July our training shorts were so tight that little was left to the imagination, and another time we weren't sent enough smaller-sized kits, meaning that the squad's skinnies had to run around with Stanley Matthews-style shorts flapping around their knees.

The lads' biggest gripe was when the waterproofs arrived two weeks late – as was often the case – which prompted a flurry of prima donna hissy-fits whenever the heavens opened. This was a nightmare for those players with blow-dried Patrick Swayze mullets who after yet another Mancunian downpour ended up looking more like a rat-tailed Peter Stringfellow.

Occasionally, some of the senior squad members would wangle a big-money sponsorship deal over the summer, and would make a grand entrance at the training ground sporting their branded shell suits, T-shirts, socks, boots and holdalls. These visions in Day-Glo would provoke wolf-whistles and comments of 'oooh, get *her* . . .' from me and the rest of the raggy-arsed brigade as we tried to conceal our envy. I remember us all lapping it up when our goalie, Perry Suckling, spent the first day prancing round the pitch in his shiny new Hummel boots, only to turn up the following morning hobbling like an old man, his feet studded with raw blisters.

'Heyyyyy, Bertie big bollocks,' we heckled. 'You'd better get your slippers on 'cause you won't be able to put your swanky boots on for a fortnight, will you?'

Then there were the close-season signings to size up. Our new recruits always elicited a degree of wariness (particularly if they played in your position) and we'd try to suss out whether they were going to be one of the lads or a pain in the neck. For the first fortnight we'd usually give them the benefit of the doubt, though, and would try to make everyone feel as welcome as possible. During my entire time at City I only ever took umbrage to one new arrival, a lad called Robert Hopkins. He treated the young professionals with utter contempt, and we did cartwheels around the training ground when he was offloaded to West Brom.

Making up the numbers would be the annual intake of 16-year-old apprentices who, on day one, would troop in like the 'fresh fish' newcomers in *The Shawshank Redemption*. Experiencing their first proper pre-season was quite a culture shock for most trainees, coming as they did from the comfort of home and school straight to the purgatory of summer training. The majority of the young 'uns would opt for a discreet, low-key arrival, getting on with their dogsbody tasks of loading up drinks crates and hanging the right kit on the correct hook. Those apprentices who turned up with a swagger and an attitude would be immediately earmarked by the older lads for some special attention, particularly if they possessed any distinguishing features. Big noses, bad acne, bowl-head haircuts and bum-fluff moustaches were seen as fair game for the seniors who took great delight in bringing these upstarts down a peg or two.

'Come 'ere, Spotty Muldoon, I'll squeeze that zit for you ...' would be a typical remark, or 'let me blow your nose for you, I'm nearer ...'

As a teenage trainee I had the misfortune of looking a bit like one of those Mr Potato Head toys ('you've not quite grown into your features yet, Paul,' was how someone once diplomatically put it). I recall being teased mercilessly during a communal meal, by our captain, Mick McCarthy, who wedged some pitta bread over both ears and yelled 'anyone seen Lakey?' at the top of his voice. I went scarlet with embarrassment but did my best to brush it off, smiling and shrugging my shoulders until the laughter subsided. But that's all you could do when you were an apprentice. Batting away such remarks by your superiors was the only viable option, because you'd never have heard the last of it if you'd had an adolescent strop or – heaven forbid – dared to retaliate.

This ribbing was mild in comparison to some of the other stuff that went on, much of which could be pretty brutal. Back in the late 1970s and early 80s there was an unwritten rule that the YTS lads had to earn the right to enter the first team changing room, and that the correct protocol was to knock on the door and wait outside until someone answered. Any cocksure apprentice who sauntered in with a player's boots or a freshly laundered training top would be given a right-hook by Joe Corrigan – City's burly goalkeeper – before being slung out of the door.

I also remember one fellow trainee receiving a birthday 'present' from the first teamers that involved stripping him down to his underpants, bundling him into a basket skip, drenching it under a cold shower and then abandoning the locked casket on the Maine Road forecourt with the traumatised player still inside.

'H-h-happy f-f-f***ing b-b-birthday . . .' he whimpered to himself when the senior lads eventually surrendered the key and allowed us to unshackle him, watched as we did so by a bemused elderly lady who'd been prodding the talking skip with her walking stick.

City's official pre-season weigh-in had its own humiliations. There was nothing worse than a public assessment to cruelly expose someone's summer bingeing, and players turning up on the first day looking like they were sponsored by Burger King would be singled out for ridicule by their team-mates. It wasn't a laughing matter for the coaching staff, though. Anyone waddling into the training complex with a Jocky Wilson beer gut conveyed the message that he wasn't prepared or wasn't bothered – or both – and was hauled in to the manager's office for a confessional ('forgive me, Gaffer, for I have sinned; it's been six weeks since my last salad . . .'). The said player would have his cards well and truly marked, and would spend the next three weeks being forced to train in a bin bag in order to sweat his flab off. And worse still, his team-mates would single him out for some serious ragging for weeks on end. Being a fat figure of fun for a squad of mickey-taking footballers was never a pleasant experience; thankfully my skinny build meant that I was never a target.

Half of me dreaded the prospect of a physically gruelling pre-season; the other half welcomed the opportunity to push my body to its limits and smash the pain barrier until my heart pounded and my muscles burned. The first couple of weeks were always the most demanding, with just a smidgeon of football amid strenuous back-to-back fitness sessions.

Such an exhausting training regime knocked the stuffing out of the best of us; even natural-born athletes like Earl 'Kip Keino' Barrett, Bob 'Olympic Spawn' Brightwell and Paul 'Road Runner' Moulden would be totally wiped out by the end of the day.

Suffering on the sidelines would also be the teenage apprentices who, mistakenly assuming that their youthful zest and innate fitness would carry them through July's trials, would find themselves chucking up their Frosties after yet another stomach-turning session. Come four o'clock, every single one of us would be collapsed on the grass, groaning in agony.

The shared pain of pre-season training definitely helped the squad to bond, but it also produced a few powder-keg moments sparked off by our frayed nerves and fatigued bodies. A notorious endurance discipline called the Snake Run was the cause of many a pitch-side scuffle. This punishing task always took place towards the end of the afternoon, and involved already flagging lads having to jump over team-mates lying horizontally round the pitch like human hurdles. All it took was a trailing leg or an 'accidental' stamp for tempers to flare, and players would often have to be separated as they wearily traded blows. Tensions could be equally as high in the dressing room. Some of the senior pros, many of whom had played at the top level for ten years or more, considered themselves experts in training strategies and enjoyed putting the world to rights if things weren't to their liking.

The 1987 close season saw our manager, Mel Machin, placing the emphasis on arduous, stamina-based work in the first fortnight. This wasn't popular with everyone, however, particularly those who preferred to let the ball do the work during five-a-side matches or skills sessions. Certain players bemoaned the fact that their short'n'sharp 20-yard passing game was being disregarded in favour of mini-marathons.

'This club treats us like shire horses, not race horses,' one commented following an afternoon of cross-country running. I managed to tolerate the five-mile slogs, though, convincing myself as I squelched through another muddy ditch that all this suffering would return me to my fighting weight. With each passing day my fitness levels climbed, the feel-good factor rose, and the needle on the scales crept gratifyingly anticlockwise. As my strength increased so too did the surge of endorphins, to such an extent that when August arrived I was bouncing around like Tigger, excitedly ticking off the days until the start of the new season.

At the beginning of August we'd upped sticks from Camp Wythenshawe and headed back to Platt Lane, the club's official training ground, where the emphasis had shifted to more tactical work in preparation for the new season. Analysing from the touchline and debating behind closed doors, the backroom staff now had the tough task of finalising their starting first team line-up. Being scrutinised at such close quarters could be unnerving.

'Believe you me, we're watching *everything*,' warned coach Tony Book.

All of us were well aware that one immaculate pass or one clumsy tackle could make the difference between a first team pick or a reserve team run-out. And although everyone in the squad remained hopeful of that final nod of approval, I don't think any of us believed we had the divine right to selection. Even dead certs such as Paul Stewart and Paul Simpson glanced nervously over their shoulders, well aware that there were plenty of frisky young colts ready to take their place.

Our concentration on the training pitch wasn't helped by the fact that Platt Lane was a meeting point for a noisy troupe of local winos who, when they weren't bothering passers-by in Moss Side, lurched down to our HQ to hassle us instead. They often congregated behind the mesh perimeter fence and spewed out a torrent of abuse as we ran out each morning.

'Yer all f***in' wankers, the lot of yer,' was probably as polite as it got.

These fellas revelled in creating as much disturbance as possible and because security at Platt Lane was non-existent, they often hung around for the entire session. Try as we might, it was hard to ignore our resident drunkards, particularly since we had to jog right past them whenever we did laps of the pitch (I remember one particularly creepy-looking guy who tried to put us off our stride as we completed each circuit by smiling menacingly and slowly rubbing his crotch up and down the netting.) The ball frequently got smashed high over the fence – especially if Imre Varadi was having target practice – and one unfortunate soul would have to go and retrieve it, often having to wrest it from the grasp of some

Rab C. Nesbitt lookalike with his arse cheeks hanging out of his pants.

'Wonder whether Bryan Robson has to cope with this at the Cliff?' we laughed as the ball was lobbed back into play.

Believing that I'd given a pretty good account of myself during pre-season, I was absolutely gutted not to figure in Mel Machin's side for the opening game against Plymouth Argyle. I watched forlornly as the player-coach, John Deehan, pinned up the squad line-up on the dressing-room wall, and ordered myself to keep my pecker up and my frustration hidden.

'Don't worry, son, your time will come,' reassured Dad when I returned home that afternoon with a face like a wet weekend. 'Just be patient.'

It was an injury to Kenny Clements that eventually provided the opening for me, and I slotted into the role of centre-half against Shrewsbury Town in September 1987. I went on to feature in the back-to-back goalfests against Millwall (4–0) and Stoke (3–0) and must have done all right because I kept my place even when Kenny regained full fitness, regularly appearing alongside him until he left the club the following March.

But, while everything seemed to be going pretty well for me on the pitch, I soon discovered that the gaffer wasn't entirely happy with everything off it.

'Can I have a quick word?' he asked me one Saturday evening, pulling me to one side on the coach back from a

League Cup tie in Wolverhampton. 'Now don't take this personally, Lakey,' he whispered, 'but I think you need to smarten yourself up a bit.'

For some unknown reason, my Nick Heyward-style Arran jumper and my nearly new cords from Affleck's Palace were unacceptable for first team travel, and Mel told me I needed to invest in a proper suit. Although I hated wearing formal gear, I heeded his advice and paid a visit to Slater's Menswear in Manchester, subjecting myself to the old tape measure and 'suits you, sir' treatment.

My youthful passion remained undimmed, though. One of my favourite city-centre hangouts, Affleck's Palace was a rickety old building on the corner of Church Street and Oldham Street that housed an odd mixture of high fashion and second-hand tat; the only place in town where you could buy designer tops and dead men's trousers all under one roof. It was also a renowned music mecca where you could spend ages browsing the little record concessions for rare vinyl and memorabilia. I was a keen collector of obscure 12-inches and picture discs, and used to love rummaging in the bargain bins and unearthing little-known gems by Echo and the Bunnymen, Spear of Destiny and Blue Rondo à la Turk (they don't name 'em like they used to, eh).

Despite his intense loathing of the place, I regularly dragged my pal Millsy to Affleck's after training. Millsy loved his King Street boutiques and 'casual' labels and hated having to mingle with the hippies, goths and Morrissey clones that Affleck's generally attracted.

'I need a bloody shower after coming here,' he'd grumble, brushing imaginary dust off his Ralph Lauren sweater before grudgingly joining me in the top-floor café for a Colombian coffee, a wholemeal flapjack and a (passive) lungful of ganja.

Kitted out in my new match-day outfit of black suit, cream shirt, orange tie and black patent winklepickers, I reckoned I was finally projecting the right professional image. With a few more first team games under my belt, I also felt I was beginning to understand the extra-curricular responsibilities that came with playing for Manchester City, namely conducting myself sensibly, representing my football club in the best possible way and acting as a role model to others. All in all, I thought I was doing all right for a new recruit. And then John Gidman went and put a spanner in the works.

A highly experienced and well-regarded pro, John 'Giddy' Gidman had signed for City from Manchester United in 1986, following in the footsteps of Denis Law, Peter Barnes and Brian Kidd by becoming one of the select few to have played for both the Reds and the Blues. A sharp and sarky Scouser, he was a popular figure in the dressing room and was admired by the lads for being the only player to drive a Porsche, as well as being one of the first to own a hands-free car phone.

His rugged, perma-tanned features and brown corkscrew curls may well have given him housewives' favourite status, but beneath the handsome exterior lay a rock-hard centre. No other player inspired greater fear among the apprentices

than Giddy. A fiery, hot-headed character, he would cheer-
fully smack any young whippersnapper who had the cheek
to overtake him during a training run.

'No one makes me look f***in' slow . . .' he'd hiss as he
elbowed you in the face.

Prior to our away game at Swindon in October 1987, the
physio Roy Bailey had informed me of a change to the
schedule which meant that I'd be rooming with Giddy
instead of my usual mucker, Bob Brightwell. No problem, I
thought. Giddy's a sound bloke, if maybe a tad on the tetchy
side, but I'm sure we'll get along just fine.

As we unpacked our suitcases in the hotel room following
our evening meal, I knew I was in for a bad night when Giddy
told me to sort the drinks out. I duly obliged, filling up the
plastic kettle and giving him first refusal on the complimentary packet of Highland Shortbread.

'What are you f***in' doing?' he demanded.

'I'm brewing up, mate,' I replied as the kettle started to
boil.

'I want a Scotch, not a friggin' sauna,' he barked. 'Get that
mini-bar open, you lanky Manc t**t, and let's have a wind-
down . . .'

An hour and three miniature bottles of Famous Grouse
later, I found myself hiding in the bathroom, trying to avoid
the mad fella on the other side of the wall intent on plying
me with alcohol. Giddy, you see, was one of those old-school
footballers who could neck half a bottle of whisky on a Friday
night and still be in fine fettle in time for the following day's

kick-off. I, in contrast, never touched a drop on the eve of a game and thought that any players who did so were bang out of order. But I was too in awe of Giddy to stand up for myself, and what was intended as a nightcap for him turned into a skinful for me.

Giddy proceeded to drag me out of the bathroom, informing me that he'd ordered us a bite to eat from the hotel kitchen, and that I had to go and collect it. At this time of night – by now it was pushing 11-ish – my other team-mates would have been tucked up in bed with a mug of cocoa, either playing on their Atari consoles or watching *Platoon* on video. Yet here was I, half-cut, creeping through the hotel to pick up an illicit late-night snack that I didn't even want. A snack, it turned out, that consisted of two gigantic plates of cod, chips and peas, handed over by a puzzled-looking chef in an anorak, presumably just about to clock off his shift.

Balancing the huge metal tray upon my palms, I sneaked past the trio of City coaches sat chatting at the bar and headed towards the lift. I stood there, swaying slightly, trying to focus on the blurry red numbers above the door as they counted down each level. 4, *ping*. 3, *ping*. 2, *ping*. 1, *ping*. 0, *ping*. 'Ground floor,' announced the lift's automated voice as the doors opened. *Oh f****, said a panicky voice in my head, as out stepped chairman Peter Swales, manager Mel Machin and one of the directors.

'Bit peckish are we, Lakey?' said Mel staring at the pair of steaming fish suppers. 'Both for you, eh?'

I nodded, not wanting to land Giddy in the shit.

'I couldn't eat the evening meal,' I lied, gritting my teeth like a ventriloquist to contain my whisky-breath, 'and I didn't think it was a good idea to go to bed on an empty stomach.'

With a face like thunder, the director – a fearsome scrap metal dealer by the name of Freddie Pye – demanded that I tell him who I was rooming with, nodding knowingly when I reluctantly admitted that it was Giddy. There then followed a long, awkward silence, after which an unsmiling gaffer told me that it was very late, and that we'd continue this conversation the next morning.

'But I will say this, Lakey, I'm not happy,' he said sternly, 'not happy at all.'

I had a terrible sleepless night. Wracked with guilt and worry, I was absolutely petrified that this slipping of standards was going to get me fired from the side and fined to high heaven. Also keeping me awake was the fact that Giddy – who'd knocked himself out with two sleeping pills – was lying on top of the TV controls which meant that every time he shifted in his sleep, the TV would either turn off or on. I didn't dare get up to retrieve the remote – let sleeping Scousers lie, I always say – and there was no way I was going to go fumbling under his backside. I was in enough trouble as it was.

At 10.25 the next morning, a bright-eyed Giddy was on the phone to his wife, exchanging small talk about the family and the weather and whatnot. Hurry up mate, I thought, we've got to be downstairs for our pre-match walk in five minutes.

Don't make us late, for Christ's sake, or else the boss will have our guts for garters.

The clock read 10.31 when we finally reached the foyer, just in time to see the back end of the team bus as it drove off in the direction of a local park. I groaned and held my head in my hands, wondering whether my own journey further and further down Shit Street was ever going to come to an end. Giddy remained as calm as you like, though, turning to me and saying 'don't worry, Lakey, I'll f***in' sort this, the bastards.'

We were still mooching around the reception area when the coach party returned an hour later.

'All the best, la',' chortled Steve Redmond as he and the rest of the team filed past us, trailed by a furious-looking Mel Machin. The manager marched over and, just as he was about to dole out a spectacular bollocking, in leapt Giddy.

'I want a f***in' word with you,' he growled, taking the wind right out of Mel's sails. 'In private, away from the lads, right now.'

Startled, he followed us into the hotel lounge and, as the door shut behind us, Giddy started.

'How f***in' *dare* you drive off without us?' was his opening salvo, which he followed up with a heart-rending story about how his missus had been seriously ill for the past week, how he'd had a sleepless night worrying about her and how he'd spent ages comforting her on the phone after breakfast, hence our late arrival for the bus.

'And as for him,' said Giddy, gesturing in my direction,

'this poor lad has done f*** all wrong, other than wanting some fish and chips last night and waiting around for me this morning. And I'll tell you this for nothing, Gaffer; if you think that me and Lakey are going to play for *you* today, you can f***in' think again.'

At which point I nearly wet my pants.

Thanks to Giddy's tissue of whoppers, though, not only did Mel immediately and profusely apologise to the pair of us, but he also agreed not to take things further. Our names remained on the team sheet and, with the air cleared and our arses saved, both Giddy and I played our part in beating Swindon 4–3 later that day.

I never got another chance to room with the long-haired livewire from Liverpool as Giddy moved to Stoke City at the end of the season. Though I've never seen or heard from him since, I'll never forget the mischievous wink that he gave me as we boarded the coach back home.

By the beginning of November 1987, City were firmly wedged mid-table in the Second Division. Our progress was being hampered by patchy, unpredictable form which led to victories over Leicester City and Bradford City being cancelled out by defeats by Hull City and Ipswich Town. A lack of goals wasn't the problem; even I managed to score one away at Valley Parade. It was our shaky, leaky defending that was clearly letting the side down.

In the circumstances, the 20,000 or so supporters who headed for Maine Road on Saturday 7 November for City versus Huddersfield Town probably wouldn't have been bursting with excitement. We certainly hadn't been setting the world alight and Malcolm Macdonald's men were down in the Second Division doldrums, so a mass feeling of apathy amongst our fans would have been more than understandable.

The match started off as a tight, tense and evenly matched affair until Neil McNab broke the deadlock in the 12th minute with a scorching left-foot strike. The players embraced our number 10 while the home fans celebrated in the stands, none of us possibly knowing that we were on the verge of one of City's most celebrated scorelines. Neily's netbuster had effectively opened the floodgates, and by the interval we were 4–0, courtesy of further goals from Paul Stewart, Tony Adcock and David White. The fans enjoying their half-time Bovril must have been delighted with proceedings. However, I wouldn't have blamed any of them having a flutter on a score draw at one of the nearby betting stands, such was our inconsistency at that time.

As it happened, anyone waging a tenner on a 10–1 thrashing would have collected a tidy little windfall. The second half was the most one-sided 45 minutes that I've ever played in, a masterclass of neat passing, sublime touches, blistering pace and superb finishing. Huddersfield simply crumbled under the pressure, unable to withstand the onslaught from a City team on fire. Eric Nixon in goal was rarely troubled but remained steadfast. Ahead of him, Reddo and Giddy kept us rock-solid in defence. Further upfield,

Paul Simpson was our chief linchpin, controlling the midfield brilliantly and acting as provider extraordinaire. And spearheading the attack was our top-notch trio of White (great pace), Stewart (great power) and Adcock (great touch), whose well-deserved hat-tricks helped us coast our way to double figures. As the match neared its conclusion, a chant of 'we want 11' rang out from the Kippax Stand.

I felt awful for our opponents as the final whistle blew. It was great to participate in such an exhilarating goal rush, but I didn't enjoy witnessing the humiliation of fellow professionals. The Huddersfield players seemed utterly shell-shocked as they traipsed off the pitch – goalkeeper Brian Cox looked inconsolable – and their post-match changing room must have had all the atmosphere of your average funeral parlour. I remember City's commercial manager, Geoff Durbin (a man rarely lost for words) admitting he didn't know what the hell to say to his ashen-faced Huddersfield counterpart when they met up after the game.

In contrast, the travelling Terriers fans seemed to have an absolute blast, celebrating wildly when Andy May – City's former midfielder – converted their consolation penalty, and doing the conga around the Platt Lane Stand when we notched up our tenth.

Our goalfest dominated the back pages the next day. PERFECT 10 and BLUES BLAZE TO 10–1 WIN boomed the headlines, with most newspapers featuring a photo of our hat-trick heroes gripping the lucky match ball. The club took full advantage of our feat by rushing out in the space of a week a commemorative 10–1 video to flog in the souvenir shop. And, with our confidence buoyed, three days later we thrashed Plymouth 6–2 in the first round of the Simod Cup, and went on to clinch consecutive wins against Reading, Watford and Birmingham City.

The Watford game, a fourth-round Littlewoods Cup tie, was a turning point in my career. We'd convincingly beat the Hornets 3–1, and it had proved to be one of those Midas touch matches in which everything had seemed to go right for me. Neily and I had dictated the midfield throughout, and I'd capped off an accomplished performance by skinning two Watford defenders, sidestepping the keeper and laying on Whitey's second goal.

In the days that followed, many nice things were written about me in the media. I'd been used to receiving a moderate amount of attention from the *Denton Reporter* and the *Manchester Evening News*, but attracting rave reviews in the national press was a different kettle of fish altogether. Seeing my name headlined in Dad's *Sunday Mirror* and reading the legendary Malcolm Allison describe me as 'the big talent at Maine Road' in the *Daily Express* was a bit bizarre, to be honest, but nice all the same.

Before long, stories began to circulate that City's youngsters were attracting the attention of the country's top clubs. One article, headed THE BARNES BABES, featured photographs of me, Bob Brightwell, David White, Steve Redmond and Paul Simpson with price tags slapped onto our foreheads – I was valued highest at £600,000 – and rumour had it that Liverpool boss Kenny Dalglish and his Spurs counterpart, Terry Venables, were making undercover scouting missions to check us out. Although very flattering, this paper talk never distracted me. I was blissfully happy with my lot at Maine Road, and fleeing the nest was the last thing on my mind.

Mr Dalglish got another chance to watch us at Maine Road (this time without his Groucho Marx disguise) when, later that season, we were paired up against Liverpool in the quarter-final of the FA Cup. It had been quite an eventful journey to the last eight, not least the fourth-round tie against Blackpool at Bloomfield Road in which I scored the flukiest goal of my career, an injury-time equaliser that earned us a home replay. I remember bustling in the ball through a muddy scrum of players, and somehow managing to squeeze it between a defender and the post from five yards out.

There were scenes of confusion after the final whistle as a couple of my team-mates tried to claim that theirs had been the final touch, not mine. I was having none of it, though. Goals for me were rarer than golden nuggets, and I wasn't having this one nicked right from under my nose. I stated my case in the simplest terms possible ('Oi! I f***in' scored that!') until the cheeky sods agreed that my name should go down as the goalscorer.

Back in the 1980s, sometimes the only way a scrambled goal could be accredited (especially if the referee's view had been obscured) was by relying on good old-fashioned player honesty. Before BSkyB entered the sporting fray, there weren't any zoom-lens cameras tracking us from every angle. Without the benefit of close-ups and instant replays (and before the days of names on shirts to aid identification) it would often boil down to a team-mate saying 'yep, it was me,' or admitting 'nah, it was him,' to determine the goalscorer.

Sadly but inevitably, Liverpool snuffed out our FA Cup dreams by trouncing us 4–0 at Maine Road. My misery was compounded by a controversial penalty decision early in the second half. Craig Johnston – a brilliant player who possessed whippet-like pace and a poodle-perm hairdo – had launched yet another Liverpool counter-attack. As he penetrated the penalty area I'd managed to get my foot in front of him and hook the ball away, but in doing so my flailing arm had inadvertently knocked into the small of his back. Johnston fell to the ground as if he'd been shot, the referee pointed to the penalty spot, and Peter Beardsley calmly slotted it past our on-loan goalie, Mike Stowell, to make it 2–0. It was pretty much game over from then on. Despite our young, fit and competitive side being well up for the challenge, we were never realistically going to claw back a two-goal deficit against the Team of the Decade.

But I learned a lot that day. I learned how it felt to play against a side who knew instinctively how to keep the ball, who were incredibly economical with their passing, who knew how to frustrate their opponents, and who were capable of changing the tempo of the game in an instant. I learned the importance of having experience in your team, with old heads like Alan Hansen and Mark Lawrenson displaying the know-how to absorb early pressure and slowly take control of a game. I learned that, to stand a chance against freakishly talented maestros such as John Barnes and Peter Beardsley, I'd have to be 100 per cent on top of my game, since any slip-up would be punished. I learned that there was a huge gap between the First and Second Divisions, and that we needed to get our act together, big time, in order to secure promotion.

Aside from the penalty fiasco, I felt that I'd done okay against Liverpool, and a variety of pundits and pressmen appeared to agree. It seemed that my reputation was growing and my stock was rising – borne out by a Barclays Young Eagle award in January 1988 – but thankfully I could always rely on the City fans to keep my feet on the ground and my head out of the clouds.

Recovering from a bout of 'flu, I was sidelined for the game against Reading on Easter Monday. I wrapped myself up and went to watch my team-mates in action, opting (for purely nostalgic reasons) to sit in the Main Stand instead of schmoozing with the suited-and-booted in a hospitality lounge. As the teams kicked off, I climbed the steps to the rear of H Block and was met with a few friendly greetings of 'All right, Lakey,' as I squeezed past the line of City fans' laps to reach a spare seat.

It wasn't the greatest of games, and the natives were starting to get a little restless as half-time approached. Sitting right in front of me was a white-haired old fella who, whenever a City attack broke down, muttered angrily to himself and whacked his knee with a rolled-up programme. After one particularly wayward pass he threw his paper baton to the floor in frustration, pointed at the home dugout and yelled, 'Get Lake off, Machin! Get bloody Lake off! The lad's crap!' As the fans either side of me stifled their giggles, I tapped Old Man Steptoe on the shoulder.

'I *am* off, mate,' I said.

He turned around, squinted at me, glanced back at the pitch, and turned around again.

'Blimey, that's the fastest you've moved all bloody season,' he said, before muttering something about getting confused with all the young players that were on City's books these days. Showing more front than Blackpool, he then asked me to sign his battered programme. It was the least I could do, considering that he'd given me one of the biggest laughs in ages.

It was an anti-climactic end to the 1987–88 campaign. Our inconsistent form and concentration lapses had scuppered any chance of promotion, and we finished a disappointing but deserved ninth in the table. I was also forced to miss the last three games of the season due to a nasty injury sustained against Bradford City, when some lumbering muppet had stamped on my right knee and damaged my medial ligament. It could have been worse – at least I hadn't broken my leg – but it still meant having to undergo surgery in Manchester to repair the damage, followed by a three-month block of physiotherapy at the National Sports Rehabilitation Centre based in Lilleshall, Shropshire.

To add insult to injury, I'd had no option but to withdraw from two England under-21 matches – I'd been selected to play against Italy and Sweden – and had to sit out City's summer tours to Australia and Scandinavia. This pissed me off no end. In between my treatments I could be found either moping around the gardens listening to The Smiths on my Discman, nursing a lukewarm coffee at the bar or watching Lilleshall-based Desmond Douglas practise his table tennis skills.

The most exciting moment of my stay in Shropshire was witnessing TV babe Anneka Rice jump from a helicopter onto our practice pitch during a speed session. Wearing a much appreciated skin-tight catsuit, she ran off in hot pursuit of a magic clue for Channel 4's *Treasure Hunt* game show.

Lilleshall, for all its downsides, was the best place for me to focus on my fitness and rehab. As well as being a distraction-free zone (apart from Anneka's peachy buttocks) it also boasted the best physiotherapy team in the country. I was lucky enough to be under the supervision of Grant Downey and Phil Newton, two fantastic physios. While treating my troublesome knee, Grant offered me his considered opinion.

'Lakey, I don't think it's just your medial ligament,' he said, furrowing his brow. 'I think you may have slightly tweaked your cruciate ligament as well, mate.'

It was a prophetic statement. Grant and Phil had identified instabilities in my knee that should have, in hindsight, been picked up, addressed and remedied at the time of surgery. Unbeknownst to me that day, this would be the first of many trips to Lilleshall.

Fortunately my summer toils paid off, and I was fit enough to report for duty at the start of the 1988–89 league campaign. As well as hooking up with my old pals at Maine Road, it was nice to meet some new faces, notably Andy Dibble, Brian Gayle, Wayne Biggins and Nigel Gleghorn.

As with all new set-ups, it took a good few weeks for us to gel as a team. Our first home game of the season ended in a humiliating 4–1 defeat by Oldham Athletic, a match which I can safely say was one of my worst ever performances in a blue shirt. I had an absolute stinker. Despite scoring our only goal, I was at fault for two of our opponents' and had to apologise to everyone in the post-match dressing room for the foolish risks and the blind back passes of which I'd been guilty. I like to think that one of the strengths of my game was my ability to learn from my mistakes; I know I definitely did that day.

September, thankfully, was a more consistent month, and we found ourselves edging towards the top half of the table after a five-game winning streak that included a 3–1 defeat of promotion favourites Chelsea. Our good form continued into 1989, the first two months of the year seeing us undefeated in the League.

The game against Hull City on 21 January was a particularly memorable experience for me, thanks to the presence of one of football's most notorious hard-men. Billy

Whitehurst, the Tigers' centre-forward, was a 6-foot man-mountain who looked like he could burst a ball with his fist, let alone his boot. He was a guy you really didn't want to mess with.

The match was about five minutes old when I won a clean header. As I did so, however, I drew my elbows back for leverage and felt them connect, as hard as is humanly possible, with the bridge of another player's nose. When I looked over, to my horror I realised that the victim was none other than William Whitehurst Esq. Oh Christ, I thought, anybody but that f***in' monster. I nervously glanced over to my centre-half partner, Brian Gayle, who just smiled, made the sign of the cross and jogged off.

Billy sank to his knees, holding his face for what seemed like an eternity as he tried to stem a nosebleed. He eventually regained his composure and the game restarted. However, as the resulting throw-in took place, I felt a presence at my left shoulder; someone literally breathing down my neck. I turned round to see Billy grinning menacingly at me, baring a set of bloodstained teeth.

'Well done, kid,' he growled, 'I like it rough.'

Damn right he did. Before the match was through my nemesis sought his revenge in every way possible, ripping my shorts, kneeing me in the groin, embedding his studs in my shin, thigh and temples and, for good measure, sinking his teeth hard into my shoulder, causing rivulets of blood to trickle down my arm. After the game – which we won 4–1 – Billy jogged over to shake my hand.

'Tougher than you look, aren't you?' he said, eyeing the enormous red stain seeping through my shirt. 'Oh, and sorry 'bout the little nibble, son.'

Apart from the odd bloodsucking footballer, my career was on an upward trajectory. Off the field things were looking good, too, as I'd started going out with a girl called Janine. We'd met in the Little B pub in Sale (a popular footballer's haunt at the time) and had hit it off immediately. So with a nice girlfriend, a few quid in the bank and a great future ahead of me, life was great. In fact, life was bloody fantastic. How would I have known that, within a few months, I'd be knocking at death's door?

I woke up dazed, confused and spread-eagled on a bed in Maine Road's first aid room. As I opened my eyes, a trio of women gradually came into focus – Mum, Janine and City's receptionist Libby – all with tears streaming down their faces. The first thought that entered my head was who's died?, and it was only when Mum wailed 'Thank God, we thought we'd lost you, love,' that I realised that the person they were crying over was *me*. And then, like some corny line in *Casualty*, I murmured, 'Where am I, Mum? What happened?'

What had happened was that, on Saturday 11 March 1989, I'd nearly popped my clogs in front of 20,000 people. It was during the first half of our game against Leicester City that I'd gone up to head away a corner, clashed heads with Paul Ramsey and hit the deck like a sack of spuds. Not only did the sheer impact knock me unconscious, but it also caused me to swallow my tongue. What followed next was five minutes of life-or-death drama, played out on the pitch in front of a hushed Maine Road crowd and captured in its entirety by the television cameras.

The TV footage (which I watched through my fingers a few days later) showed me lying there lifelessly for a few seconds before suddenly going into a violent spasm, my body squirming, my legs twitching, and my lips turning blue due to the lack of oxygen. A panicking Steve Redmond gestured madly to the physio Roy Bailey, yelling, 'Oh, f***ing hell . . . Roy, get here quick . . .' as I continued to convulse on the ground. It was all too sickening to watch for the other players, most of whom turned away looking decidedly green at the gills.

Roy sprinted onto the pitch with his medical bag and, assisted by the Leicester City physio, tried to clear my airway. You could have heard a pin drop, apparently; even big Helen stopped ringing her bell. Meanwhile, as crucial seconds ticked by, the club doctor, Norman Luft, frantically pushed his way to the pitch from his seat in the directors' box. Dr Luft arrived just in time to give Roy some vital guidance, helping him to hook out my lolling tongue with a pair of bandage scissors. I remained unconscious the whole time.

Mum and Dad were watching the events unfold from the Main Stand that day, and I can only imagine what must have been going through their minds. I found out after that Mum instantly knew that something was seriously wrong, and she remembers screaming at the top of her voice for someone to come to my aid, and quick. Desperate to reach me, she managed to fight her way down to the advertising hoardings before being shepherded to the first aid room by a steward. My dad was frozen with shock and remained rooted to his seat, and it was only when I was stretchered off the pitch, to a backdrop of thunderous applause from the City fans, that he went to find his wife and son.

Many supporters have since told me that the atmosphere in the stadium was really eerie once I'd exited the pitch. No one knew whether I was out for the count or in the clear – dead or alive, even – and as a result many fans were too distracted to give much attention to the outcome of the game (the final score was 4–2 to City, incidentally, with Trevor Morley scoring his first hat-trick for the club).

Thankfully, I came round just before half-time. This was good news for two reasons. Firstly, I hadn't kicked the bucket; and secondly, had I not made such a swift recovery, the game might well have been abandoned at the interval with City heading for an important win. (This was corroborated when I bumped into that day's referee, Ron Bridges, at the City of Manchester Stadium a few years ago. He told me that both captains had agreed not to bring their teams out until they knew for sure that I'd regained consciousness.)

I vaguely remember lying in the emergency ambulance and seeing Dad hovering above me, ordering me not to speak or move my head and telling me that I was being taken to hospital for tests and brain scans. Luckily the results came back clear, and by the next morning I was sitting up in bed in pretty good spirits (or 'joking with the nurses', as they say in the papers). The only after-effect of the previous day's shenanigans was a banging headache. I couldn't recall anything of the incident – a blessing, I suppose – and listened open-mouthed as Mum and Dad gave me a blow-by-blow account of the whole frightening episode.

I was swamped with cards and flowers from friends, fans and well-wishers, and remember feeling incredibly touched by the hundreds of heartfelt messages. The following Monday I also received a visit from a noisy entourage of team-mates. Among them was Trevor Morley, who handed me a gigantic card in a shiny silver envelope.

'I'm glad you're on the mend,' Trev had scrawled inside, 'and thanks for overshadowing my first City hat-trick, you selfish bastard.'

In the aftermath of my tongue-swallowing, Mum was deluged with media requests for interviews. She readily obliged, revealing to a procession of reporters how relieved she felt that her son was still alive and kicking, and how grateful she was to Norman Luft and Roy Bailey for getting me out of danger. She also seized upon the opportunity to urge football clubs to improve club doctors' access to the field of play by installing them in the dugout rather than high up in the directors' box, thus avoiding a repeat of Dr Luft's worryingly long delay in reaching the pitch.

It seems that Mum's mini-crusade helped sway opinion, as shortly afterwards the FA tightened their guidelines, decreeing it mandatory for all club doctors to be at pitch-side. I wasn't the only tongue-swallowing casualty in football

– something similar had happened to Bryan Robson earlier that season – but I think it was my particular case, followed by Mrs Lake's one-woman media campaign that spurred them into action.

I will, of course, remain eternally grateful to the medical team for saving my life that day, because that's what they did when all's said and done.

'The boy didn't have much time left . . .' admitted Dr Luft to the media shortly afterwards, acknowledging the severity of the situation. I know the incident traumatised Roy in particular – he broke down in tears during the post-match press conference – but he can take comfort in the knowledge that, thanks to his cool head and prompt actions that day, I'm still here to tell the tale.

Life's fragility was highlighted for me again when, a few weeks later, the dreadful events at Hillsborough unfolded. I was resting at home that day – a groin strain had put me out of contention for City's game at Blackburn on 15 April 1989 – and I vividly remember the feeling of deep shock as the news filtered through from Sheffield.

On the 20th anniversary of the disaster, I sat down with my eldest son, Zac, to watch a special BBC documentary about that fateful day. As moving as it was harrowing, the film was a sober reminder of how the beautiful game can seem trivial in the face of such appalling human tragedy. And how a near-death experience like mine can fade into insignificance when compared with the horror of 96 lives lost.

4

24-hour Party People

Like most footballers, I enjoyed relaxing with a few drinks after a game. I was never what you'd call a party animal, though, so no weekend benders or dentist-chair games for me; a few bevvies in my local rounded off with a trip to a nearby nightclub was about as wild as it got.

Whenever we had a Saturday match, most of us would do the right thing and steer clear of alcohol from Wednesday onwards. Being more of a weekend drinker, I never found it a problem. This wasn't the case for one or two of my colleagues, though, who'd find it really hard to stay off the booze and would occasionally risk a couple of midweek pints. It was something that you could get away with if you pulled your tripe out at Platt Lane the next morning, and put in a good performance the following match day. But if there were ever any tell-tale signs of lethargy during a keep-ball session, or if your form dipped over the weekend, questions would be asked about those sneaky beers in the Crown that a mate of the gaffer's had just happened to witness.

Our food intake was less of an issue. In my day, football clubs didn't have a platoon of nutritionists and sports scientists to dish out dietary advice (being told by the physio to avoid curry and chips on a Friday night was as scientific as it got) and we were generally at liberty to eat what we liked. What's more, the absence of a canteen at Maine Road meant that the City players would usually grab their post-training lunch from one of the fast-food joints dotted around Moss Side and Rusholme. Jason Beckford and I would regularly queue up for Jamaican patties from Alvino's on Great Western Street which, delicious though they were, would have sent any dietician running for their calorie counter.

Since the club didn't have the facilities to allow us to dine together, our pre-match meal would be whatever we decided to knock up for ourselves at home. In fact, we only ever ate en masse when we stayed overnight at a hotel before an away game, and even then we'd have a pretty free rein on the menu, tucking into huge mixed grills and gulping down mugs of builder's tea. English football clubs hadn't yet cottoned on to continental-style health regimes and, as far as they were concerned, food was merely fuel. At City, anyway, the rationale seemed to be the more meat protein you could shovel down, the better. I remember, prior to a match at Ipswich, struggling my way through a leathery steak and finding myself still gnawing on a lump of gristle at half-time.

I'd always make amends for my midweek abstinence every Saturday and Sunday night, though. After a home game I'd honour my post-match commitments of socialising with opponents in the players' lounge and chatting to sponsors in the executive suites, but would do my utmost to be out of the club by 6.30 p.m. so that I could be in the Fletchers Arms in Denton within the hour. There I'd meet up with Kevin the plasterer, Carl the painter, John the policeman, Jason the footballer and my brother Mike and his pals. After wetting our whistles with bottles of Sol we'd hail a taxi to one of the region's many nightclubs, where I'd occasionally bump into some of my City team-mates.

I suppose I had a split personality when it came to clubbing. Some Saturday nights would find me donning a smart suit and tie and schmoozing down to suburban 'nitespots' with names like Quaffers, Smokies and Yesterdays. In stark contrast, the following week would see me pulling on my baggy Joe Bloggs jeans and smiley-face T-shirt, and sauntering into Manchester city centre to hang out at rave joints like the Venue or the Haçienda.

Of the more mainstream, out-of-town nightclubs, the best of the bunch was definitely Fridays in Didsbury. It got my vote because it offered its punters the option of three differently themed dance rooms, each with its own specific play list. This musical apartheid meant that you could shoulder-shimmy to Orange Juice on the middle indie dance floor, thus avoiding Public Enemy in the R&B/hip-hop room to your left and Sister Sledge in the disco/chart room to your right.

Cheesy though it was, I had some great times at Fridays. I can still picture Jason commandeering the dance floor with his MC Hammer routine, and John making us fall about with his spookily accurate Rick Astley take-offs. One of my favourite Fridays' moments, however, involved Andy 'The Cat' Dibble, City's larger-than-life goalkeeper.

One summer night in 1990, Jason, Andy and I had decided to treat our respective girlfriends to a 'Dine 'n' Disco', a deal which got you a three-course meal and entry into the club for less than £20. It had been only a few weeks since Andy's infamous howler at the City Ground – featured in most Football Bloopers DVDs – that saw Nottingham Forest's Gary Crosby mischievously heading the ball out of our goalie's hands to score one of the cheekiest goals in sporting history.

After ordering our food from the waitress, the lads and I strode up to the bar to get the drinks in. A couple of City fans were supping their pints when we got there and, after a friendly chat, one of them offered to buy us a round, which we gratefully accepted. He duly handed Jason and me our bottles of Stella but, just as he was about to give Andy his, paused for a moment, balanced the bottle on the palm of his hand and nudged it with his forehead *à la* Gary Crosby.

'Eh, does this ring a bell, Andy?' he grinned, as Jase and I collapsed in hysterics at the sheer audacity of it all. The Cat didn't see the funny side of this cheeky *Phoenix from the Flames* re-enactment, however, and loudly told the fan that he was bang out of order, or words to that effect. Hearing raised voices, a posse of brawny bouncers suddenly appeared out of nowhere, yanked the three of us by our collars and bundled us out of the front door. Andy's attempts at an explanation fell on deaf ears, and we all had to skulk off to a nearby pub to wait for the girls as they polished off their double portions of chicken-in-a-basket.

'Cheeky bastards, those fans,' said Andy as we got another round of drinks in. 'Don't think I'll ever live that Crosby thing down, will I?'

Fridays would always be packed to the rafters with pretty girls, but copping off with someone was never the be all and end all for me. Sad as it sounds, I loved a good dance more than anything else, and often couldn't be bothered with the whole chatting up rigmarole. In my younger days I was a bit awkward with the ladies – I improved with age – unlike my more confident mates who would hold court on a shiny leather sofa with a lurid cocktail in their hand and a giggly girl on their lap.

Knowing full well that it added to their magnetism, some of the City lads would openly flaunt their footballer status. It was something that I never felt comfortable with, though. I was not one to give it the big 'I am' and I only ever owned up to being a City player if a third party happened to mention the fact. Inevitably, though, you'd get female groupies latching on to you just for the supposed prestige of copping off with a footballer. I remember getting it together with one such girl, a very well-to-do City fan from Wilmslow. She was stunning, with hair down to her waist and legs up to her armpits, and I couldn't believe my luck when she made a play for me one night. The relationship was short-lived, however; I had to give her the old heave-ho when she uttered the immortal line 'we must do brunch, Paul, darling; I'll fax you.' Somehow I don't think a Cheshire yuppie would have gone down a storm in Denton. Besides, I didn't have a fax machine.

Then there were the jealous boyfriends to contend with. You'd only need to glance at a girl in a bar (or vice versa) for some Rottweiler of a fiancé to skulk out of the shadows and start giving you daggers. Quite literally, as it happened, as I once had a knife pulled out on me in the Puss in Boots pub in Stockport because some half-wit United fan mistakenly thought I was hitting on his girlfriend.

Have-a-go headbangers came with the territory when you were a semi-famous footballer. I remember celebrating my 24th birthday in a club in Sale and being violently attacked by a bouncer who, from out of nowhere, grabbed me by the throat and accused me of swearing at one of the bar staff. Total bullshit, of course, but he'd obviously identified me as some kind of big-time Charlie who needed roughing up and turfing out. The next day, nursing a badly bruised neck and barely able to speak, I received a call from a deeply apologetic nightclub boss who informed me that he'd sacked the bouncer in question and wanted to offer me free entry and drinks on the house when I next visited. As if I was going to show my face in there again.

The following Monday, however, as I was getting changed

after training, a team-mate gave me the glad tidings that there was a slightly peeved bouncer waiting for me in the car park. I didn't fancy the idea of my teeth being rammed down my black 'n' blue throat, so I spent most of the afternoon barricaded in one of the admin offices. I only dared to venture out once Colin the Barbarian had got bored and finally driven away in his Ford Transit, thankfully never to be seen again.

It wasn't the only occasion I'd had a run-in with bouncers – they're not always the easiest people to warm to, let's face it – and many Saturday nights out were almost ruined because of their crap attitude. Many of my friends were black – including Jason and his brother, Darren, who'd also played for Manchester City – and they'd often have huge problems getting into certain clubs. Unlike the white lads among us who, oddly enough, would rarely encounter such trouble.

'Not tonight, lads,' became an all too familiar spiel as admission would be denied for such phony reasons as having the wrong haircut or wearing the wrong shoes.

'Mate, I'm a painter and decorator with a wife and four kids,' protested my pal Carl when one of these bully boys took exception to his shaven head, implying that he was some hardened Moss Side gangster. They would relent once they realised a few of us were footballers – that's how shallow they were – and would reluctantly usher us through.

By rights we should have told these meat-heads where to shove their poxy clubs but, if I'm honest, in those days we were more bothered about pursuing some after-hours drinking and dancing than storming off home as a matter of principle. But it always left a sour taste in my mouth. There were far too many venues in Cheshire and South Manchester that employed DJs to play wall-to-wall black music like soul and Motown yet – totally oblivious to the irony – hired door staff to treat non-white people like outcasts. Racism, I'm sorry to say, was alive and well in suburbia.

The quickest way to sober up on a Sunday morning, I discovered, was the realisation that I had to be at a Junior Blues' meeting by 10 a.m. After a heavy night on the town, nothing instilled greater dread than the knowledge that, in an hour's time I'd be dressed as a chicken and doing the 'Birdie Song' in front of 200 kids at City's Social Club.

One of Maine Road's oldest and most respected institutions, the Junior Blues was established in the early 1970s with the aim of nurturing thousands of young supporters. Babies born into true blue families would often be enrolled before they left the maternity ward – sometimes just minutes after Dad had cut the cord – and for the next 16 years little Johnny or Julie would qualify for discounted tickets, behind-the-scenes tours, regular glossy magazines and entry to the monthly Sunday-morning get-togethers. The organisation blazed a trail for junior supporters' clubs and was rightly held in great esteem by chairman Peter Swales, so much so that he'd insist on five or six players attending each meeting. He rarely forsook his Sunday-morning brekkie in bed to come himself, though. Funny, that.

These player appearances were managed on a strict rota basis, with the big-name stars required to turn up to two or three meetings per season and the younger lads about four or five. Attendance was compulsory (any no-shows would receive a hefty fine) even for those players who routinely went home to Scotland or the Midlands after a game. If these fellas were ever earmarked for JB's duty they'd have to get up at the crack of dawn on a Sunday morning, no doubt cursing those pesky kids as they hit the road at sunrise.

If truth be told, I found these Sunday-morning gatherings an ordeal in my younger, more self-conscious days, although I changed my attitude a little as I got older, one day even becoming the organisation's president. Meeting and greeting a roomful of Junior Blues and their parents wasn't the problem. It was more the fact that every single player was coerced into taking part in the on-stage entertainment, which could be anything from a song and dance number to a 'comedy' routine. I'd much rather have sat through a sermon at nearby St Crispin's than make such a public tit of myself, but I really had no choice in the matter.

I was always a bag of nerves backstage, petrified at what lay in wait for me on the other side of the velvet curtain. I remember once having to perform the actions to that god-awful 'Music Man' song, playing an imaginary pia-pia-piano while Andy May pretended to bang on a big bass drum and Mark Lillis did a half-hearted trombonist impression (just look at what you missed out on, Giggsy).

As the kids pelted us with Chewits and their parents

laughed and pointed I died a thousand deaths inside, counting down the minutes until I could flee to the refuge of my Escort. And what made it worse was that the Social Club's stage lights were more like sun lamps. Sub-tropical heat was the last thing you needed when you were hungover, and I'd stand there, sweaty and nauseous, frightened to death that I was going to vomit over the Dawson family in the front row.

At least I never had to pretend to be a ventriloquist's dummy on stage, unlike poor Jim Tolmie, a City striker from the mid-1980s and one of the shyest blokes you could ever meet. I remember the wee Scot being forced to sit on some old fella's knee, who then proceeded to shove his arm up his jumper and jerk him to-and-fro like a Ray Allan and Lord Charles tribute act. I seriously thought Jim was going to burst into tears at one point.

In direct contrast, though, you'd get some of the more extrovert players who would quite happily perform their party pieces under the spotlight, like Earl Barrett who wowed the kids with his body-popping and his Michael Jackson moonwalk as part of the annual Junior Blues' pantomime. I managed to wriggle out of a solo performance that Christmas, convincing the director that my recital of Pam Ayres's 'Oh I Wish I'd Looked After Me Teeth' probably wouldn't bring the house down.

When it came to Manchester's cluster of rave clubs, the Haçienda was beyond compare. Spearheaded by Factory Records boss Tony Wilson and bankrolled by the band New

Order, the Haç had been a fixture since 1982 – Madonna performed her first ever British gig there – and had transformed the city's clubbing scene by offering an alternative to grotty student dives and grab-a-granny nights. However, it wasn't until the explosion of the so-called 'Madchester' music scene in the late 1980s that it truly came to the fore.

I was a regular there during the so-called 'Second Summer of Love', a period straddling 1988 and 1989 in which the city of Manchester became the place to be. You couldn't turn on MTV or flick through *The Face* without seeing scowling Manc bands sporting baggy jeans, floppy hats and 'curtains' fringes. I remember watching that infamous November 1989 edition of *Top of the Pops* when both the Roses and the Mondays made their debuts, a wild-eyed Ian Brown swaggering around to 'Fools Gold' and a bog-eyed Shaun Ryder staggering about to 'Hallelujah'. Both bands had been introduced by Jenny Powell and Jakki Brambles, two squeaky-clean hosts who, judging by their bewildered expressions, hadn't had much previous contact with drug-ravaged Mancunians. You could see the relief on their faces when those nice boys from the Fine Young Cannibals took to the stage with their short haircuts and neatly pressed chinos.

People who'd once looked down on England's second city were now looking north for inspiration. Our music revolution had blown apart all the stereotypes of a city defined by *Coronation Street*, spindly men with whippets, dark satanic mills and podgy northern comedians. It was Mancunians, not Londoners, who were now setting the pace, with our friends in the south having to contend with the focus shifting elsewhere for a change.

For me, being in the middle of all this was thrilling, and I had a real sense of being in the right place at the right time. Not only was I living and clubbing in the coolest city in the world, I was also privileged enough to be playing for one of its football teams. The fact that I was realising the dream of thousands of young Mancunians made me cherish my charmed existence all the more. To echo the local buzz-word of the day, I was well and truly *sorted*.

On a Saturday night, the queue outside the Haçienda snaked all the way down Whitworth Street, all sharing the common desire to get waved through by the notoriously discerning bouncers. Occasionally, though, one of the doormen would spot me in the queue and beckon me over.

'What are you queuing for, Lakey man? Grab yer mates and I'll walk you all straight in.'

This blatant queue hopping used to make me cringe, but my mates would lap it up.

'This can't be bad,' they'd say as we waltzed to the front to a chorus of tuts. 'The Red Stripes are on us, big fella . . .'

The Haçienda's interior was awesome, modelled as it was on a huge industrial warehouse complete with steel girders and stark lighting. But the thing that really set it apart from the rest was the fact that you went there for the music. No lairy lads in shiny suits, no stiletto-shod girls dancing around handbags, just brilliant rave and retro tracks spun by brilliant DJs like Mike Pickering and Dave Haslam. Their sets would work up the throng of wide-eyed, Ecstasy-fuelled clubbers into a frenzy, and even though I didn't do drugs, I always had a blast. I can still conjure up memories of me and my mates going wild whenever A Guy Called Gerald's 'Voodoo Ray' came on. No other track better captured the mad-for-it mood at that time, and I still get goose-bumps whenever its intro booms out from my iPod.

Plenty of City fans hit the Haç on a Saturday, most of them giving me a quick nod and a 'hiya, Lakey' before letting me get on with my Bez-style freaky dancing. This was in direct contrast to the glitzier venues in town, where you'd spend the whole night being tailgated by supporters wanting to talk about that day's game or debate some dodgy refereeing decision. Don't get me wrong, I didn't mind bantering with fans at any other time of the week, but on a Saturday night I just wanted to chill out with my mates. At the Haç, there was no such circus. No one gave a toss that you were a footballer, and that's just how I liked it.

What really fascinated me about the Madchester club culture was its gradual infiltration of the City terraces. Suddenly, for a whole faction of fashion-conscious young Blues, going to the match was no longer just about football; it was also about the clothes and the attitude. As I pulled up to Maine Road on a match day I'd pass groups of lads and lasses walking down Lloyd Street dressed in their unisex uniforms of flared jeans, fishing hats and Kickers. From what I could see, the distinction between club wear and match day clobber was becoming blurred; what was being worn to the Venue on a Friday night was also being worn to the game the following day.

The effects of this cultural crossover meant that football tops, especially City shirts, became high-fashion items in their own right. Pre-Madchester, replica kits had largely been the preserve of diehard fans or football-crazy kids and weren't often seen away from the terraces. However, in the late 1980s they started cropping up in a variety of city-centre dance and indie clubs, as well as gracing the window displays of menswear style emporiums like Hurleys, near Piccadilly station.

Broadening the shirt's appeal was the parading of Blue allegiances by influential members of the Manchester music scene. A decade earlier it seemed that only middle-aged actors and comedians came out as City fans, but now the likes of The Smiths' Johnny Marr, The Stone Roses' Reni and The Cult's Billy Duffy were revealing their true colours.

Meanwhile, over in the Mancunian suburb of Burnage, two City-daft, music-mad brothers were lying in their bedrooms dreaming of fame and fortune. Within a couple of years their group, Oasis, would become the most successful rock 'n' roll band on the planet, and Noel and Liam Gallagher would be renowned as City's starriest fans. Their proud endorsement of the City shirt – donned in countless gigs and photoshoots around the world – would add massively to its kudos.

Mum and Dad's wedding day, 1955.

Left to right: David, me, Tracey and Michael, 1973. Fringes courtesy of Pyrex pudding bowls.

The St Mary's RC Primary School team at Wembley in June 1980, prior to the Smiths Crisps six-a-side final. I'm flanked by our manager, John Mercer, and the ex-Chelsea and Arsenal star John Hollins.

The victorious St Mary's side, together with silverware. The 'grass' that we're standing on was our home pitch, believe it or not.

Manchester City's feeder team, otherwise known as Blue Star FC. My team mates included Steve Redmond (top row, second left) and Andy Hinchcliffe (end of bottom row)

Celebrating in the dressing room after winning the FA Youth Cup in 1986. Our coaches, the great Tony 'Skip' Book and Glyn Pardoe, are in the background.

Reddo and I, in our YTS apprentice days, being put through our paces at City's Platt Lane training ground.

Home grown lads together. Left to right: Me, Andy Hinchcliffe, Ian 'Bob' Brightwell, Steve Redmond, David White and Paul Moulden.

Being stretchered off against Bradford in 1987. The start of all of my problems.

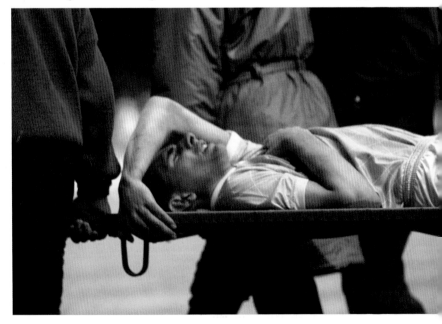

Denton's footballing Lake brothers. At that time I was playing for City, Michael for Macclesfield Town and David for semi-pro club Droylsden FC.

The Lakes en masse at my elder sister Susan's wedding.

The England under-21 XI, lining up in Albania, March 1989.
Back row, left to right: Me, Steve Bull, Stuart Ripley, Nigel Martyn, Paul Ince, David Burrows. Front: David Smith, Michael Thomas, Steve Chettle, Steve Redmond, Steve Sedgley.

My only appearance for the England 'B' side. It was always an honour to play for my country.

The tongue-swallowing incident of March 1989. You can see the players screaming for the club doctor as physio Roy Bailey tries to clear my airway.

Mum and Dad enjoying a night out.

With a pair of City mascots, Mark and Dan Thomas, before a home game at Maine Road.

Hoisting up Ian Bishop after goal three of our 5-1 rout of Manchester United. September 23rd 1989 was, without doubt, one of the best days of my life.

(*Left*) Here's my favourite ever City kit, worn when I was at the peak of my game…

…and here's my least favourite, worn just once against Arsenal in 1989. (*Right*)

Umbro's garish City away strips of the late 1980s – as opposed to the minimalist sky blue home shirts – became iconic clubbing tops in Manchester. Particularly coveted was the 1988 maroon-and-white striped design with the blue collar, as well as the plain maroon top that was produced two years later. Both had City sponsors Brother's name emblazoned on the front and both looked – to coin a slogan of the time – 'cool as f***' teamed up with jeans and Adidas Gazelles.

I had a real soft spot for the 1990 kit, probably because I'm sporting it in one of my favourite action photos. This shot – one of the few to adorn my walls at home – was taken during a pre-season game in Norway when I was at the peak of my career and playing the best football of my life. I look in tip-top condition, the kit looks classy as hell and, most importantly, my Shaun Ryder-style fringe looks the dog's bollocks.

In October 1989 City's infamous canary-yellow third kit was introduced, arguably the gaudiest City strip of all time. We wore it only once, away to Arsenal – they thrashed us 4–0 – and ran onto the pitch looking like Fyffes Bananas FC, to chants of 'are you Norwich in disguise?' and 'who the f***in' hell are you?' filling the stadium. Yet, while this custard-hued shirt looked hideous on the pitch, it would have made perfect clubbing wear for the smiley-face brigade at the Haçienda or in Ibiza. However, for some reason Umbro decided not to mass-produce it for the fans and by doing so, I reckon, missed a trick and lost out on a potential fortune. The 13 yellow City shirts worn at Highbury were the only ones ever to be manufactured, I gather, and have since become collector's items which go for a song on eBay. I didn't have the foresight to keep my top, unfortunately, so if someone's got the yellow one with the number 11, can I have it back please, mate?

There were other indications that the loved-up Madchester vibes were transmitting to Maine Road. I'm not saying that everyone in the Kippax was blowing whistles and popping Ecstasy, but there was a real sense of uninhibited fun among our supporters towards the end of the 1980s, in spite of the monotony of Second Division football. Nothing embodied this better than the infamous inflatable craze which, according to Manchester historian and author Gary James, caught on when a bloke called Frank Newton took the first inflatable banana to Oldham v City at the beginning of the 1987–88 season. No one really knows why; it was just one of those bizarre things that City fans did.

As the season progressed more bananas appeared, but it wasn't until the 1988–89 campaign that thousands of people began coming to matches armed with inflatables of all shapes and sizes, from hammers to beach balls, from giraffes to dinosaurs. During one match – I think it was away to West Brom – I remember spotting two huge Frankenstein's monsters having a fight in the City end. The crowd seemed more entertained by this inflatable boxing bout than by the game itself, singing 'Frankie, Frankie, give us a wave' and totally ignoring my team-mate Brian Gayle as he cleared his defensive lines.

The biggest love-in of all was, without doubt, the 1988 Boxing Day fixture at Stoke City. A group of City fans, heavily influenced by a City fanzine of the time, *Blue Print*, had decided to celebrate the festive season by going to the Victoria Ground in fancy dress, and the idea spread like wildfire. Costume hire shops were plundered, wives' wardrobes were ransacked, and City's diehards would yet again brighten up the football world with their unique brand of lunacy.

As our team coach drove up to the stadium that day it wasn't the usual sea of blue-shirted fans that parted for us; instead it was a swaying mob of Draculas, Nazis, Mr Blobbies, Mother Superiors, Tommy Coopers, pantomime horses, Bernie Clifton ostriches and lots of hairy cross-dressers. Total mayhem. The decision to stage a mass fancy-dress party in the Potteries was quite a brave one; Stoke could be a menacing town on a match day and, in the 1980s, was notorious for its special brand of 'hospitality' to visiting supporters.

In keeping with the party atmosphere, the club made us run out onto the pitch carrying our own inflatables to launch into the away end. We weren't exactly thrilled by the idea – I remember Neil McNab spewing out a stream of Scottish expletives when he was handed a huge blow-up banana – but we did as we were told.

If our woeful performance was anything to go by, it should have been us City players who turned up in fancy-dress costumes that day. Eleven clowns' outfits would have sufficed for the farce that culminated in a 3–1 defeat, a result which no doubt put a dampener on all the revelling on the terraces. There was a feeling of deep embarrassment on the team coach as we headed back up the M6, all of us lamenting our lacklustre display. Twelve thousand fabulous fans had gone to all that trouble to create a carnival atmosphere, yet our response had been to truly rain on their parade.

By the end of February 1989 we were topping the league, thanks to a purple patch of six consecutive wins with Wayne Biggins and Nigel Gleghorn scoring a lot of goals. Our comfy 11-point cushion made automatic promotion a distinct possibility but despite our lofty position we weren't donning the blinkers. We were very conscious that there were some tough games ahead and some decent sides waiting to knock us off our perch; fellow First Division wannabes such as Chelsea, West Brom and Crystal Palace all had the promised land in their sights and were ominously hitting form at the right time.

My comeback game after the tongue-swallowing trauma saw second-place Chelsea visiting Maine Road. A crowd of 40,000 – our biggest gate of the season – witnessed our team being totally out-thought by a side brimming with confidence and experience. Bobby Campbell's men fully deserved their eventual 3–2 victory and duly leapfrogged us to the top spot. Despite this setback, we managed to garner enough points during March and April to enable us to remain in automatic promotion contention. However, a dismal home defeat by underdogs Barnsley on 22 April caught us unawares, and in an instant the atmosphere in the dressing room changed from upbeat to downcast. It seemed that we were losing our nerve in the crucial final stages of the season, and questions started to be asked about our resolve. Any more points dropped like this and we were going to be in serious danger of missing out on a top-two place and – horror of horrors! – condemning ourselves to another season in the second tier.

A concerned gaffer and his assistant, John 'Dixie' Deehan, sought to allay any doubts and convened a post-training pow-wow, hammering it home to us that we really did have the willpower and firepower to haul ourselves up a division and that yes, we really were good enough to rub shoulders with Liverpool and Arsenal. With their battle cries ringing in our ears, the following Saturday we went down to the Manor Ground and demolished Oxford United, playing out a 4–2 victory to a backdrop of 'we're going up' chants from the away end. On the coach back home, Mel and Dixie did the maths and relayed the good news that all we needed to secure promotion was one win from three games. This was the psychological boost that we needed. It would take a collapse of monumental proportions to screw this one up, surely.

On the first day of May we came up against arch-rivals Crystal Palace who, now that Chelsea's champions' status had been sealed, were our sole challengers. Only two days earlier the gaffer had gently broken the news that he was giving me, as Brian Gayle's replacement in central defence, the responsibility of marking the great Ian Wright. (It was by no means the first time that my role had been shuffled around. I played in every outfield position during that 1988–89 campaign, and ended up wearing eight different shirt numbers in one season.)

Wrighty, with his incredible eye for goal, was the best attacker in the division, bar none. If the prospect of shadowing him wasn't daunting enough, his partner up front just happened to be the sublime Mark Bright. Not since the great Liverpool double-act of Kevin Keegan and John Toshack had two strikers displayed such telepathy. Steve Redmond and I had to psych ourselves up more than ever that day; it was our job to contain the league's deadliest duo and the outcome of the game was probably going to rest upon our shoulders.

For the most part we succeeded in putting the brakes on the Wright 'n' Bright roadshow, and by half-time we were 1–0 up. But, as is the case when you're up against top-class marksmen, you can't give them an inch, whether it's in the first minute, the 41st minute or the last minute. With only a quarter of an hour of the game remaining I made the fatal mistake of allowing Wrighty to peel off me. He was able to swivel and whack the ball into the top corner, past the outspread arms of makeshift goalie Nigel Gleghorn who, ten minutes before half-time, had been forced to replace an injured Andy Dibble between the sticks. Final score: 1–1.

I was furious after the game, punching the wall and

berating myself for being at fault for an equaliser that had caused us to drop two valuable points. It was Neil McNab who calmly sat me down and tried to put everything into perspective, telling me not to beat myself up about a daft yet uncharacteristic error.

'You had the better of a quality striker for most of the game, Lakey, and you've just got to learn from it.'

'But if I'd have kept a tighter check on Wrighty we'd be as good as up by now . . .'

'Listen, mate. You and Reddo kept their chances to pretty much one shot, and that was with Gleggy in nets, don't forget. Don't be too hard on yourself. I know you're feeling like shit. But use your anger as a positive, if you can. Do whatever it takes so you don't have to feel like this again.'

I managed to exorcise my demons in time for the following game against Bournemouth at Maine Road. An assured first-half performance was capped with a brace of goals from Paul Moulden and a poacher's strike from Trevor Morley. Our promotion was almost within touching distance, and so buoyant was our mood that we almost danced a Highland fling up the tunnel at half-time. Adding to our glee was the fact that the club had promised us an immediate, no-expense-spared holiday abroad if we were to secure the three points, and as such were prepared to field a second-string side for what would be a meaningless final game of the season.

As we back-slapped each other in the dressing room and mentally packed our suitcases, a typically low-key Mel Machin expressed caution and warned us against complacency. But then a mischievous grin played across his face as he informed us that he'd arranged for one of his pals to give us a quick motivational pep-talk. What do we need this for? We're three up, for chrissakes, I remember thinking, wondering which former colleague of the gaffer's was going to get wheeled out.

From the direction of Roy Bailey's physio room toddled Eddie Large, the Mancunian funnyman and City fanatic who, in those days, was a huge primetime TV star along with his weedy sidekick, 'Supersonic' Syd Little. What followed was the most surreal half-time team talk I've ever experienced. Eddie, wearing a shiny grey showbiz suit with rolled-up sleeves, proceeded to dole out individual advice to each of the players using his well-known repertoire of celebrity impersonations. So Deputy Dawg ordered me to keep tight in defence; Frank Carson told Neily to use the width and pace of Whitey; Cliff Richard advised Trevor Morley to shoot on sight; Harold Wilson told Bob Brightwell to keep it simple and Benny from *Crossroads* told Andy Dibble to stay awake.

If only the Cat had heeded Benny's advice. He conceded three goals in the second half (no thanks to a defensive horror show in the final ten minutes, and a Bournemouth midfielder by the name of Ian Bishop running rings round us) and the sure-fire win that we'd assumed at the interval finished up as a sorry score draw. Mel's mystifying decision to take off in-form Paul Moulden at the interval probably hadn't helped matters, but we were all to blame for a pathetic second-half display. After the match we sat in the changing rooms, dumbstruck, half expecting Eddie Large to come back in and do his Oliver Hardy impression.

'Well boys, that's another fine mess you've got yourselves into . . .'

I suppose we were just carrying on the time-honoured City tradition of doing things the hard way. Our hot 'n' cold, harum-scarum form meant that the significant lead we'd had weeks earlier had been whittled away and we were now in need of a single point from our last game to earn promotion. Our Day of Destiny – the away match against Bradford City on 13 May 1989 – loomed large. In true football lingo, it was going to the wire.

On the morning of the big match, I got out of bed at eight o'clock and made myself my regulation breakfast of scrambled eggs on toast, swilled down with a mug of PG Tips. On any other Saturday my mum would have been there to prepare the brekkie and pour the tea, but she and Dad had left for London in the early hours. My brother Mike was playing for Macclesfield Town in the final of the FA Challenge Trophy – against Telford United – and my parents had been faced with the awful dilemma of having to decide between watching me at Bradford or Mike at Wembley. The latter prevailed, of course. It wasn't every day that you got to see your son play in a Wembley cup final and I completely understood their decision.

'But we'll be keeping tabs on your game on the radio, son,' assured Dad. 'We're banking on a double celebration, aren't we, Sheila . . .'

Once I'd washed, dried and put away the dishes I went upstairs to read the *Daily Mirror* on the loo for 20 minutes. After a quick shower and a shave, I pressed my new Reiss suit (the threadbare Slaters suit had since walked itself down to my local Oxfam), polished my shoes, knotted my tie and carefully gelled my hair. Once I was all primped and preened I went outside to check the car's oil, water and petrol levels, my mind playing tricks as I envisioned the scenario of a breakdown causing me to miss the most important match of my life. DOZY LAKE'S NO SHOW screamed an imaginary newspaper headline as I checked the tyres for nails and the engine for a car bomb. I then returned indoors and re-polished my shoes, undid and re-knotted my tie and re-gelled my hair.

Nervous? *Me?*

All this OCD behaviour was an attempt to reduce any kind of thinking space which, for me, usually bred anxiety. Like most of my team-mates, I had far too much 'me time' for my own good. In a normal week, roughly 20 per cent of my daytime schedule would be devoted to playing or training, but the remainder would invariably be spent at home watching *Blackadder* videos, mooching around Manchester city centre or whiling away long, boring coach journeys.

It was during these periods of respite that I was more likely to mull things over and plague myself with worry and paranoia. Do the fans like me? Will we win on Saturday? Do the other lads respect me? Am I justifying my place? Does the manager rate me? Will I get back in the side if I get injured?

Will I have a nightmare game and have 30,000 supporters on my back? All these doom-laden thoughts often whirled around my head when I had just my Hitachi VHS toploader for company.

That morning I didn't want to give myself a chance to feel any such insecurity, hence all this unnecessary fannying around. Luckily, however, my nerves started to settle once I put the key in the ignition and reversed off the drive. As the engine revved up, so did I, it seemed.

'One last big effort, Lakey,' I declared out loud as I began the short journey to the Finglands coach depot in Rusholme. 'C'mon. C'mon. *C'mon!*' I yelled, slamming my palms against the steering wheel.

I climbed onto the Bradford-bound coach and took my seat near to Bob, Mouldy, Hinchy, Whitey and Gerry Taggart. Senior players including Neily, Trevor Morley and Gary Megson had taken their usual places at the back and were already guarding their poker hands. Mel, Dixie and the rest of the coaching staff occupied the front rows, along with a select band of journalists who were permitted to travel with us to matches.

The conversation may have been trivial (I remember Gerry and I chuckling at the infamous farm that stubbornly bisects the M62) but, beneath the surface it was very much a case of squeaky bums and churning stomachs. We were hours away from one of the most important games of our lives, a game that we *had* to win or draw since Crystal Palace were still very much in with a shout. The facts were simple. If we were to lose at Valley Parade, and Palace were able to beat a relegated, demoralised Birmingham City by a margin of four goals, we'd be doomed to the play-offs.

Of great comfort to the younger lads was the fact that Tony Book and Glyn Pardoe were travelling with us that day. Just their mere presence had a soothing effect. Usually involved with the reserves or youth team on a Saturday, my former mentors had been given special dispensation to accompany us on this journey and it was strangely relaxing to hear their friendly, familiar voices chatting about this, that and every-thing. The gaffer, like a Trappist monk, remained silent and contemplative the whole time. He'd spent the lead-up to the game talking tactics and lifting spirits and, as far as he was concerned, he'd said all that needed to be said.

'Stay focused, lads,' he'd stressed earlier that week, drumming into us the importance of remaining mentally strong and steadfast. 'I can't tell you how vital it is that you keep your mind on the game.'

That, as it transpired, was easier said than done as we made our way to Bradford. Maintaining a state of calm proved to be virtually impossible when all we could see out of the coach window was a convoy of Blues in full-blown party mode, with carfuls of fans honking their horns, hanging out of their windows, singing City songs and waving their blow-up toys. I remember seeing a Vauxhall Nova covered in inflatable fried eggs go racing by. Then a Chrysler Sunbeam with a quartet of rubber dolls pressed against each window. Followed by a Volvo estate with a tyrannosaurus rex strapped to the roof-rack. I'd never taken LSD but this was probably the closest thing to an acid trip I was ever likely to experience.

We did our damndest to remain poker-faced, many of us having to stifle snorts and giggles as this mad motorcade crawled by. The last thing we wanted to do was incur the manager's wrath on this most important of days. But only someone with a heart of stone and a sense of humour by-pass would have not chuckled at the sight of a grinning City fan sitting in a paddling pool on a pick-up truck. Whoever you are, mate, you made me spit my brew out all over Gerry Taggart.

Massive congestion problems near the Yorkshire border didn't help our concentration, either. At one point it didn't look as though we were going to make it in time for kick-off, and a police escort had to be dispatched to help Derek the driver worm his way through the traffic. Luckily this did the trick and, by 1.30 p.m., we were walking out into the warm spring sunshine to assess the Valley Parade pitch. It wasn't in the best condition, to put it mildly. We surveyed the dry, dusty and cratered surface with heavy hearts, knowing that it would severely hamper our usual brand of flowing attacking football.

Hovering around the tunnel area with a camera crew in tow was ex-City boss John Bond, who had been dispatched by Granada TV's *Kick Off* to report on the match. Mr Bond had spent the majority of the season slating us in the media and failing to recognise that his former club, on a shoestring budget and featuring a crop of youngsters, had done fantastically well to get to the verge of promotion. His scornful style of punditry hadn't made him many friends at Maine Road – only the night before he'd been on television saying that City's young players were nowhere near top-flight standard – and as a result his presence in Bradford that afternoon wasn't welcomed by us (or the City faithful, for that matter).

'I'm not doing an interview with that ****,' was the general consensus among the players, and we all proceeded to snub him as he waved his microphone in our direction.

'Er, lads, can I have a quick word?

'You can have two, John. F*** and Off.'

The City fans, as vociferous as ever, were packed behind the goal as we defended in the first half. Like many sides with nothing much to play for, a relaxed Bradford City started the brighter. There was no demob-happy, end-of-term party with this lot, though, especially with manager Terry Yorath and coach Norman Hunter – two famous winners – egging them on from the dugout. In contrast, we spent the opening minutes beset with nerves. In those early stages we were definitely guilty of thinking far too much about the result, instead of concentrating on the job in hand and heeding the gaffer's advice to approach it as just another game.

As we'd suspected, the pock-marked pitch didn't do us any favours, and the simplest passes ricocheted off the surface at random angles. It was one such dodgy divot that gave Bradford a lucky break in the 24th minute. Mark Ellis pinged a shot across the box, and one fluky bounce and six bobbles later the ball trickled over Paul Cooper's goal-line to make it 1–0. Strange though it may seem, this goal didn't send us into a flap; quite the reverse, in fact. It actually woke us up and galvanised us all into action. As half-time approached, we'd already seen several goalscoring chances go begging, with Nigel and Mouldy coming tantalisingly close. In the dressing room, an extraordinarily calm Mel Machin sat us down and, speaking in quiet, measured tones, told us to hold our nerve and not trouble ourselves with negative thoughts.

'It will come, lads,' he insisted. 'It will come.'

The ensuing second half was like the Alamo, save a couple of breakaway attacks from Bradford. Time and time again we'd create a good opportunity in front of goal, only for a bad bounce to skew the end result. The home side, to their credit, scrapped like tigers and soon realised that the only way to knock us off our stride would be to increase the physical nature of their game.

'Let's piss on their chips and shut that lot up,' I heard one of their players shout as he gestured to the legions of rowdy, banana-waving City fans. As a consequence, hard cases like Peter Jackson, Brian Tinnion and Mark Leonard started to make their (stud) mark on the game. Nigel Gleghorn was the first to get scythed down but, luckily for us, remained in one piece. Gleghorn and McNab had been our star performers on the day, the former jinking, checking and bombarding the box with quality balls, and the latter changing defence into attack with his hallmark killer passes.

It was only a matter of time before our equaliser arrived.

Hand on heart, that's how confident we felt. And this was in spite of the news filtering through to us from the stands and the dugout that the nightmare scenario of Crystal Palace thrashing Birmingham was coming to fruition. I was getting back into position when, from the corner of my eye, I saw a City fan running onto the pitch. Sporting a shaggy brown mullet and dressed top to toe in stonewashed denim, he looked like an escapee from a Status Quo tour bus. God knows how he'd managed to hurdle over the hoardings because the lad seemed completely bladdered. He suddenly started remonstrating with Reddo, so I sprinted over to try to calm the situation down. The fan then turned his attentions to me, grabbing my waist and squaring up to me, eyeball to eyeball.

'Lakey, Lakey, Palace are stuffing Birmingham 5–0,' he slurred (he'd actually been given some duff information; it was 4–1 at the time).

'If it stays like this we won't go up, mate. You've gotta tell everyone to pull their fingers out . . .'

'We are doing, pal, we are,' I said, guiding him towards the touchline. He then mumbled something about once playing against me when he was a kid, before a steward frogmarched him off the pitch.

Contrary to popular myth, it wasn't this fan's intervention alone that changed the course of the game. While the break in play certainly gave us a couple of minutes to regroup and refocus, it was our unrelenting pressure and self-belief that finally did the trick. The hallowed equaliser came in the 86th minute, a superbly worked piece of skill by Paul Moulden who hooked a perfectly flighted pass into the channel. David White, on the left side of the pitch and on his wrong peg, managed to steal a yard and whip a precision cross onto the incoming foot of Trevor Morley, who slid the ball past keeper Paul Tomlinson.

Back of the net. Back where we belonged. And back home to Manchester for the mother of all parties.

5

True Faith

It was 1977 – Silver Jubilee year. In common with the rest of Great Britain (well, apart from the Sex Pistols and Arthur Scargill) we staged our own street party to honour Her Majesty. The dads of Bowker Avenue tied Union flag bunting to lampposts and rigged up trestle tables, which the mums draped with red, white and blue tablecloths. Then out came the party food, a mouth-watering feast of sausages on sticks, potted meat sarnies, fairy cakes, iced gems and the *pièce de résistance*, an Arctic Roll served up on a commemorative plate. As the men cracked open the Watneys Party Seven and the women sipped their Cinzanos, us kids toasted Queen Elizabeth II with tumblers of American cream soda topped with a scoop of vanilla ice-cream and a sprinkling of hundreds-and-thousands.

Yet amidst all this patriotism, it was to be another Royle – Joe Royle – who would capture my attention that year (sorry, Ma'am). Manchester City were having a cracking season and

Genial Joe, our star striker, had played a pivotal part in our surge up the First Division. Maine Road was treated to some really stylish football around that time, possibly the best I've ever seen from a City team. Classy players like Dave Watson, Asa Hartford and Brian Kidd were a joy to behold, the latter sending me and Albert the milkman wild when he banged in four during a memorable game against Leicester City. Come May, I was distraught to see us finish an agonising point behind table-toppers Liverpool, with Mum's consoling words of 'It's only a game, love,' cutting no ice whatsoever.

This was also the first year in which I entered the furnace of a Manchester derby. City thumped United 3–1 in September, and I remember bouncing up and down on my blue plastic seat as Mick Channon – the scorer of our third – galloped past the Main Stand doing his trademark windmill celebration. I couldn't wait to get to school the following Monday, marching proudly into the classroom with my 'Man City Are Magic' badge pinned to my blazer.

Denton was a traditional stamping ground for Blues but there were a smattering of United fans in my form, albeit of the part-time variety who didn't know their McCreerys from their Macaris. There was nothing worse than having to endure non-stop Red gloating whenever they took the spoils, and I'd often try to silence them, asking 'When did you last go to Old Trafford, then? Or d'you prefer a comfy armchair in front of the TV?'

I remember once having a fight in the school playground with a couple of Reds, the day after City had inexplicably sold

Peter Barnes to West Brom. Barnes's exit, in July 1979, had come as the result of Malcolm Allison's infamous cull of fans' favourites that had already seen the departure of Gary Owen and Asa Hartford.

'You're goin' down without Barnes, down without Barnes ...' these lads had taunted as I'd tried to batter them senseless with my sky blue sports bag, my eyes stinging with tears. The news of these transfers had left me devastated. I hero-worshipped Barnes in particular and loved the way he niftily ran down the wing while flailing his left arm about like a baton-waving conductor.

The United fans at that time probably irritated me more than the team itself which, to be fair, contained some fabulous players. Steve Coppell, Joe Jordan and Sammy McIlroy were top-drawer professionals at the peak of their game and, as a fledgling footballer myself, I had the utmost respect for them. That said, my deep-seated City allegiances meant that I'd feel comfortable praising these players only when they turned out for their national sides. Somehow it seemed more acceptable and less disloyal for me to applaud a timely tackle or a perfect pass when they wore the white of England, the blue of Scotland or the green of Northern Ireland rather than the red of Manchester United.

I might well have seen these Old Trafford favourites in the flesh had I accepted United's offer to join their youth team set-up. I was about 14 at the time – not long before I was due to sign schoolboy forms for City – and Dad and I had gone to watch my brother Mike play for Nova Juniors, a local feeder side with links to a number of First Division clubs. As we stood chatting on the sidelines, a bloke in a red and black Adidas coat walked over.

'I'm glad I've caught you,' he told Dad, 'because I've been meaning to speak to you about Paul.'

It transpired that he was a United scout, and he'd been handed a brief to persuade me to jump ship in order to join their youth team on a tour of Spain. The club had been keeping tabs on me for some time, apparently; they'd been watching me play for Tameside Boys and were hopeful that they could lure me away from City with the promise of a cast-iron schoolboy contract. Dad politely thanked him for his interest and said that we'd talk about it when we got home, but he and I both knew that there was nothing to discuss. I was Blue to the core, and it was definitely a case of thanks, but no thanks.

The Manchester derby, one of the most keenly anticipated events on the sporting calendar, has thrown up some scintillating tussles over the decades. From City's 5–0 drubbing of United in 1955 to the Reds 5–1 pasting of the Blues in 1960, and from the 3–3 thriller at Maine Road in 1971 to the Old Trafford showdown three years later (when Denis Law's back-heel condemned United to the Second Division), the fixture has always been packed with incident and excitement.

In September 1989, at the age of 20, I found myself facing the thrilling prospect of playing in my first ever league derby.

United hadn't visited Maine Road for two years – our demotion had deprived us of our usual derby quota – and the old feudal rivalries were about to be renewed with a vengeance.

The animosity between City and United fans always intensified during the lead up to these head-to-heads but this time round it felt as if emotions were running higher than usual. The Reds' supporters, with their 'let's all laugh at City' mindset, no doubt saw the match as another opportunity to belittle their downtrodden neighbours. As far as the Blues were concerned, though, this was more than just a game. It was a perfect chance to settle some scores, redress the balance and restore our reputation. The previous two seasons, after all, had been pretty grim for all involved. Plying our trade in a lower division had meant enduring soul-sapping journeys to Gay Meadow and Home Park, being wellied from pillar to post by bruisers at Hull and Bradford, and suffering piss-taking chants ('you're the shit of Manchester') from mocking supporters.

Adding to our torment were the reams of compare-and-contrast newspaper articles that weighed the down-at-heel penny-pinchers from Moss Side against the upwardly mobile big-spenders from Old Trafford. I don't think I was the only person who'd had their fill of all this 'poor relations' sniping, and who saw a dream victory over United as the perfect way to salvage some pride and silence our critics.

Like many other Mancunian suburbs, Haughton Green was gripped with derby fever as the big day approached. It seemed that everywhere I went, from corner shops to garage forecourts, there'd be fans of either persuasion waiting to pass comment. Being ambushed by expectant City fans as I ordered a fish supper from The Village Chippy was fine, of course. Not so great was being waylaid by United punters in the newsagents.

'Next week you'll be reading about your lot getting f***ing stuffed, won't you, eh . . .?' goaded a red-shirted Einstein as I bought my paper one morning. I never used to rise to the bait though, and would just bite my lip and flick a V-sign in my pocket.

My family would get loads of hassle from United fans, too, none more so than Mum who sometimes worked behind the bar at the local Conservative Club.

'Paul, love, I hope you're going to win this derby,' she said wearily after returning from a shift one evening. 'There are some loudmouths back there who need shutting up.'

The bookmakers installed Manchester United as the clear favourites to win. This was to be expected, of course, bearing in mind that we were freshly promoted and were experiencing the worst start to a season for ages. We'd only managed four points from a possible 18 and, to cap it all, had suffered an embarrassing away defeat to Third Division Brentford in the League Cup. United, more surprisingly, were also enduring a similarly awful run of results, but stacking the odds firmly in their favour was the spending spree in which the club had forked out millions for the quartet of Gary Pallister, Paul Ince, Neil Webb and Danny

Wallace. Pallister alone had cost a monster £2.3 million, which at that time was an English record for a defender.

City had also delved into the transfer market, albeit on a much more modest scale. Peter Swales had produced his moth-eaten chequebook in August to sign Clive Allen from Bordeaux for £1 million and Ian Bishop from Bournemouth for £750,000. Our chairman, for a change, had conducted a very astute bit of business. In Clive, he'd brought in a highly experienced goal-poacher who inspired and invigorated our other strikers. Bish proved to be one of the most balanced footballers I've ever played with, and he was unrivalled when it came to delivering a pinpoint pass with either foot.

The bookies also paid scant attention to the fact that we'd beaten the Reds 2–0 at Old Trafford a month previously. Granted, it may only have been a close-season friendly for Mike Duxbury's testimonial, but it was still a highly unexpected victory which had given us a welcome shot in the arm. United's star-spangled side, led out by Alex Ferguson, had been way below par that afternoon. Laboured and lethargic, they just couldn't match our work-rate and were nowhere near their usual competitive selves. United's cause wasn't helped by the fact that three or four of their players seemed to be nursing monumental hangovers, their every move accompanied by a potent whiff of stale beer.

Not that our opponents' meekness took the sheen off the final outcome, though, because we were chuffed to bits to get one over on United at Old Trafford. Our coaches, Skip and Glyn, themselves derby veterans, had always told us that any fixture against 'them across the road' mattered, whether it was a youth team game or a friendly match. And this one really, really mattered. In hindsight, it helped to rekindle a certain derby-winning mentality, which was nice, considering that the first team hadn't won one since 1981.

Saturday 23 September 1989. The morning of the 111th league Manchester derby. I was en route to Moss Side, with music blaring from my stereo, when I pulled up at the traffic lights at the junction of Stockport Road and Dickenson Road. Standing at the adjacent bus stop was a City fan with his arm around his young son, both of them kitted out in replica tops and wearing the traditional-style sky blue and white scarves. Having clocked me sitting there in my car, this bloke nudged his lad and then did something that will stay with me for ever. Pressing his palms together as if in prayer, he looked at me beseechingly and mouthed three simple words.

'Please. Please. *Please.*'

The lights turned to green and I drove off towards the ground, my eyes welling up with tears and my bottom lip a-quiver. It was the fella's haunted expression that had done me in. Here was a man who'd probably been wearied by years of taunts and jibes from United fans, a life-long Blue aching for one tiny chink of light to keep his hope afloat and his pride intact. I felt as though I owed him one. We *had* to beat United.

Our preparations for the game hadn't exactly gone to plan. Niggling injuries to Andy Dibble and Clive Allen, coupled with an illness to Neil McNab, meant that all three were going to be sidelined for this key game. It was a huge setback for us. Without the spine of our team, we'd be lacking a large chunk of experience, always so vital in a derby. Mel Machin had no option but to reshuffle his pack of players. Paul Cooper was drafted in to replace Dibs in goal, Ian Brightwell and David Oldfield were slotted into midfield and attack respectively, and Gary Megson and Jason Beckford were on the substitutes' bench.

Significantly, this change in personnel meant that half the squad was now made up of home-grown former youth teamers. So, with Redmond, Hinchcliffe, Brightwell, White, Beckford and myself all figuring on the team sheet, there were six boyhood Blues champing at the bit to play in their first ever competitive derby.

With just hours to go before kick-off, anyone spying through the keyhole of our dressing room would have seen six hyperactive 20-somethings bouncing on benches, sprinting on the spot and prowling around like caged tigers. Our non-Mancunian team-mates – particularly Ian Bishop, David Oldfield, Gary Fleming and captain Brian Gayle – were completely taken aback by our strength of feeling.

'You're a Scouser . . . you'll *never* know how much a Manchester derby means,' I remember joking to Bish, who just smiled and shrugged his shoulders.

It didn't take long for our spirit and enthusiasm to rub off though, because come two o'clock the atmosphere was electric. Everyone was up for it. Even mild-mannered old heads such as

Coops and Meggo were roaming around like men possessed, psyching themselves up and pumping their fists in preparation for the battle ahead. I got a little *too* fired up that day, if truth be told, losing my cool when an apprentice waltzed into the dressing room sporting a bright red tie.

'Get that f***ing thing off,' I shrieked at the poor lad. 'Why are you wearing *that* colour, today of all days? Have you got shit for brains or what?'

Totally uncalled for, I admit (and I'm really sorry, pal, if you're reading this) but all this intense derby frenzy had clearly messed with my head.

Helping to get us totally 'in the zone' that day was Tony Book. Mel Machin was more of a tactician than a talker and, after giving us the briefest of pep-ups, he passed the baton on to Skip. Maine Road's resident warhorse cranked it up big time, with Mel nodding in agreement beside him.

'You'll need to win your own personal battles today, lads,' he said sternly, pointing at us like the bloke in that 'Your Country Needs You' poster. 'So take care with your first touch, your first pass, your first tackle. Do the simple things well and the rest will follow.'

He went on to lecture us on the art of self-control – no rash tackles, no miscontrolled balls, no letting the occasion get the better of us – before ending his speech with a rally-cry.

'We all know that United are going to come at us fast and hard, so just keep your f***in' composure and trust the players around you. You all know your jobs, you all know what this game means. Don't let yourselves down.'

Skip then made a beeline for me, Whitey and the rest of the young 'uns – his 'boys' – and shook our hands, his eyes glinting. *You're ready,* he seemed to be saying to us. *I've prepared you for days like this.*

As I crossed the white line on that sunny autumn afternoon – the last to emerge, as my superstition dictated – I was confronted with a swathe of sky blue shirts covering the Kippax, North and Main Stands. Every man, woman and child seemed to be sporting their colours. This spectacular sight, combined with the sound of 40,000 City fans belting out 'we're the pride of Manchester', made me come over all giddy and light-headed. The last thing I needed was to get wobbly-legged, so I asked Trevor Morley to help calm me down by firing some balls to my feet, which he did while the usual photos and handshakes were taking place in the centre circle.

I was going to be operating behind Trev as a left-sided midfielder that afternoon. It wasn't my most natural role – I felt far more comfortable playing on the right – but I wasn't complaining; I was just grateful to have been picked. I'd have pulled on some gloves and gone in goal if it meant guaranteeing my place in this derby day line-up.

It was United who started the game the stronger, despite the fact that, like us, they were missing a trio of integral players. Bryan Robson, Steve Bruce and Neil Webb were all out injured which was fantastic news for us. Robson, in particular, was the heartbeat of United's team and we knew that his presence was going to be sorely missed.

Not that Alex Ferguson's side were a one-man show, though, judging by the cut-and-thrust of the opening five minutes. Mark Hughes and Brian McClair immediately stamped their authority on the game, linking well and showing great fluidity of movement. Danny Wallace went on a couple of dangerous-looking sorties, and Paul Ince justified his £1 million price tag with some strong runs and incisive passing. Though we'd fully expected United to grab the game by the scruff of the neck from the outset, we were in serious danger of being steamrollered out of it. As we desperately tried to stave off their threat and get a foothold in the match, Skip's orders rang out from the dugout.

'Pick up . . . stay with your maaaan . . .' he brayed in his Somerset twang. 'Know where they aaaaare . . .'

Unexpected events in the North Stand gave us some timely respite from the pressure. A group of United fans had foolishly infiltrated the home support and, after a bit of argy-bargy, started to spill out onto the perimeter area. As a precaution, referee Neil Midgley decided to take both teams off the field of play in order to let the stewards and police deal with the incident. So, while the Reds' fans were escorted to their rightful place in the Platt Lane Stand, both teams were told to return to the dressing room.

This time-out gave us a chance to calm ourselves down and, in between muscle stretches and swigs of energy drinks, we were able to get our heads back into gear. Mel and Skip were quick to analyse how the match was developing, telling us to adapt our game by getting tighter, moving the ball more quickly, and not allowing United to settle.

Those errant United fans had definitely done us a big favour. After our eight-minute breather it was a far more self-assured City team that the ref led out for the second time.

It would be wrong of me to write about this game without paying tribute to the late Neil Midgley, who was both a fabulous referee and a fantastic bloke. No one could control a game and communicate with players like Midge. His unpretentious character, combined with an innate sense of fairness, made him one of the most popular and well-respected officials on the circuit. You wouldn't see Midge being swayed by a crowd, an occasion, a manager or a player. And you'd never witness him flourishing a yellow card for an exuberant celebration or some throwaway dissent when a good talking-to (spiced with his own industrial-strength language) would suffice. Back in the days when refs were permitted a sense of humour, Midge would deploy his famous wit to defuse many tinderbox situations, of which there were plenty in this particular derby clash. One potential flashpoint had seen Trevor Morley and Paul Ince squaring up to each other following a clumsy challenge. True to form, Midge had dealt with things brilliantly.

'Lads, lads, calm down, will yer?' he'd bellowed in his broad Salford accent. 'Anyone would think this was an important f***ing derby match ...'

The players grinned and shook hands, an incident was

averted and the game's flow continued. Common-sense refereeing like it ought to be. Rest in peace, Midge.

Galvanised after our impromptu break, we started to move forward with more confidence and successfully managed to peg United back into their own half. Our build-up play paid dividends in the 11th minute when a marauding Trevor Morley was fouled near the halfway line. The resulting free-kick, a 60-yarder expertly dispatched by Andy Hinchcliffe, met the feet of David White whose quality first touch allowed him to whip the ball across the box. Gary Pallister was caught in two minds and uncharacteristically failed to clear. An unmarked David Oldfield, hovering on the brink of the six-yard box, pivoted and smashed a first-time strike into the roof of the net. It was a goal of which Clive Allen, sitting watching in the stands, would have been rightly proud.

If David's spectacular opener stunned United, the second one – scored a minute later – knocked them for six. Trevor Morley's fierce shot from the edge of the box was parried out by United's keeper, Jim Leighton, to the left channel. I managed to pick it up and feigned to shoot twice, confusing the persistent Viv Anderson, before taking a shot at goal. Leighton blocked it again and, although the ball landed between three United players, it was tricky Trev who reacted first and forced it home. Cue chants of 'we love you City' from the Blue faithful, closely followed by catcalls of 'Fergie, Fergie, what's the score . . .'

This two-goal cushion not only boosted our confidence but allowed our game plan to take shape, and we started to put into practice Skip's principles of responsibility, trust and support. We worked our arses off, doubling up and filling in, winning our second balls, our knock-downs and our tackles, and being alive and aware at set pieces. Earlier that week the gaffer had taken great pains to highlight the aerial threat of Pallister and Anderson and, as it happened, United's two best chances in the first half had stemmed from soaring corners. Some stout defending – particularly from Gary Fleming, who had at least one goal-line clearance – kept us out of danger until half-time. Flem, a Northern Ireland right-back whom Mel had signed from Nottingham Forest was, for my money, our team's unsung hero that day. His knack of reading situations, identifying danger and being in the right place at the right time contributed to a faultless display at the back.

The yawning gap left by Bryan Robson's absence was ever more apparent as the first half went on. United's midfield play became hurried and ragged and we began to dominate the zone that Robbo usually marshalled so assuredly. And with Steve Redmond and Brian Gayle commanding the centre of our defence, we were able to manage the menace of McClair and Hughes.

Suffering a particularly nightmarish game was Gary Pallister, whose hesitancy led to our third goal. Reddo brought the ball out of defence and clipped it into the path of Oldfield. After out-thinking and outpacing United's number 6, Dave laid on the perfect cross for Ian Bishop, whose brave, diving header, left the hapless Leighton in no man's land.

This is incredible, I thought, as I rushed over to congratulate our goalscorer.

'*Now* do you know how it feels, you f***in' beauty?' I yelled, before grabbing him by the waist and hoisting him up to face the rejoicing City fans. Little did I know that this euphoric image of Bish punching the air with his fist as I held him aloft would go on to achieve something of an iconic status in City's history. The photograph of our goal celebration has featured in countless books and articles, and was once blown up to huge proportions to occupy one whole wall of Maine Road's souvenir shop. Every picture tells a story, they say, and I think this one captured the joy and passion that Bish and I felt at that precise moment.

Goal number three marked a watershed for us. 'It's gonna be our day,' became the dominant mindset and we actually started to relax and enjoy the game, knocking the ball around freely and second-guessing United's every move. We felt pretty safe in the knowledge that we weren't going to surrender a three-goal lead in such a crucial match – we'd learned our lesson against Bournemouth the previous season – but this still didn't stop Skip and Dixie Deehan screeching, 'F***in' focus! Don't switch off!' from the dugout. There's no pleasing some people.

'Keep the same tempo,' said a customarily chilled-out Mel Machin at half-time. 'Be safe, be cautious, stay firm and solid and you'll see the game through,' he told us as we towelled ourselves down and geed ourselves up. Skip had the final word, though.

'Keep the ball, and let them f****in' chase shadows,' he growled.

The United lads ran back out onto the pitch with added purpose, having probably been at the rough end of Ferguson's legendary hairdryer. No doubt he'd convinced them that the game was still winnable and, sure enough, within five minutes of the restart they managed to pull a goal back. And what a phenomenal strike it was. Russell Beardsmore got the better of Hinchy, for once, and dispatched a great cross to the far post. It was latched onto by an airborne Mark Hughes who, with superb control and agility, unleashed a bicycle kick which rocketed past Paul Cooper.

Here was our big test. Now was the time to steel ourselves and keep our cool. As the strains of 'c'mon you Reds' floated across from the away end, I could sense some nervous tension in the City stands as a stream of United half-chances went begging. Luckily, our fans' conviction was restored when we grabbed our fourth. With United's back line once again in disarray, a crunching tackle involving Trevor Morley thrust the ball in my direction, hitting me in the stomach. The United players claimed handball and, as they stopped in their tracks, I was given the space to have a shot on goal. Leighton desperately half-blocked, landing the ball at my feet once again. I contemplated having a tight-angled shot, but hesitated when I saw Mike Duxbury moving in to thwart it at the near post, deciding instead to square the ball to David Oldfield. Dave, who was loitering with intent near the goalmouth, rolled it in and killed off the game for good. Goodnight Vienna. Or catch yer later, as we say in Manchester.

As David's shot hit the back of the net, I wheeled round to the Platt Lane Stand with my arms outstretched. Not the wisest of moves when all's said and done, because I suddenly found myself face-to-face with 3,000 seething United fans baying for my blood. I was just about to scurry back upfield when, to my amazement, among the crowd I spotted one of my old United-supporting classmates from school. I couldn't believe it. I hadn't seen this lad for years, yet here he was at Maine Road, ranting and raving and brandishing the middle finger. So what else could I do but flash him a grin, pump my fist and yell 'get in there'? In response he gave me a mouthful of abuse and aimed a gobful of phlegm in my direction. Like I cared. His team were being outshone in a derby and, like many of his comrades, he didn't appear to be coping terribly well.

My old school pal's agony continued, because a few minutes later we banged in our fifth. Some clever interplay between Trev and Bish in the middle of the park culminated in the latter pinging a 40-yard ball that soared over the head of United's Mike Duxbury. David White half-volleyed it with one of the best first-time crosses I've ever seen, planting the ball perfectly onto the head of Andy Hinchcliffe, who steamed in with an unstoppable header that nearly scorched a hole in the top left-hand corner. It was a brilliant goal. Jim Leighton, scooping yet another ball from the back of the net, looked crushed. Behind him, a mass exodus of United fans was taking place, chants of 'Fergie Out!' echoing around the away end as they vacated their seats and trudged towards the stadium exits. 'Fergie In!' countered the Blues as they partied in the aisles.

Now that we'd more or less won the game, it was all about staying professional and maintaining some decorum. As full-time edged ever closer, the temptation to start grinning like a Cheshire cat was almost unbearable. With ten minutes to go, however, any hint of a smile was wiped off my face when a bulldozing, spleen-venting tackle from Mike Phelan left me with a shinful of stud marks. Despite my protestations, there was no way I could stay on the field. As physio Roy Bailey slowly led me back towards the Main Stand I received a standing ovation. Already running onto the pitch as my replacement was Jason Beckford. It was a bittersweet moment for me. Whilst I was totally gutted to be limping off in such a momentous game, I was pleased as Punch for my big mate. I knew that notching up his first derby appearance would mean the world to Jase, and I was delighted that he was going to have the chance to savour that magnificent atmosphere.

'Well done, Lakey,' smiled Mel as I hobbled towards the tunnel. Skip leant back in the dugout, dragged on his cigarette, and gave me a knowing wink that said job well done. On the adjacent bench sat an ashen-faced Alex Ferguson, next to him an equally downcast Brian Kidd. Behind them, United's Russell Beardsmore – himself a native Manc – looked on the verge of tears.

I was lying on the treatment table clutching an ice pack to

my leg when the final whistle went, and the huge roar from the stadium almost levitated me to the ceiling. Before long my team-mates piled in, happy and glorious, and the dressing room erupted.

Once the celebrations had died down, I gave a champagne-fuelled interview to BBC Radio Manchester's Ian Cheeseman.

'So what was the secret of today's victory, Paul?' he asked.

'I ate raw meat for breakfast,' I said, baring my teeth. Ian has since told me it's his top favourite response to one of his questions.

A week or so after the derby, while shopping in the city centre, I happened to spot my old school 'friend' (a.k.a. the Platt Lane spitter) browsing through a rail of clothes.

'Lakey! All right, mate?'

'Yeah, fine.'

'I saw you at the derby.'

'I know, pal. I saw you, too.'

'I gobbed at you.'

'Yeah, and you missed.'

'You know what, mate, I feel really bad about that.'

'It's all forgotten about. Don't worry.'

'But I want to make it up to you.'

'Honestly, it's not a problem . . .'

'I tell you what, Lakey, pick anything out of this shop – anything at all – and I'll nick it for you.'

I made my excuses and left (as the papers say), chuckling to myself.

*

The aftermath of the 5–1 saw things panning out very differently for the respective managers. With legions of disgruntled Reds calling for the head of Alex Ferguson, many football pundits were predicting a humiliating exit for the United boss. He dug his heels in, though and, with the aid of a supportive chairman and some of his trademark Glaswegian grit, he successfully managed to weather the storm.

Some say the 1989 derby drubbing – 'the most embarrassing defeat of my career', admitted Ferguson – was the catalyst that shocked the Reds' boss into making wholesale changes at Old Trafford. In due course he turned things around and, as we all know, gradually amassed a side of world-beaters and masterminded an amazing haul of trophies. A few years later, I happened to be drinking in a bar when a United fan swaggered over. He wanted to thank me for having a hand in the 5–1, purely because it 'helped us on our way to glory.' The pleasure was all mine, pal, all mine.

In contrast, Mel Machin's fortunes took a nosedive. Securing our promotion to the First Division and engineering our best derby result for years ended up counting for nothing when, on 26 November, Peter Swales gave him the Cuban-heeled boot. Two league wins in two months had cast us adrift at the foot of the table, and the gaffer was, as they say in football, 'relieved of his managerial duties'. His departure was hastened by a variety of reasons, but the quality of his coaching wasn't one of them. You couldn't really fault Mel's technical knowledge and expertise, especially when it was attack-minded, and his methods were actually seen as quite innovative at the time.

One tactic Mel had always advocated, odd as it sounds, was to give certain on-field moves their own pet names. It followed a similar tack to those cryptic phrases that rugby players shout before line-outs. So 'Jack', for example, indicated a step-over, 'Sid' meant that you were planning a flick and 'Fred' signified a back-heel. We had to learn all these code words off by heart, Mel being of the opinion that they would outwit our opponents and improve our communication. Sometimes it helped; mostly, it hindered.

'What the f*** was that, Lakey?'

'It was a Jack, wasn't it?'

'I don't care if it was Tom, Dick or f***in' Harry, it was supposed to be to a blue shirt, you tit.'

Yet, for all his tactical abilities, it was Mel's lack of off-field interaction that became his Achilles heel. Some players – myself included – perceived the gaffer as naturally shy and introverted, and didn't let it bother us. Others, however, thought him intentionally cold and aloof and couldn't take to his reserved managerial style.

Whichever side of the fence you occupied, it was clear that Mel had real difficulty in expressing himself and connecting with us. Banter and small-talk simply weren't his style (he left that to Dixie and Frizz) and he would seldom join in any post-match drinks or coach-trip card games. It was this detachment that bred mistrust and resentment among some players, and meant that our boss never truly commanded the dressing room during his two-year spell.

'He had no repartee,' said a befuddled Peter Swales after the sacking, clearly meaning to say 'rapport'.

Mel seemed to find it especially hard to deal with the 30-something, been-there-done-it brigade. Wily old pros such as Neil McNab and John Gidman would regularly disrupt training sessions ('I'm not having this "Jack, Sid and Fred" crap . . .') and never really bought into his brand of strike-orientated fantasy football which, while exciting to watch, would often leave us exposed defensively. As a consequence, it wasn't unusual to see senior players barging into the manager's office on a Monday morning armed with a long list of grievances.

I was saddened, but not surprised, to see Mel's reign come to an end. It had reached the point where he'd become a bit out of his depth, I feel, and he probably didn't possess the gravitas to be a first team manager in a top-flight setting. Yet, although things didn't ultimately work out for him at Maine Road, it's only fair that his contribution to Manchester City is rightfully acknowledged. Mel Machin may not rank as one of the most flamboyant managers in City's history, but without him I might never have experienced the joys of the Huddersfield win, the Bradford promotion, or the United tonking.

And for that, Gaffer, I thank you.

In December 1989, word had it that one of my former City heroes was being lined up to fill Mel Machin's shoes. Joe

Royle, at that time successfully managing Oldham Athletic, was top of City's hit list, Peter Swales having made some very public overtures to try to lure him to Maine Road.

Not for the first time, though, our chairman ended up with egg on his face. Following a concerted 'Don't Go' campaign by the Latics' fans, Big Joe surprised everyone by deciding to stay put at Boundary Park. An embarrassed Swales had to change tack quickly, and within days had persuaded Howard Kendall to take on the job.

Most of us were really excited at the prospect of being managed by the revered former Everton, Blackburn and Atletico Bilbao coach. Others, like Ian Bishop, seemed more apprehensive, though, concerned that their style of play wouldn't fit in with Kendall's tactics and would render them surplus to requirements.

'Well, that's me off, then,' confided Bish as the news filtered through.

'What makes you so sure, mate?'

'Howard didn't rate me when I was at Everton, Lakey, and I just don't think I'm his kind of player. Sooner or later I'll be offski, just you wait and see . . .'

After wading through the encampment of reporters, photographers and camera crews on the Maine Road fore-court, Howard reported for duty on Friday 8 December. We played Southampton at the Dell the following day, with Tony Book assuming pitch-side duties while our new boss watched, hawk-eyed, from the stands. The lads and I knew that we were on trial, and the pressure to make an impact and get noticed was intense. We were playing for our City careers as well as for the three points.

As it turned out we got beaten 2–1, but it wasn't a bad performance by any means, and we were unfortunate not to come away with a draw. I was lucky enough to put in a decent showing, gradually settling into the game and almost forgetting the close scrutiny that I was under. The *Manchester Evening News* gave me the thumbs-up as well, rating me eight out of ten and voting me their Man of the Match. I never took much notice of newspaper player ratings – some were so off-beam you wondered whether the reporters had actually been to the game – but I was more than happy to see this one in black and white.

It wasn't until Monday's training session that we met Howard formally for the first time. As he stood before us in his crisp new City shell-suit, I was at once struck by his cool and calm demeanour.

'I'm not worried, lads,' he said. 'Just a few little tweaks here and there and we'll get it right, I promise you.'

With the gaffer's arrival came much upheaval, though, and over the next few weeks we witnessed an unprecedented evacuation of playing staff. Before the year was out, a ruthless Howard had offloaded Brian Gayle, Gary Fleming, David Oldfield, Neil McNab, Andy Hinchcliffe, Trevor Morley and Ian Bishop. Bish's premonition had been correct, and I was really sad to see him and the other boys leave Maine Road.

Surviving the cull was a select band of young squad members, like myself, Whitey and Bob, plus a couple of older hands in the guise of Colin Hendry and Gary Megson. Needing to steady his ship with some age and experience, Howard immediately swooped for the signature of QPR's Peter Reid, the hardy midfielder and his former Everton henchman. It was an excellent signing. Reidy may have been approaching the twilight of his career, but his unrivalled experience and influence would help to halt our run of bad form.

Howard made another intuitive signing a few weeks later, scooping up Irish international Niall Quinn from Arsenal and rescuing him from reserve team football. Quinny – who immediately endeared himself by arriving at Maine Road in a battered old Jag that he'd won in a bet – was a fabulous acquisition, his skill and stature bringing an added dimension to the side. Both Quinny and Reidy, with their engaging personalities and muck-in attitude, would become as popular off the pitch as they were on it. They were, and remain, two of the nicest guys in football.

Controversially, Howard also decided to plunder his old Everton squad, luring Adrian Heath, Wayne Clarke, Mark Ward and Alan Harper over to Maine Road. This brazen smash 'n' grab caused much consternation on both sides of the Mersey. The sudden departure of fans' favourites like Bishop and Morley enraged many City supporters, who saw the Scouse influx as an old pals' act gone too far. The Everton fans were equally aggrieved, cursing their former manager as half their team upped sticks and did a runner down the East Lancs Road.

The logic of all this soon became evident, however, because only one of the gaffer's first eight league games ended in defeat. By instilling confidence to a young side depleted of self-belief, by injecting experience into a team with spirit but without much know-how, and by sorting out a ramshackle rearguard that had been haemorrhaging goals, Howard had got us back on an even keel. We'd go on to lose only three more games before the end of the season, and would finish the campaign comfortably safe from the drop zone, level on the same points as Manchester United (our 14th spot was our highest league position for eight seasons, in fact).

By raising standards and changing mindsets, Howard had transformed us from dithering wrecks into disciplined warriors. Eager to be part of the Kendall revolution, we all began to work our socks off in training in order to catch the boss's eye, each of us desperate to be on his team sheet and in his good books. There was, it must be said, a considerable trade-off for the daily toils at Platt Lane. The gaffer subscribed to the 'work hard, play hard' ethos and would organise some serious downtime in which we were encouraged to let off steam and relax. Rumours of a burgeoning drinking culture at the club certainly contained an element of truth.

It was no secret that Howard was partial to a tipple or two like many top managers at that time. The ex-Everton lads had said as much, regaling us with tales about his half-time 'refreshments' at Goodison Park, as well as his weekly 'team-building exercises' hosted in a variety of Liverpool watering holes. Not that this was particularly outlandish; alcohol was still very much part and parcel of professional football in the 1980s.

Howard's *joie de vivre* was very much in evidence during the squad's end-of-season trip to Tenerife in May 1990. His composure was unaffected by the non-stop flow of booze, and each night he'd entertain us all with a medley of football anecdotes. One evening, much to our amusement, he didn't bat an eyelid when a mischief-making Gary Megson ordered him a neat tumbler of Bacardi from the bar, topped up with a thimbleful of Coke. Howard proceeded to take a huge gulp before licking his lips.

'Hey, you can go again, Meggy,' he'd smiled.

His early-morning perkiness in Tenerife put us all to shame, too. Most of us would be bedbound until noon with blinding hangovers but Howard would be up and at 'em after just a couple of hours' kip, tucking hungrily into a full breakfast and striding purposefully to the hotel's tennis courts, where he'd trounce a bleary-eyed Mark Ward in a three-setter.

Most afternoons would see the gaffer cracking open more champagne by the poolside and, in order to sidestep the carnage of yet another daytime session ('I'll be going home in a box if I try to keep up,' moaned one team-mate), we'd do our utmost to try to avoid him. Like something out of *Mission Impossible*, we'd don our dark glasses and baseball caps, hiding behind strategically placed lilos or using unsuspecting families as decoys. Then, with the coast clear, we'd sneak onto the beach to top up our tans and rest our livers.

To Howard, though, alcohol was more than just about the lads glugging loopy juice and getting legless; I'm convinced that it also played a significant part in his brand of footballing psychology. He was a canny man-manager and a deep thinker – a 'people person' of the highest order – and he never underestimated the power and influence of team spirit. And if a squad's solidarity had to be induced by booze, well so be it. The aftermath of our game against Charlton – our first home defeat since his arrival – was a case in point.

It was a match that we should have won comfortably and a granite-faced Howard stormed out of the ground, after the final whistle, without saying a word. We all trooped forlornly into Maine Road the following Monday, expecting a punishing training session followed by some fire and brimstone treatment from a livid manager. What we got, though, was a toothy grin from Howard, a pat on the back from our coach, Bobby Saxton, and a comically lightweight training schedule comprising head tennis in the gym under the stand and runaround ping-pong in the weights room. No mention whatsoever was made of the game. It was weird. I remember the lads looking askance at each other, thinking what the hell's going on?

After the session Howard sat us all down.

'Lads, you were bloody dreadful on Saturday, and I think you know how I felt after the match. You let bad habits seep back into your game and I won't stand for it. But you've all had a lot to contend with since I've been here. Some of your mates have been sold. Some of you young lads have had to step up to the plate in trying times. You've all had to adapt to lots of change. And I have to admit, you've done fantastically well for me. So cheers for that.'

He then nodded at Bobby, who went into the gaffer's office and brought out two crates of lager.

'Let's just forget Saturday's game,' said Howard. 'Have a couple of beers on me, and let's crack on till the end of the season, eh?'

He'd spectacularly wrong-footed us, turning a negative into a positive and expertly turning our dimmer switches back to full beam.

Even when it came down to disciplining players, Howard used booze as currency. The Monday following the Old Trafford derby (it had ended honours-even after Ian Brightwell's memorable 'I just wellied it' equaliser) we were summoned to a meeting room at the training ground. As we walked in, I clocked half a dozen bottles of Bollinger under Howard's chair. He's starting early, I thought.

'Right, then,' he said. 'The club has had a complaint from Greater Manchester Police that one of our players swore at some United fans on Saturday' (cue some Muttley-like sniggering from the lads), 'and I want whoever it is to own up now.'

Silence.

'C'mon, lads. Whoever it is, they're going to pay for this

vintage champers out of their wages so, I'll ask again, who's the big mouth?'

Silence.

'All right then, there are two more cases of Bolly in my office that also need paying for, so you can *all* stick your hands in your pockets if—'

And with that, a bashful Andy Hinchcliffe coyly raised his hand.

'It was me, Gaffer. Sorry 'bout that. Just got a bit wound up, that's all.'

After making Hinchy cough up his fine, our smiling boss cracked open the champagne and poured out the lunchtime aperitifs, using paper cups so as to conceal the drink's identity from any passing pressmen.

Howard organised his legendary weekly 'socials' on Wednesday afternoons. After training, we'd pile down to a city-centre bar, hijack a couple of tables and spend the entire afternoon downing drinks and singing songs. The gaffer loved nothing more than a good, beery singalong, and would encourage *a cappella* karaoke sessions in which each player would have to belt out his favourite tune for everyone else's amusement. It was an absolute blast. Adrian Heath would usually be first up with his rendition of 'Sweet Caroline', followed by David White's ultra-Mancunian take on 'American Pie'.

Much further down the running order, and after swigging a couple of Grolsch's for Dutch courage, I'd murder a Beatles classic like 'Ticket To Ride' or 'Norwegian Wood'. The lads would often bail me out by joining in with the chorus, mercifully drowning out my shaky Larry the Lamb-style vocals. Funnily enough, I was ten times more nervous doing these turns in front of my team-mates than I was playing in front of 35,000 fans.

Looking back, I can see Howard's ulterior motives for convening these get-togethers. He was acutely aware that any problems between players were often ironed out during our alcohol-soaked afternoons and, by egging on the timid players who needed bringing out of their shell, as well as exposing the gobby players who needed putting in their place, our socials were seen as the ideal leveller.

He knew, for example, that a young player struggling with self-confidence would feel more at ease with his senior colleagues after a couple of beers, chatting freely when he may have not done so sober. This breaking down of barriers, Howard no doubt hoped, would then be transferred to the training pitch, whereupon the lad would no longer be scared to open his mouth and scream 'man on!' to the seasoned pro he was only laughing and joking with the previous Wednesday.

On the other hand, if a trouble-causing player was deemed to be rocking the boat, our boozy sessions would often bring matters to a head. With inhibitions loosened and tongues slackened, opinions were always more forthcoming. By taking players away from the confines of the training ground and encouraging them to relax, Howard was basically providing us with a platform upon which we could freely air our views about tactics or team-mates. This would often lead to the occasional handbags-at-dawn, but would usually have the desired effect of a player realising the error of his ways, or a 'bad apple' having a strop and demanding a transfer the following week.

I remember one particular get-together going a bit haywire. Some of the long-term City lads were very suspicious of Howard's Everton recruits – there's no denying that it had bred some resentment – and Howard was keen to reduce any tension between the Manc and Scouse factions. With this in mind, he organised a particularly boisterous drinking session. This peace-making attempt turned pear-shaped, however, when a team-mate took the opportunity to make a few near-the-knuckle comments about the recent changes in personnel.

'F*** me, lads, looking round the changing room these days I'm not sure what shade of blue I should be wearing. Jobs for the boys, eh . . .' All hell let loose. Insults were hurled, the session was abandoned, and the player's cards were well and truly marked.

Despite Howard's success on the pitch, it was no secret that some club officials weren't impressed with the behind-the-scenes approach by our maverick gaffer. But I can safely say that I never felt more connected with a manager than I did with Howard. As far as I was concerned, the guy was a coaching genius and a master communicator who performed wonders at Maine Road.

He was, without question, the best boss I ever had.

6

Moving On Up

Maybe I shouldn't have bothered turning up to school on Wednesday 16 June 1982.

'Will you be joining us today, Lake?' my biology teacher asked sarcastically, slamming down her board rubber in frustration as she'd caught me staring out of the classroom window. On any other day I'd have probably paid much more attention to her carefully chalked diagram of an amoeba, but on that particular afternoon there was only one thing on my mind.

I'd woken up thinking about it. I'd pulled on my uniform thinking about it. I'd munched on my cornflakes thinking about it. I'd dawdled to school thinking about it. I'd spent the whole of dinnertime thinking about it. Nothing else in my life mattered that day. My body may have been in Denton, Manchester, but my soul was over in Bilbao, Spain, where England were due to commence their World Cup campaign against France.

At half-past three – 45 minutes before the big kick-off – I joined the crush of kids swarming out of the school gates, before running down Town Lane towards the bus stop. There was always a short wait for the 204, so to pass the time I dug out my dog-eared World Cup '82 Panini cards and pored over details that had been etched upon my brain for weeks.

Hans Krankl, Austria. Age: 29. Position: Striker. Club: Rapid Vienna.
Franco Causio, Italy. Age: 33. Position: Midfield. Club: Udinese.
Junior, Brazil. Age: 27. Position: Defender. Club: Flamengo.

I felt like a close personal friend of these players, so familiar were their names, faces and statistics, and the prospect of being able to watch Hans, Franco and Junior in action was almost too much to bear. I'd not been so excited about watching telly since Brian Jacks's attempt to break the world squat thrust record on *Superstars*.

Soon enough the orange double-decker came around the corner, and I quickly stuffed my Paninis back into my left blazer pocket and then rummaged for the 12p fare in the right. I needn't have bothered, as the steamy-windowed bus, packed to the gills with expectant football fans, whistled straight past without stopping.

Flamin' Nora. I had no option but to tackle the mile-long route on foot, running as fast as my navy blue Pods would carry me. Blotting out the pain of a chafing bag-strap, I sprinted down the home straight of Bowker Avenue, reaching the finish line – our patent red front step – at exactly 4.14 p.m. I banged on the front door, barged past my mum, dumped my bag in the hall, kicked off my shoes, charged into the lounge and switched on BBC1, just in time to see Bryan Robson driving a left-footed volley past Jean-Luc Ettori.

'Twenty-seven seconds . . . the fastest goal in World Cup history . . .' screamed John Motson as Mum emerged from the kitchen with a celebratory beaker of orange squash. Against all odds – France were much-touted finalists – England went on to achieve a comfortable 3–1 victory, with Robson and Trevor Francis at the heart of a majestic performance (Francis was still officially a City player, though he would soon be Sampdoria-bound). Two more wins – against Czechoslovakia (2–0) and Kuwait (1–0) secured our top spot in the table and guaranteed our entry into the second group stage.

As per usual, the entire country went England-mad at the merest whiff of success. Fans from Penrith to Penzance were sent into a tizzy at the prospect of Ron Greenwood's boys – deemed by many as the best national team in ages – hoisting aloft the World Cup trophy for the first time since 1966. I too got swept away by all this England-mania, skateboarding down to Taylor Sports in Denton and splurging my pocket money on some red and white England wristbands (my spends of £1.50 a week – earned by bottling up the Skol and Guinness at my uncle Jim's pub – didn't stretch to the full Admiral kit).

The shock result against France was to be the pinnacle of England's tournament, sadly. Goalless draws against West Germany and Spain in Group B snuffed out any hopes of progression, and our World Cup came to a sad premature end. Luckily my Maine Road upbringing had primed me to cope with disappointment and underachievement and, as Captain Marvel and the lads boarded their 747 back to Blighty, I just did a Gallic shrug of the shoulders and switched my allegiances to France instead.

Les Bleus easily overcame Austria and Northern Ireland in the second stage, turning on the style and flaunting their unique brand of flair football. Theirs was a side bursting with charisma, whether it was the grace of Michel Platini, the speed of Jean Tigana, the precision of Alain Giresse or the panache of Didier Six. I followed them every step of the way to that riveting semi-final against Germany, notorious for the dramatic Battiston versus Schumacher set-to when the French defender was brutally scythed down by the opposing goalie.

'That's GBH, that is,' shouted Dad, theatrically leaping out of his armchair and upending his ashtray as my brothers and I scrutinised the action replay. Whilst it was by far the most cynical foul that I'd ever seen, I secretly lapped up the heroes-and-villains drama unfolding before me. This marvellous game ended 3–3, with the Germans knocking out the French in a penalty shoot-out.

Two players particularly caught my eye that tournament. Paolo Rossi, for his golden-booted finesse and for the way he led the line in the final, helping Italy to a formidable win against the German bad guys. Also Norman Whiteside, Manchester United and Northern Ireland's 17-year-old man-child, whose effortless transition from Old Trafford to the world stage was nothing short of inspirational.

I can trace my first World Cup memories right back to 1978, the year that Argentina memorably staged the tournament. This unexplored territory of top-class foreign players and wall-mounted fixture charts hit me like a thunderbolt. I couldn't get enough of the fanatical crowds, the tickertape receptions and the technicolour kits, not forgetting the glamorous stars with lyrical names that begged to be said out loud. Mario Kempes. Karl-Heinz Rummenigge. Leopaldo Luque. Willy van der Kerkhof. And best of all, Daniel Passarella.

My brothers and I were transfixed by this footballing fiesta and would marvel at the slick passing, lightning-paced attacks and wonder-strikes that were beamed over from South America. It wasn't unusual for us to watch three matches in a row, especially over the weekend. We always preferred the BBC's coverage, though, partly due to its lack of adverts, but also because its World Cup theme was far catchier than ITV's. This upbeat little tune – called 'Argentine Melody' – never failed to get me fizzing with excitement. Its jingly-jangly tune was always the cue for me to take my place on the sofa as the cameras panned in on Frank Bough and Jimmy Hill in the studio.

'Good evening and welcome to World Cup *Grandstand*,' Boughie would smile, 'and thanks for joining us for Brazil versus Sweden . . .'

During these televised games I would insist on scampering upstairs to update my *Shoot!* wall-chart whenever a match stat needed logging.

'Can't you wait till after the game, son? You're missing all the action . . .' Dad would yell up as I carefully pencilled in the exact time of Reinaldo's equaliser.

Realising how much this TV heaven meant to her boys, Mum turned a blind eye to our obsessive-compulsive viewing disorder. It was the only time she ever let us eat our tea on our laps, and we'd graze on our corned beef hash without once taking our eyes off the screen. My sisters weren't as tolerant, though. Our month-long encampment in the lounge irritated the hell out of Sue and Tracey, who would invariably have to slope upstairs to watch their weekly dose of *Dallas* on the portable, fiddling with the flimsy aerial until Sue Ellen staggered into view.

This was yet another example of football ruling the roost when I was a kid. It totally dominated our household, with weekends monopolised by our fixtures, radiators draped with steaming kits and platefuls of calorie-stuffed carbs for Mum's growing lads. Nowadays my sisters will joke about having their noses pushed out by Dave, Mike and I, but I can well imagine how niggled they must have felt. I'm the first to admit that, as I floated through childhood in my football bubble, I never really gave much thought to this state of affairs. However, as I've grown older, I look back at those times with some degree of guilt. Sue and Tracey's formative years were eclipsed by football, and I can totally understand why they have no interest in the game these days.

My sisters could therefore be forgiven for not giving two hoots that England had failed to qualify for Argentina '78. Though I mourned the absence of our lads, my ardour for the Finals wasn't dampened in the slightest; it just meant that all my hopes now rested on Ally McLeod's Scotland to do the business. In common with many Sassenach households, the Lakes became honorary Scots for a month. The presence in the team of City stalwarts Asa Hartford and Willie Donachie made it a complete no-brainer for me, coupled with the fact that, according to Dad, we had more than enough Celtic blood coursing through our veins to claim kinship.

'Your mum's from a family of McGintys, and that sounds Scottish enough for me,' he told us as we watched a tartan-clad bloke belting out their world cup song on *Top of the Pops*.

We're on the march wi' Ally's Army, he sang, his sporran swinging in time with the music, ' . . . *we're going tae the Argentine . . .*'

The Scots' match against Holland on 11 June was one of the most eagerly anticipated games of the tournament. Mike and I were only allowed to watch the first half, since it was kicking off on a Sunday evening and we had school the next day (David, being just that bit older, was allowed to watch the whole game). It was all-square at the interval, Kenny

Dalglish having equalised a minute before the half-time whistle.

'Right, up you go, boys,' said Mum, no doubt expecting the usual whines of 'awww . . . can't we stay up for a bit longer?' Instead, Mike and I nodded meekly and padded upstairs, Mum's orders uncontested only because we'd already planned to have a sly listen to the second half on Radio 2.

My elder brother and I shared a small bedroom, competing for space with a coffin-sized Grundig radiogram that was so huge we could only move around the room sideways. The display panel of this sound system was a work of art, comprising a variety of knobs and switches and a metre-long window dial featuring hundreds of far-flung services such as Radio Belgrade and Voice of America. By and large our listening habits were confined to just three or four stations; Radio Luxembourg or Radio 1 for the pop music (including the sacred Sunday-night chart rundown) and Radio 2 or Manchester-based Piccadilly 261 for the sports shows.

In those days, overseas match commentaries were transmitted down fuzzy phone lines. This, together with the ebb and flow of the night-time medium wave signal, meant that chunks of the Scotland v Holland game that summer night were barely audible and we could only keep tabs on the game by pressing our ears against the vibrating fabric speakers. The crackly commentary by BBC's Peter Jones evoked a real sense of distance as Mike and I sat in our little bedroom, straining to hear the match action against a background of muffled chants and muted salsa bands.

We could hardly contain ourselves when, with about 20 minutes to go, Archie Gemmill, Scotland's balding, barrel-chested midfielder, scored what sounded like a wondrous goal to make it 3–1, having already upped their tally with a penalty after the break. We had to stifle our cheers into our pillows, fearful that Mum and Dad would hear us and get wind of our crafty ruse.

The following day I trooped down to the park to hook up with my friends for our after-school World Cup kickabout. Each day of the tournament would find us faithfully re-enacting a specific match, replaying the full 90 minutes and replicating all the action in minute detail to include scorers, bookings and substitutions. The previous week we'd staged end-to-end thrillers like Tunisia v Mexico and Italy v Hungary, yet the excitement was reaching fever pitch for that afternoon's Scotland–Holland showdown. After the usual team-selection arguments ('no *way* am I being Alan Rough . . .'), I finally won the fight to be Archie Gemmill.

'Gooooooaaaaaalllllll!' went the cries round Haughton Green Park after I played a one–two with Steve Archibald (i.e. our Mike), nutmegged Johan Neeskens (alias Simon Whelan), and skilfully lifted the ball over the legs of the despairing Jan Jongbloed (aka Brendan Hourihan). I clenched my fist as the winner went in, shouting 'get in therrrre' in my best Irn-Bru accent.

Then, as was the custom, we all reached into our tracksuit

pockets to throw shredded toilet paper up into the air, our makeshift version of the tickertape that we'd seen fluttering over Córdoba and Buenos Aires.

A decade later, the fantasy became reality. I pulled on an England shirt for the first time in September 1988, making my international under-21's debut in a friendly against Denmark. I'd been called up before, but injury or illness had always prevented me from appearing. This time, fortunately, I was fit, well and raring to go.

Prior to the kick-off at Vicarage Road, I joined the gaggle of team-mates in the main reception and made my way to the dressing room. There, beneath my peg, lay a pure, white, pristine number 8 England shirt. It might as well have been lowered down on a silver platter by a host of angels for the profound effect that it had on me. I carefully unfolded the crisp cotton shirt and gingerly pulled it on. As my head popped out of the top, I happened to look in the mirror and caught a glimpse of those three embroidered lions on my chest. Had I not been in a roomful of fellow professionals I'm sure I'd have punched the air and jumped for joy.

The customary pre-match get-together had taken place at Bisham Abbey, a training complex situated in rural Buckinghamshire. Travelling with me down the M1 were my City team-mates Bob Brightwell, Steve Redmond and Andy Hinchcliffe, who'd also been picked for the squad. As reassuring as it was to be with some friendly faces, it was also nice to meet up with different players from other teams, many of whom I'd come up against on numerous occasions wearing my City colours. Unsurprisingly, there was plenty of club-versus-club banter, much of it of the north-south divide variety.

'Nice to see you Manc wannabes getting a taste of southern style,' joked Steve Sedgeley as me, Bob, Reddo and Hinchy arrived at the HQ.

Despite the presence of many up-and-coming starlets, there was a refreshing absence of egos within the squad. Michael Thomas, who was making a big name for himself at Arsenal, struck me as a very level-headed guy with no edge to him whatsoever. His Gunners team-mate, Paul Merson, was a laugh-a-minute nutcase, and I got on famously with lads like Stuart Ripley from Blackburn Rovers and Coventry's Dave Smith.

Although we quickly bonded as a unit, the competition between us remained intense. The 1990 World Cup in Italy was looming on the horizon, and the Denmark game was seen as a shop window in which to showcase our skills. It was our chance to impress the big cheeses in the England set-up, from our passionate under-21s coach, Dave Sexton, to the head honcho, Bobby Robson.

The game, watched from the directors' box by Mr Robson as well as Messrs Dalglish, Graham and Souness, went pretty much according to plan for me. Beforehand, however, I'd had to deal with my usual bout of pre-match tension, an inner conflict that made my head buzz with excitement and my knees knock with nerves. I needed to chill out, big time, so I spent a few minutes' solitary confinement in the dressing-room toilets. Hunched in a cubicle, I drummed into myself all the fundamentals that I'd learned over the years. As often happened in these circumstances, I closed my eyes and sought Tony Book's counsel.

Keep level-headed, Lakey; stay focused and do those simple things well . . . I visualised him saying, narrowing his eyes and jabbing his bony finger.

So that's what I did. Keeping it simple, and avoiding silly mistakes in those first 15 minutes, did my confidence the world of good and had a real calming effect on my game. Once my nerves had settled, everything I did in the first half seemed to come off – my passing, my positioning and my setting up of chances – and Vinny Samways and I set the tempo for the game.

A whack on the calf ruled me out of the second-half action. Though I was upset to have to leave the pitch, I felt pretty pleased with my display. My appearance, albeit brief, had showed me that not only could I hold my own with players at this level, but I could actually go out there and shine.

Something that I hadn't foreseen in the aftermath of my England call-up was the dramatic increase in my fan mail. What had previously been a trickle of post turned into a torrent, as supporters from all over the UK began to write into the club to request autographs and signed memorabilia. One afternoon I noticed a brown Jiffy bag wedged into my pigeonhole.

'Maybe it's your first pair of knickers to sign, Lakey,' laughed Nigel Gleghorn as I tentatively groped the squashy packet. 'Open it, mate, let's have a butchers . . .'

I was taken aback when I pulled out its contents. There, in all its blue velvet, gold-tasselled glory, was my first England cap. Before then I'd only considered the cap in an abstract, statistical kind of way, but seeing the tangible proof took my breath away.

'That's quality, Lakey. One to show the grandchildren, eh,' said Nigel as I balanced it on my index finger and studied the embossed lettering. Part of me felt the urge to put it on, drive to my old school in Denton and yell 'librarian my arse!' at that careers adviser who'd doubted my football ambitions. Instead, though, I walked across the stadium forecourt towards my car, with my treasured package under my arm, reminding myself of the importance of keeping my size 11s firmly grounded.

You're only as good as your last match, son; never forget that, I imagined Dad warning me. *Don't be getting' all bloody high and mighty, now . . .*

Still, I did try my posh cap on when I got home, staging a camp fashion parade around the lounge for my giggling mum. But, high jinks over, I then returned it to its padded beige envelope and switched my priorities to that Saturday's game.

The magnitude of representing your country only truly hits home when you're standing tall, puffing out your chest and belting out the national anthem. Even more so when you're playing overseas. The first time I sang 'God Save The Queen' on foreign soil was on 7 March 1989, prior to a UEFA under-21s championship tie in Shkroda, Albania. As the music reached its climax, I felt a tremendous upswelling of patriotism and had to steel myself to keep the tears at bay.

The match that ensued was in effect a curtain-raiser for the England v Albania World Cup qualifier due to take place in the capital, Tirana, the next day. Indeed, Bryan Robson, Paul Gascoigne and the rest of the lads were in the crowd that night. Just being able to share the flight over with them had been enough for me, yet here they were, sitting yards away from the touchline, watching our every move. It was the perfect morale-booster.

Our opponents were the oldest-looking under-21s I'd ever seen in my life, with leathery complexions, glossy beards and thickets of chest hair sprouting over the top of their shirts. It was like an Academy XI coming up against a Veterans XI. The Albanians were technically able and physically imposing but, thanks to some stoic defending from the two Steves (Chettle and Redmond) alongside some effective link play between me and Stu Ripley, we controlled the game and fully deserved our 2–1 victory. Had it not been for our wayward finishing the goal margin would have been much wider, but it was a good result nonetheless.

Following the final whistle, my Albanian counterpart jogged over, shook my hand and gestured for me to swap jerseys. The prospect of forsaking my prized red away shirt for a white, sweaty polyester number didn't exactly fill me with joy but, as protocol demanded, I peeled it off and reluctantly handed it over. However, before fulfilling his side of the bargain this fella suddenly turned on his heel and legged it, Carl Lewis-style, out of the stadium, still clad in his own shirt. I was left standing there, red of face and cold of nipple, with the laughter of ten team-mates ringing in my ears.

'They've only got one strip, you Manc muppet. They never do swaps,' cackled Michael Thomas. 'Oh, and nice tits, by the way . . .' he shouted as I stormed off in the direction of the home dressing room to reclaim my shirt.

I arrived there to be informed via basic Albanian sign language that my arch-enemy had already fled into the night. I then found myself being slowly backed into a corner by a dozen Teen Wolf lookalikes wearing 'whatcha gonna do 'bout it?' expressions.

I wish I'd known the Albanian for 'I'll get me coat.'

Venturing beyond the Iron Curtain for the first time had been a huge culture shock for me, and I found the stark contrast between this Communist outpost and my cushy Western lifestyle extremely unsettling. Our hotel was a case in point. The room I shared with Steve Redmond, with its dull decor and barred windows, was like a prison cell. Its open plan layout meant that we could almost touch the bath from our beds, and were within sniffing distance of a Balkans-style hole-in-the-ground toilet. This was a completely new concept to me and, as I stared into its stagnant abyss, I found myself yearning for my pine-fresh Armitage Shanks loo at home.

'It's a good job we're mates, Lakey,' Reddo said, squatting over the hole of doom and taking aim as I averted my gaze to the polystyrene ceiling.

Making this sorry situation even worse was the fact that, having been advised by our medical team not to touch Albanian food with a bargepole, we'd flown over our own supplies from England. So we arrived laden with bread, jam, chicken, potatoes, Mars bars and Ambrosia rice pudding. And a crateful of Heinz baked beans. Tin upon tin of Heinz baked beans, supposedly to maintain our carbohydrate quota and to keep us regular. With this as our staple diet, and with a prehistoric bog in which to deposit its outcome, it's no wonder that our hotel room ended up smelling like the elephant house at Chester Zoo.

Travelling to watch the seniors play in Tirana was an enlightening experience. Our driver was friendly enough – the three lions cardboard cut-out that he'd glued to the windscreen was a lovely touch – but the coach itself was a knackered old rust-bucket with cracked headlights and a sagging exhaust pipe. Inside, the seats were threadbare, the ashtrays overflowed with fag ends and the curtains were so rank that they'd probably have disintegrated had we tried to pull them shut.

Tirana itself was a concrete jungle of slate-grey factories and high-rise apartment blocks, interspersed with areas of barren wasteland. It made Denton look like Disneyland. Its citizens, however, were anything but drab. As if somehow compensating for their austere surroundings, they paced the pavements dressed in stack heels, bell bottoms with Bay City Rollers-style turn-ups and those short tartan jackets with the furry collars. It was like stepping back into the 1970s and seeing your childhood clothes being worn by adults.

England won the match 2–0, coasting to victory with goals from John Barnes and Bryan Robson. Within an hour of the final whistle we were aboard a coach hurtling towards Tirana airport, delirious at the prospect of seeing our families and sleeping in our own beds. Two days in Albania had been quite enough.

As I queued at the check-in desk, sitting astride my suitcase, I gazed over at our big-name players signing autographs and posing for pictures with a noisy group of England fans. It was abundantly clear who the main attraction was. At the hub of the scrummage was Paul Gascoigne, basking in the spotlight and chatting with the supporters as if they were bosom buddies. It was fascinating to behold. In fact, I was staring so intently that I happened to catch his eye and, before I knew it, Gazza was ambling over to me.

'Howay, Lakey?' he said in his Geordie twang.

'Er, not bad, Gazza,' I stammered. I'd never really spoken to him before, and assumed that I was about to become a target for one of his wind-ups. A few of the under-21 lads had already fallen victim to his trademark pranks.

'Just to say I thought you were quality the other day, man.

You took the piss going forward. And I f***in' *loved* the nutmegs.'

'Thanks, Gazza.'

'S'all right. But don't get too good, mind. I'm not having you nickin' *my* f***in' place,' he said, giving me a playful wink before bounding back to his adoring fans.

Blimey. I could have flapped my arms and flown myself back to London at that very moment, such was the uplifting effect of Gazza's ringing words.

And, if I didn't think it was possible to get any more starstruck, none other than Bryan Robson offered me and Reddo a lift back to Manchester after we touched down at Gatwick. I spent the journey home perched on the back seat of his chauffeur-driven Mercedes, pinching myself that I was cadging a ride with the England captain, the very same midfield maestro that I'd watched score that early-doors pile-driver seven years previously.

As his driver bombed up the fast lane of the M6 (the police booked him not once, but twice for speeding) Bryan spoke freely about his career in football, offering up snapshots of life at Old Trafford and talking about his time as an international.

What a great bloke, I thought to myself as I hit the sack later that night, cocooned in my comfy duvet, delighted to be back home in Haughton Green.

Later that year I found myself jetting off to Eastern Europe again, for the final group tie of the under-21 championships in Poland. I was particularly keen to impress in this game, having seriously annoyed Dave Sexton during the home leg at Plymouth. I'd been supplied a horror pass 20 yards from goal with a Polish player breathing down my neck. Displaying remarkable stupidity, I'd nutmegged him on the edge of the box, before passing the ball out of defence.

Afterwards, I'd received a proper cockney ear-bashing from the manager.

'Lake, my son, If I ever see you f***ing nutmegging a centre-forward in the box when we're 2–1 up with five minutes to go, I'll drag you off and rip that f***ing shirt off your back. What gives you the f***ing right to take chances like that for your country?'

As our coach almost literally tore a strip off me, Paul Merson did his utmost to try to make me laugh, standing behind Sexton and gurning theatrically. I had to dig my fingernails deep into my thighs to stop myself from guffawing. The last thing I wanted to do was to show disrespect because, in the cold light of day, Sexton was spot on. Over-confidence can lead to recklessness, and I didn't blame him for wanting to make an example of me.

In a small town called Jastrzebie, in a tiny university stadium, we beat Poland 2–1. The Poles posed a greater threat than the Albanians – they were considerably more organised and creative – but our perseverance and spirit prevailed that day with the magnificent Merson as our talisman. Victory wasn't enough for us to progress to the next round, though; that honour went to Sweden, a team I'd not been able to play against due to injury.

*

In January 1990, hours before City's third-round FA Cup match at Millwall, I took a phone call in my hotel room. On the line was an official from Lancaster Gate, the FA's headquarters.

'Mr Robson has announced his provisional World Cup squad today,' he said, 'and I'm pleased to inform you, Paul, that you'll be flying the flag for Manchester City.'

I felt like screaming my glad tidings from the rooftops, but I needed to stay focused on the cup tie, so I decided to keep schtum until after the match. With an added spring in my step, I went on to have a great game, keeping the Millwall wide-men in check and scoring probably my best ever goal for City, a 20-yard volley that whistled through a crowded penalty area and soared into the top corner. My strike wasn't enough to prevent us being booted out of the cup, though, as the home side rode out 2–1 victors.

'It's no more than you deserve, Lakey,' said my mate Neil McNab when I revealed my good news to him on the coach back to Manchester. 'This is your chance to really go and express yourself. And I'm not just saying this, pal, but there's no one in the England set-up as versatile as you.'

Lilleshall was the venue for our 48-hour get-together. I was shitting bricks as I drove down to Shropshire that cold January morning, convinced that I would somehow make a fool of myself among England's elite. Also playing on my mind was how I would cope without the fraternal support of Bob, Reddo and the other lads in the under-21 set-up.

I parked up, and started on the half-mile trek towards Lilleshall Hall. It needn't have been such a schlep, had I not decided to park my little Vauxhall behind the tennis HQ so as to avoid the embarrassment of pitching it up next to a gleaming fleet of Mercs, Jags and Porsches. A month previously I'd been delighted to take delivery of my new black Astra GTE (sponsored by a local plant-hire firm), but I just didn't feel comfortable rolling up alongside all these turbo-charged mean machines.

As I checked in at reception, I was told that I'd be rooming with the Wolverhampton Wanderers' striker Steve Bull. I walked in to find him reclined on the bed reading a newspaper, and before long we were having a good chat over a cup of tea. He seemed a really grounded guy, expressing his excitement at being picked as well as his determination not to become overawed by the big-name players.

'We've got as much right to be here as them,' he stressed in his Black Country tones, 'so let's give a good account of ourselves. Just because they drive Jags doesn't make them any better than us.'

Unusually, there were to be no practice matches during our two-day meet. Instead, Bobby Robson had scheduled an intense programme of fitness sessions and skills training. With everyone desperate to make their mark, the competition and rivalry were predictably fierce. Gary Stevens, the Everton full-back, was in pole position after the final assessments, closely followed by Aston Villa's David Platt. Despite my nerves getting the better of me I didn't fare too badly, finishing about halfway down the pecking order.

That evening we were treated to a luxurious meal at a nearby stately home. There were 15 of us to each banqueting table, and I was sandwiched in between Steve Bull and Mike Newell, and facing Gary Lineker, Bryan Robson and Paul Gascoigne. I was as quiet as a mouse at first, nodding politely and only speaking when I was spoken to. I felt socially inept among all these mega-famous, super-confident players and was paranoid that I was going to start blushing – or worse, stuttering – if I attempted conversation.

Gazza – who was genuinely hilarious – held court the whole time, playing the fool with Lineker as his willing straight man. Lineker, much to my embarrassment, decided to raise the subject of the City versus Spurs game the previous August, which had seen Gazza mocking me throughout by pulling out his ears, provoking me to retaliate by mimicking a fat belly (the newspapers had been full of our spat the next day). I cringed as the whole episode was relived to all and sundry.

'I'd take that as a compliment,' grinned Bryan Robson. 'He only does that to players who give him the runaround.'

'F*** off, Robbo, no one's got the better of me this season . . .' retorted Gazza. He probably had a point.

John Barnes and Peter Beardsley cottoned on to my shyness and went out of their way to make me feel at ease, chatting enthusiastically about Liverpool and conceding that City had given them a real run for their money when we'd visited Anfield on the opening day of the season.

'You certainly kept Rushy quiet,' said Beardsley, recalling how Liverpool's number 9 had hardly got a sniff that afternoon.

As the conversation (and the alcohol) started to flow I began to relax a little. I even plucked up the courage to ask them what advice they'd give someone like me at this stage in my career.

'Steer clear of Gazza,' chuckled Barnesy.

Following dessert, Bobby Robson came over to our table to say hello. With his sunny nature and unassuming manner, he struck me as a really warm, genuine person. There were gales of laughter when he addressed Gary Stevens as Trevor – confusing players' names was a famous trait of his – but the affection towards him was palpable. The England lads obviously thought the world of Bobby, and it was easy to see why.

'So how d'you think you did at Lilleshall, then?' asked Howard Kendall when I came back to Platt Lane.

'All right, I think, Gaffer.'

His features crinkled into a smile.

'I've heard you did much more than all right.'

'What d'you mean?'

'Well, let's just say I've had an interesting little chat with Bobby. Not only does he think you're the best young player he's seen for ages, Lakey, but he's talking you up as his next England captain.'

'Are you winding me up?

'Nope. Marvellous feet, great attitude, he said.'

Bloody hell.

'Don't look so surprised, son. It sounds like Bobby's got big plans for you. You've been well and truly earmarked.'

By March 1990 I'd graduated from the under-21 to the England 'B' squad and was selected for the friendly against the Republic of Ireland in Cork. Reporting for duty was a roll-call of England's young elite, amongst them Matthew Le Tissier, Tony Adams, David Batty and Dalian Atkinson. I found myself sharing a room with Nottingham Forest's Nigel Clough. We chatted briefly about how our respective seasons were going, and I asked him what it was like having Brian as a father, and how he coped with idiots like me posing very predictable questions.

'I'm proud of my dad, of course I am,' he said, 'but I'd like to make a name for myself, if I can.'

Nigel was quite a shy, softly spoken lad. Unlike my flight partner, Lee Dixon, who'd chattered so incessantly that I thought his emergency oxygen mask was going to drop down.

The Ireland game, coming a couple of months before Italia '90, was my final chance to make some kind of impression. I knew beforehand that I was going to be sitting on the bench for the first half, as Dave Sexton was keen to give us all a run-out, but this didn't overly concern me. I'd still have a good 45 minutes in which to prove my worth.

Half an hour before the game, both teams filed onto the

pitch for the customary warm-up. As I did a few heel-flicks, I was startled by a sudden, deafening cheer from the crowd. The stands erupted. And then the object of all the yelling and screaming loped towards me, having just emerged from the tunnel.

'How ya doin', Lakey?' said my Manchester City team-mate Niall Quinn, patting me on the back.

'Bloody hell, Quinny, are they always like this when you're in town?' I asked him as green-shirted fans loudly chanted his name.

'Bit mad, isn't it . . .'

'You're telling me, pal. I know what, why don't you drive round the perimeter in a Pope-mobile next time, eh?'

He grinned broadly, told me to go away in a distinctly unholy manner, and cantered back to his team-mates. The hero-worship continued unabated until the final whistle. In all my career, I don't think I ever saw such an outpouring of emotion for one player. They loved him, bejaysus.

Quinny was recovering from a thigh strain and had made himself available to the 'B' team in order to sharpen up his fitness. The Irish lads couldn't believe their luck. His aerial threat made all the difference, enabling the home side to take a 2–1 scoreline into the interval.

In the visitors' dressing room I psyched myself up, convincing myself that I could play my part in turning around our fortunes in the second half. My eagerness turned to despair, though, when Dave Sexton made a point of singling me out.

'We're a goal behind, Lakey, so I need you to be playing wide left for me, son.'

My heart sank. *Wide f***in' left?* I've played there once in three years. I'm an in-form full-back-cum-midfielder, for f***'s sake, not a winger. My head pounded with anger. Some shop window, eh. I felt like doing a sit-down protest I was that pissed off, but ultimately I was pulling on an England shirt and had to quickly regain my composure.

I ran out of the tunnel shaking my head, staggered that Sexton was prepared to deploy me in an unfamiliar role just because we were lagging behind in a meaningless friendly. I tried my best to approach the game professionally, getting my head down and cracking on with it, but my mind was all over the place. I'd never felt so angry and frustrated on a football pitch, and as such was never going to produce a vintage performance. We lost 4–1 in the end, Quinny's brace sending his disciples crazy.

I kept my mouth shut in the dressing room afterwards, but everyone knew I was absolutely steaming. I respected Dave Sexton as a coach, but I didn't respect this decision one bit. As far as I was concerned, my trip to Cork had been a complete and utter waste of time. Meddle with a team to your heart's content if there's nothing at stake, Dave, by all means, but not when there's a coveted World Cup around the corner.

In my mind, any chances I had of making Bobby Robson's final squad had been scuppered. It was an embittering experience that, I'm sad to say, demeaned the value of my

England 'B' cap. I don't think I even took it out of its envelope when it arrived in my pigeonhole a few weeks later.

I returned to Manchester feeling utterly deflated. I sought solace in the bosom of Maine Road, though, putting any disappointment on the backburner and focusing on all things domestic. I also took time out to buy my first property, a three-bedroom townhouse in the Stockport suburb of Heaton Mersey. I'd been prompted to do so by a top football agent who'd set up a meeting in Brown's, a chic London club, to discuss my future options. In between some serious people-watching – George Michael, Andrew Ridgeley and Pepsi 'n' Shirlie were partying there that night – I listened to the agent as he advised me to take advantage of my ascendant career by investing my surplus cash into bricks and mortar.

Towards the end of April, a grim-faced Howard called me into his office to inform me that Bobby Robson had decided not to include me in his World Cup squad. In hindsight, I don't think that the Cork fiasco had much bearing on the final judgement. The fact that I was a relative newcomer to the England set-up, and was seen as something of a gamble, probably sealed my fate rather than anything else. Manchester United's Paul Parker, who was selected in my place, was older and more experienced than me and represented a much safer bet.

'I'm really sorry, Paul,' said Mr Robson when he rang me shortly after the official squad announcement. 'I've had to go for an out-and-out defender for Italy but, I'm telling you now, your time will come, son. Keep playing well, keep yourself fit, and I'll be seeing you again, mark my words.'

I appreciated the phone call and accepted his decision. But that didn't mean to say that I wasn't gutted beyond belief.

Watching Italia '90 on television was never going to be an easy experience for me. Being within touching distance of playing on those glorious pitches and competing with the best footballers in the world did my head in, frankly. I certainly wasn't running upstairs to fill in a World Cup wall-chart, put it that way.

One of the hardest aspects was having to endure New Order's 'World in Motion' song. Not that I didn't rate it – I thought both the single and the video were fantastic – but its blanket media coverage meant that it was a constant reminder of my non-attendance. The video in particular perfectly captured the spirit and character of the England squad – Gazza's impishness, John Barnes's style, Stuart Pearce's passion – and only served to make me want to be there even more. And as for Pavarotti and his Nessun bloody Dorma . . .

I wallowed even deeper in self-pity when my nephew Chris ran into the lounge wielding a Paul Lake Italia '90 Panini sticker. Old Mr Panini, it seems, had cranked up his printing presses shortly after our Lilleshall get-together. On one side was a head-and-shoulders shot of me in an England shirt and on the other was printed a list of statistics next to a quote attributed to Lawrie McMenemy.

'Always seemed to be injured at the time of important under-21s call-ups,' it said. Cheers, Lawrie. Kick a man while he's down, why don't you.

My disappointment evaporated as the tournament progressed. By the time England had reached the last 16, I'd really begun to enjoy the football and got wholeheartedly behind the lads, the living proof being my child-like whoop when David Platt scored his late winner against Belgium. My joy would be short-lived, unfortunately. A week later, not only did I have to witness the sight of Paul Gascoigne's blotchy, tear-streaked face, I also had to stomach England's semi-final defeat at the hands of Germany. Gazza's ability on the pitch (and antics off it) had made him the star attraction of the tournament, and seeing his reaction to being yellow-carded, and potentially missing out on the final, was unbearable.

As it happened, the German penalty machine put paid to our hopes and dreams, although I don't think I was alone in thinking that a final without Gazza just wouldn't have been the same.

Rip-roaring holidays in Ibiza and Tenerife helped me to overcome my World Cup woes. Playing tennis in the sunshine and dancing until dawn did me the world of good, and by the time August came my mojo was fully restored.

Just days after my appointment as City captain – one of the most pivotal and emotional moments of my career – Howard summoned me for a meeting to discuss a contract renewal. This came as a huge relief to me. Since my trip to Lilleshall, speculation concerning my City future had been unrelenting, with an exasperated Peter Swales constantly having to refute headlines linking me with various clubs. Liverpool was the name most bandied about, with reports circulating that Kenny Dalglish had tabled a £3 million bid. I tried to ignore the rumour mill and concentrate instead on my football, but sometimes it was hard to block out those voices from the Kippax that I heard questioning my loyalty. I often felt like stomping over to them to set the record straight.

'Don't believe all the rubbish you read in the papers, lads,' I wished I could have said, 'because I'm going nowhere.'

I headed to the gaffer's Maine Road office after training, feeling positive and upbeat. Howard reclined in his leather chair, and proceeded to offer me a five-year deal, which I gleefully signed on the spot.

'However,' he said, 'give me ten solid games as captain, and we'll rip that contract up and I'll make you the highest-paid player that this football club has ever seen. You're going places, Lakey,' he beamed, 'and I need you to be going places wearing a sky blue shirt.'

This was music to my ears. Not only had Howard handed me the captaincy and secured me a new contract, he was virtually guaranteeing my long-term future at Maine Road.

To mark this fact, the *Manchester Evening News* decided to organise a photoshoot the following day. I met them on the pitch after training, the snapper producing a blue and white scarf for me to hold aloft as he clicked away. After giving a couple of upbeat quotes to a local reporter I ambled out of the stadium, the scarf still round my neck, and signed a few autographs for a cluster of fans milling around the forecourt.

I soon heard a loud shout coming from the direction of the City souvenir shop.

'Over here please, Paul,' the store manager had mouthed, gesturing in a come-hither manner.

I remember walking into the shop, assuming he was about to congratulate me on my new contract, or about to ask me to sign the back of one of his home shirts for posterity.

'I'll have that scarf back, thank you very much,' he'd snapped, leaning over the counter and wresting it from my shoulders. 'Don't think I didn't see you trying to walk off with it.'

Two weeks later we were up against Aston Villa at Maine Road, only my third outing wearing the captain's armband. I'd been told that the new England manager, Graham Taylor, was in the crowd, apparently keeping tabs on me and David Platt. I felt in tip-top condition as I jogged onto the pitch, guiding the City mascot with one hand and saluting the City fans with the other. I let the little lad take a pot-shot at Andy Dibble (who over-dramatically leapt the other way) before steering him towards the centre circle for the perfunctory photos and toss of the coin. As the mascot dashed back to the tunnel to his proud parents, I took the opportunity to mobilise my back four in the final moments before kick-off.

'Remember your jobs today, lads, especially at those set pieces. Don't stop talking – communication's the key, okay – and let's try and keep ourselves switched on for 90 minutes . . .'

And, after some handclaps and backslaps, we all took up our positions, ready for battle to commence.

The first hour of the match saw us comfortably holding Villa's attack, with the two Tonys – Cascarino and Daley – failing to make much of an impact. It was after half-time, though, that we started to get more of a grip on the game. In the 65th minute I advanced towards goal in a mazy run, skinning Cascarino and Paul McGrath, nutmegging Derek Mountfield, before having the ball nicked off my toes by a diving Nigel Spink.

Then it happened.

Intercepting a pass to Cascarino, I jumped in and clipped the ball to my team-mate Mark Brennan. As I did so my right boot got stuck in the turf, my body twisted awkwardly and, with an almighty crunch, I landed in a heap on the ground. As I hit the deck I felt a weird clunk in my knee, followed by a sharp, searing pain.

I lay on the pitch in the foetal position, frozen with shock, totally unaware that my life had changed forever.

7

In a Lonely Place

I was carried off the pitch, flanked by physio Roy Bailey and the club doctor, Norman Luft, too dazed and shell-shocked to acknowledge the thousands of upstanding City fans. We headed down the tunnel to the physio room where the doc assessed my knee, swiftly concluding that it was far too swollen for any clear-cut diagnosis.

'Try to relax, Lakey,' said Roy. 'I'll pack it with ice now, and I'll have another look at it after the game. We'll probably know more in the morning, to be honest,' he added, before grabbing his medical bag and rushing back to his pitch-side duties.

I lay on the treatment table, my leg throbbing, my heart racing and my head swimming with frantic questions. What kind of injury is it? Have I broken something? Is it just a bad twist? What's Graham Taylor thinking right now? Will he think I'm injury prone? How long will I be out? Just a fortnight? Maybe a month? Please God, don't let it be the whole season . . .

Suddenly, a huge roar from the crowd made the whole room vibrate, and seconds later a tannoy announcement proclaimed that City had gone 2–1 up.

'... *and City's goal scored by number three, Neil Pointon* ...'

I spent the rest of the game clutching an ice bag to my knee, listening to all the cheers and chants as they filtered through the walls. Once the 90 minutes was up, the City fans celebrated the three points and, as per usual, the club's 'Boys in Blue' anthem blared out of the stadium speakers.

> *... blue and white they go together*
> *We will carry on for evermore* ...

My prognosis remained uncertain for several days as I waited patiently for the swelling to subside. I continued to turn up to Maine Road each morning, cadging lifts with my pal Jason, hobbling around the place on crutches and spending hours in the physio room. Following two mind-numbing days spent icing and compressing my knee, things eventually calmed down and I was sent to hospital for an x-ray.

'You'll be back around the six-week mark,' was the reckoning after the results confirmed that there was no bone damage. I was given the impression that, while it was more than just a knock, it certainly wasn't as serious as everyone had initially feared. I wouldn't need to see the consultant again, I was told, and an MRI scan of my ligaments and tendons wouldn't be necessary.

Roy tasked me with a basic rehab programme. Designed to

focus on building the strength in my hamstrings and quads, it comprised gentle, stress-limiting exercises alongside some light weight training. Now and then I felt some discomfort in my knee – it gave way on a couple of occasions – but, like most players who didn't know any better, I assumed that such setbacks were par for the course, and accepted the party line of 'you've obviously got a slight weakness there, Lakey.'

After a month or so I was told that I could have a change of scenery, a welcome development since I was becoming increasingly stir-crazy in the cramped physio room, and was sick of staring at the same four walls. I started training at Maine Road, following a more physically demanding routine that had me jogging around the perimeter of the pitch and hopping up and down the concrete steps of the Kippax terracing. I must have covered every inch of that stand, scaling Rows A to Z and back again, sweating buckets like a poor man's Rocky Balboa.

I spent my recovery time sitting in one of the wide aisles, resting my knee and sipping from a bottle of water. Sometimes I'd watch as the head groundsman, Stan Gibson, lovingly tended to his pitch, mowing the turf into wide stripes before watering it with the sprinklers. Having been at the club for decades, Stan was almost part of the furniture at Manchester City and lived with his wife, Joyce, in a little house that adjoined the souvenir shop. Short, squat and as strong as an ox, he was one of the most loyal and likeable people at Maine Road, and was held in great affection by players and staff alike.

Despite his onerous workload, Stan always came over for a chat if he spied me up in the gods.

'How's that knee of yours feeling today, Lakey?'

'Not so bad, Stanley, not so bad.'

Sometimes he'd compare my own plight with that of Colin Bell, whose battle for fitness he'd also witnessed at close quarters in the late 1970s. Colin was arguably the best player ever to have worn a City shirt, but his career was blighted and ultimately finished by a knee injury. I remember seeing him in action following his ill-fated comeback, his limping frame a heart-rending sight for all those fans who'd seen 'Nijinsky' in his prime.

Our groundsman would get choked up just talking about him.

'Colin worked like a trooper, just like you,' he'd say, his weather-worn face flushing with emotion. 'It broke my heart to see him sat alone in the stands, just like it breaks my heart seeing you sitting here now.'

'I'll be all right, don't worry about me . . .'

'Just you keep on going, pal. And even if you come back half the player, you'll still waltz into that team, y'know that, don't you?'

'Thanks, Stan.'

'And another thing . . .'

'What's that, mate?'

'Keep off my f***ing grass,' he'd say, chuckling to himself as he trundled back towards his beloved pitch.

After a month of endless running, I was given the green

light to start some proper football work. I was delighted with this, in spite of the fact that orders from the chairman had decreed that I couldn't rejoin my team-mates at Platt Lane. I wasn't to be on public display, apparently, and I was told instead to make my way to the Manchester University playing fields to train privately.

At the time I assumed that this closed-door policy was purely for my benefit, minimising distraction and helping me to focus. Looking back, though, I now think there was more to it than met the eye. Many football reporters were closely tracking my progress, and I think there was an element of twitchiness on the club's part. They were under pressure to return one of its prime assets to full fitness, and didn't want any setbacks or mishaps to become common knowledge.

It was probably a good job that, apart from the physio, no one saw my knee dramatically give way during that first on-pitch training session. Theoretically, the plan had been for me to move up a gear by attempting some sprinting, passing and tackling. Roy was also keen to work on some twisting and turning, since up until then my exercises had largely involved running up and down in straight lines.

The reality was very different, however. My knee was unable to withstand a short burst of weaving in and out of cones, and it collapsed beneath me. Seeing me lying face-down in the mud was enough for Roy to tell me to go and get changed.

'Lakey, let's call it a day. I'm taking you to see the specialist.'

I limped back to the dressing room, my head down and my spirit dented.

The following day I was booked in at a north-west hospital for investigative keyhole surgery (or an arthroscopy, to give it its proper meical name).

'You've ruptured your anterior cruciate ligament,' explained Roy after he'd spoken to the consultant. The ACL, he told me, was the criss-cross tendon in the knee that acted as a restraint to prevent damage, especially while twisting and turning. He might as well have spoken Swahili as he continued to blind me with science, because all I could think about were those three shattering words: *ruptured cruciate ligament. Ruptured cruciate ligament.* The injury that all footballers dread. The worst possible outcome.

The forward strategy, I was told, was an innovative but relatively untested technique which would involve the reconstruction of the ligament using a sliver of my own tissue, taken from the patella tendon of the same knee.

'So what's the recovery time, then?' I asked nervously.

'Well, you probably won't be playing for another six months, at least,' sighed Roy, trying to break the news as gently as possible.

Weird as it sounds, I took some solace from this faraway-sounding timeline. After weeks of uncertainty, a part of me welcomed the clarity of a specific diagnosis. The prospect of major surgery followed by a half-year lay-off wasn't ideal, of course, but at least now I had a target to aim for. My mind flicked through an imaginary calendar. December, January, February, March, April, May. If I play my cards right I could be fit by June, I thought. Get through pre-season unscathed and I might even be in the starting line-up come August. I reckoned I could live with that.

Within weeks, I was wheeled down to theatre in a private hospital, all gowned-up and ready for my big op. As the sleepy-juice was injected I chose not to recite the customary reverse countdown; instead, Bob Brightwell had dared me to reel off 'they think it's all over; it is now . . .' I got a few strange looks as I lay on the operating table, reciting Kenneth Wolstenholme's famous words from 1966, getting as far as 'over' before drifting into the land of Nod.

A few hours later, I awoke to hear a weird buzzing sound coupled with the odd sensation of someone roughly grabbing my knee. Groggily, I opened my eyes, lifted my head and saw that my leg was encased in a cage-like contraption that was automatically, and painfully, bending my knee up and down (a CPM machine, I later learned, meaning 'constant passive motion'). It wasn't the best wake-up call I've ever had in my life.

My first physiotherapy session, three days after the operation, involved trying to straighten my leg and raise it off the bed. My head was willing, but my body wasn't, yet following some mind-over-matter on my part (and some unflagging patience on the physio's) after a couple of hours

I was finally able to achieve some mobility. I continued apace over the next few days, tackling exercises which, basic though they were, represented slow-but-sure progress.

I was discharged after a couple of weeks, but was still required to attend daily out-patient sessions. My self-confidence soared as each mission was completed – walking, then running, then driving – and it was a momentous day when, after two more months of painstaking rehab, I was told that hospital intervention was no longer necessary and that I could return to my club for treatment.

City's medical team was incredibly short-staffed, however, with one part-time doctor and one physio tasked with overseeing 40 players. Bearing this in mind, the club decided that I should continue the majority of my recovery at the FA's rehabilitation centre, adhering to a schedule that would entail spending two weeks out of every three at Lilleshall.

Like a sporting version of Fame's New York School of Performing Arts, but without kids dancing on yellow cabs and singing 'High Fidelity', Lilleshall was a hive of activity. Nestled in a leafy corner of north Shropshire, this sprawling former hunting lodge housed the FA's Centre of Excellence and Medical Education Centre, and acted as the hub for a variety of sporting bodies, including British Gymnastics, National Archery GB and the English Table Tennis Association. Bizarrely enough, the venue also doubled up as a designated training centre for Her Majesty's prison wardens. No doubt these blokes felt right at home in Lilleshall's spartan residential blocks; the place wasn't called the Colditz of professional football for nothing.

I didn't like leaving Manchester at the best of times, especially when my temporary digs amounted to a small, dingy room with bare walls and fraying carpets. I remember unpacking my bags with a heavy heart on the day of my arrival, emptying out my clothes and toiletries onto an old wooden bed with a mattress that reeked of Dettol. The ensuite, while not of Eastern European standards, was still pretty grim, with an ancient toilet, a mildewy shower and an illuminated mirror that exposed every pimple and pock-mark. Seeing the Singing Detective stare back at you as you shaved each morning wasn't the best way to start your day.

My room's only saving grace was its ground-floor location, which allowed me the luxury of receiving all four channels on the wall-mounted television. The players on the lower ground floor couldn't tune into BBC2 and Channel 4 – the *Countdown* and *University Challenge* fans were livid – but it was the lads in the basement who had the real bum deal, with TV sets that could only pick up BBC1. Having telly addicts hammering on my door at night ('let us in, Lakey, *Midweek Sport Special*'s on . . .') became commonplace.

All in all, it wasn't the ideal environment for someone who needed their spirits lifting. Whenever I was at a loose end – more so at night, when all was quiet – I'd lie on the bed or pace around the room, mulling over my crappy predicament. I'd constantly replay my chequered career in my head, rewinding and pausing, searching for clues and answers, torturing myself with guilt and blame. Why am I so susceptible? Is there something wrong with my build? Did I play too much football as a child? Have I played through the pain barrier too often? Did I rush back too soon after my first injury? Is this all my fault?

I tried my best, though, to hide these innermost thoughts from my family whenever I journeyed back to Manchester. I enjoyed my regular reunions with the Lake clan, yet would dread the subject of 'our Paul's knee' being brought up during Sunday lunch.

'Are you in much pain, love?' Mum would ask, her eyes full of concern. 'I've got paracetamol in the cupboard if you need it.'

And then Dad would pose the million-dollar question.

'You'll be all right won't you, son?' he'd ask, sharpening his knives and carving the roast chicken while Mum dished out the veg. 'You're young, you're fit, there's no reason why not, eh?'

Not wanting to overly worry my family, I'd try to skirt around the issue. It was something that I would become expert at over time.

'I'll get there, Dad, but it might be a little bit longer than I thought,' I'd say, feigning nonchalance, before quickly changing the topic of conversation.

'So anyway, Mike, how's life at Macclesfield? Are those scouts still sniffing about, or what . . . ?'

During one of my visits home, I arranged to meet up with a financial adviser. In the early 1990s the UK was stuck in the mire of recession, with interest rates skyrocketing to 15 per cent. Without any appearance money or win bonuses, my income had almost halved, my bank balance had withered to nothing and I was struggling to afford the £1,000-per-month mortgage on my house in Heaton Mersey. I wasn't in a position to sell up – property prices had plummeted and I'd have found myself in negative equity – so I had no option but to rent it out to cover the monthly repayments, and use my parents' place as a base whenever I was training up in Manchester. So now I had another tribulation to add to my growing list. Injured, isolated, frustrated and skint.

I never slept well at Lilleshall, and this wasn't always as a result of my new money worries. Ever since that fateful Villa game I'd experienced horrendous recurring nightmares, the most terrifying of which involved me lying lifelessly on top of a rubbish tip like a discarded tailor's dummy. In another scary scenario I would be swimming in an Olympic-sized pool, but never be able to touch the sides because the more I ploughed on through the water, the further the pool's edges moved away. Not the hardest dreams to psychoanalyse, I imagine.

So vivid were these nightmares that I'd often jolt myself awake, the sweat bucketing off me as a full-blown panic attack took hold. Unable to get back to sleep, I'd cool myself down with a shower before clicking on the Teasmade and sitting in bed, waiting for TV-am to start. When I wasn't in the mood for a cockney rat puppet or a barmy keep-fit woman, I'd just nurse my cuppa and listen to the dawn chorus that floated in through the tiny rectangular window. Lilleshall's vast gardens were a haven for wildlife – rabbits, foxes and badgers were a frequent sight – but it was our feathered friends that held the biggest novelty value for me. I was used to the occasional tweeting sparrow or screeching starling in Manchester, but had never heard anything remotely like the stereophonic Shropshire birdsong that greeted me each morning.

Mike Hooper, the Liverpool goalkeeper and fellow Lilleshall inmate, was a keen birdwatcher who never tired of reminding us that we were in a twitcher's paradise. Whenever he heard an unusual chirrup he would stop in his tracks, even if it was slap-bang in the middle of a training session.

'Sshhhh . . . that's a lesser-crested house warbler,' he'd say with a whisper, cupping his ear to listen as the ball flew past him into the top corner.

'Yeah, and there's a great tit between the posts,' was one memorable riposte.

Awaking with the lark meant that I would be famished by breakfast. Luckily, Lilleshall's legendary English brekkie – a huge platter of crispy bacon, sizzling sausages and poached eggs, daubed liberally with tomato ketchup – dealt with the hunger pangs. The canteen was a meeting point for track-suited people of all ages, shapes and sizes, from the teenage School of Excellence wannabes to the bespectacled, 40-something archers. It was the male and female gymnasts, though – all permanent residents – who raised the bar in terms of attitude and professionalism. They'd always be down for their muesli and grapefruit juice at 7 a.m., bounding past us en route to their strenuous circuit training while we were wolfing down our third round of fried bread.

The gymnasts' astounding discipline, centred on a punishing six-days-a-week exercise regime, put us footballers to shame. My admiration for these supremely dedicated athletes knew no bounds, especially in light of the absolute pittance they received from their sporting body.

I had to report to my rehab gym at 9 a.m. sharp, Monday to Friday. Meeting me there would be a mixed bag of professional footballers, some from the various Divisions; some with complex injuries, others with more straightforward knocks and strains. The unlucky minority, such as Ian Durrant and myself, were recovering from ligament ruptures and had been sentenced to a long stretch of intensive treatment. Those suffering from less serious problems, like Vinnie Jones and Ally McCoist, were parachuted into Shropshire for much shorter stints.

Durrant, the Rangers midfielder, was a lad I got to know quite well. Our similar injuries and long-term rehab meant that we had to spend a large chunk of time together and, with his brilliant training attitude and infectious enthusiasm, I couldn't have wished for a better companion to spur me on. Ian also possessed a caustic sense of humour, and would often upset the more sensitive souls in the camp by over-dramatising their injuries.

'Has your club got a good insurance policy?' he'd ask a

nervous-looking player receiving treatment from the physio. 'Cause by the look of that ankle, you're gonna f***in' need it . . .'

Liverpool's John Barnes – who'd probably never upset a colleague in his life – spent a few weeks at Lilleshall for an Achilles tendon problem. Having had the pleasure of meeting John at the Italia '90 gathering I already knew that he was a gem of a bloke, and as such was delighted when his cheery face popped round the gym door one morning. Some of the younger lads were totally awestruck by him, but his friendly manner immediately put them at ease.

Lighting up Lilleshall with his vibrant personality for a brief spell was the one and only Vinnie Jones, who arrived from Sheffield United needing a dodgy knee attending to. In the short space of time he was there he left an indelible mark, most notably on one hapless PT instructor who was guilty of being a bit too over-familiar with the players, and who'd often get our backs up with the occasional sarcastic comment. As far as Vinnie was concerned, this Sport Billy possessed far too much swagger and needed bringing back down to earth.

'That big-time wanker needs a short, sharp f***in' shock,' Vinnie announced one day, his eyes blazing. He proceeded to haul this startled bloke out of the campus in true hod-carrying style, before bundling him into his boot and taking him for a bumpy, wheel-spinning, two-mile joyride to the front gates and back. Our PT friend emerged from Vinnie's boot white-faced and jelly-legged, and went straight to bed.

An unexpected addition to our knackers' yard was Alan Shearer. The medics treating his knee at Blackburn Rovers were among the best in their field, but he'd decided to swap Ewood Park for Lilleshall temporarily to escape the hurly-burly of a football club and allow himself more time to focus.

Alan didn't say much during the first couple of days – I think he was wisely sussing us all out – but by the third day he'd lightened up and dropped his guard. His renowned competitive streak soon became apparent, though, never more so than during the arduous 12-mile bike rides that we were regularly dispatched on. During his first group cycle, Alan made the mistake of trying to get the better of us. Being a Lilleshall novice he wasn't familiar with the route or the terrain but, as strong-minded as ever, set off far too quickly and pedalled away from the pack like billy-o. By mile ten the rest of us had easily caught him up, hurling obscenities as we glided past him before taking the sharp left through Lilleshall golf course that led us all back to base.

Alan, in his haste to outdo us, sped straight past the golf course turn-off. When he started to see signs for Wolverhampton he realised he was completely lost and had to ask for directions from a local yokel.

We were naturally out in force to give him a hero's welcome when he finally crossed the finish line half an hour later, smiling sheepishly with his arms outstretched in mock celebration. Jibes of 'here he comes, king of the mountains' would plague him for weeks, but he took it all in good humour. He was a decent lad, was Alan, and it was nice to have him around the place.

Riding highest in the popularity stakes, though, was Ally McCoist. Anyone assuming that someone as rich, famous and talented as Ally was bound to be a raving egomaniac would have been mistaken. The Rangers striker was a big hit from the minute he arrived at Lilleshall, his warmth and charm as endearing to the lads in the gym as it was to the girls on reception. Coupling a gift of the gab with a sympathetic ear, Ally was great company, and I remember having the occasional heart-to-hearts with him about my trials and tribulations. As with my good friend Niall Quinn, it was impossible not to like the guy.

The great thing about Lilleshall was that we were all treated as equals, despite the presence of many household names. Rehab, it seemed, was the supreme leveller. Marooned in the middle of nowhere, detached from our football clubs and stripped of supporter adulation and press attention, we all had the same goals: the desire to get fit and the determination to salvage our careers. I generally hated being holed up in Shropshire, but it would have been a much gloomier place without the support of Ian, Ally and the rest of the lads to help me get through the hours, days, weeks and months.

Devised by the taskmaster physios from hell, our daily rehab programme was backbreaking. But, gruelling as it was, we adopted the mindset of 'no pain, no gain', knuckling down and cracking on with the perpetual cycle of circuit training, swimming relays and cardio-vascular workouts. Some lads weren't able to cope with these marathon sessions and would get straight on the phone to their clubs, pleading to be brought home.

Our whip-crackers were well aware of our Groundhog Day existence, though, and would try to relieve the monotony by whatever means they could. Letting us play along with Simon Bates's *Golden Hour* on Radio 1 was a regular mid-morning diversion, with a forfeit for the team that hazarded the wildest guess for the featured year.

'Lakey, you plank, you said 'Dreadlock Holiday' was 1977, not 1978.'

'Chill out, lads, I was out playing football while you lot were sat watching *Cheggers Plays Pop* . . .'

The issuing of forfeits was a deadly serious business at Lilleshall. Each day would always finish with a match of sit-down volleyball or a game of boules, with the losing side liable for an immediate penalty that could be anything from 3,000 metres on the rowing machine, 40 pull-ups on the rings or a cycle sprint to the gates and back. This unwelcome addition to our workload was no laughing matter, particularly on Fridays when we were allowed to clock off earlier than usual and head home for the weekend. The pressure, therefore, to aim your boule as close as possible to the jack was intense; the last thing you wanted to do was incur a detention and become public enemy number one.

While the daily grind could be pretty hard-going, the occasional comic interlude often lightened the load. Even something as childish as one of the lads running off with Desmond Douglas's table tennis bat kept me chuckling for days. I recall the British ping-pong champion – who was a lovely bloke – spending about an hour in the canteen frantically looking for his prized possession while we sniggered at the table like a bunch of naughty schoolboys, debating how we were going to smuggle the bat back into his kitbag without being rumbled.

And then there was the memorable afternoon when an England cricket XI arrived en masse for some fitness work prior to that summer's test series against the West Indies.

'F*** me, I didn't know the Embassy world darts team were in town,' I said as we watched the hulking figures of Graham Gooch, Mike Gatting et al jogging around the pitch.

'Oi, Cliff Lazarenko, the canteen's that way,' we heckled as the nation's finest bowlers and batsmen ran past.

'Piss off, you football jessies,' came the retort.

'One hundred and *eighty*!' we all shouted in unison.

Another sportsman to become the butt of our juvenile humour was tennis star Chris Bailey, who was recovering from a cruciate ligament injury similar to my own. He and I got chatting one morning. He seemed a really nice fella and, being a keen fan of tennis, I was fascinated to learn about his life on the ATP circuit. In fact, we got on so well that Chris invited me to join him for a game of soft tennis the next day. I accepted with trepidation, thoroughly expecting to be trounced by the former British number one.

With my football mates watching from the sidelines, I gave

him a sound thrashing, pumping my fists in victory like my old hero, Roscoe 'The Bullet' Tanner. Jeers of 'call yourself a tennis player, Bailey?' echoed round the sports hall as Chris looked on, clearly distraught. The lads found this display of emotion hilarious, and duly christened him Fluffy for the rest of his stay. Lilleshall's macho environment could be quite pitiless sometimes; a place where any chinks in your armour would be mercilessly exposed and exploited.

Also helping to alleviate the boredom were our eagerly awaited Thursday nights out. A chance for us to escape the donkey work and relax with a beer, these 'socials' became the high point of our week. We tended to give the on-site sports bar a wide berth (it was crammed with local hangers-on who'd swarm round Alan and Ally like bees to a honey pot) opting instead to take a cab to Telford.

Telford was a typical new town, a bit like Runcorn but minus the glitz and glamour. I remember seeing Barnesy's face fall when we got dropped off in the bland, soulless town centre. Five minutes later he was hot-footing it away from a nearby neon-lit 'fun' pub that, within seconds of our arrival, had put 'World In Motion' on the jukebox. Being forced to rap 'you've got to hold and give, and do it at the right time' in public was evidently Barnesy's idea of hell.

We did most of our after-hours revelling in Cascades, a dingy nightclub tucked away in a shopping precinct. With plenty of game girls and dark corners this venue was perfect for a bit of ducking and diving, but, being a hopeless chat-up merchant, I'd often slope off to the indie room to take in some tunes instead. The Farm's 'Altogether Now' was played every single week, and will for ever remind me of my swanky nights in Telford central.

The doner kebab van did a roaring trade at 3 a.m. when our crew spilled out of Cascades, often with a couple of local lovelies in tow. The taxi ride home would usually involve me sitting in the front passenger seat making polite conversation with a disinterested driver while the UK's finest footballers and Telford's top totty got down to some back-seat smooching. The female gymnasts would often join in the partying when we returned to barracks, the combination of testosterone-fuelled footballers and young, nubile sportswomen leading to a flurry of Thursday-night bed-hopping and a glut of Friday-morning groin strains.

Stinking of stale alcohol and suffering from hellish hangovers, we'd all stumble into the gym a few hours later. Fully wised up to the previous night's antics, the physios would lay on extra-hard sessions as punishment. Nauseous players would dash outside to throw up after being made to perform 200 sit-ups. Other unfortunates would be forced to do 15-minute shuttle runs, leaving them dizzy, dehydrated and fit for nothing. God knows what our club paymasters would have said had they seen us in that state but, thankfully, news of any transgressions never seemed to travel very far.

As a matter of fact I had very little contact with anyone at Manchester City during my spells at Lilleshall. I sensed an 'out of sight, out of mind' vibe going on, and matters weren't helped by the fact that incoming phone calls were banned (mobiles were still the size of house bricks and were yet to become all the rage).

There was one important call that I was allowed to accept, however. On the eve of Bonfire Night in 1990, I was summoned to reception to be told that Howard Kendall was on the line, wanting to speak to me as a matter of urgency.

'Hello, Lakey,' he said quietly. 'I wanted to talk to you myself before you read it in the papers. I left Maine Road today, y'see . . .'

I listened in shocked silence as he told me that he'd decided to return to Everton to replace the recently sacked Colin Harvey. He explained how difficult the decision had been, but that the lure of his former club had been impossible to resist. He also reassured me that his Maine Road successor, my team-mate Peter Reid, shared his desire to get me back playing in a blue shirt.

'Good luck, Paul. Just keep working hard, son, and I'm sure it'll come right for you,' was how he ended the conversation.

I placed the receiver back in its cradle, sank into a nearby settee and tried to get my head around this bombshell. Howard Kendall was the manager who'd revitalised our team, who'd installed me as captain, and who'd outlined great plans for my future. And now, after less than a year in charge, he was moving on. There was no ill-feeling on my part; I respected him far too much for that. My sentiments weren't shared by City fans, however, many of whom never quite forgave Howard for jumping ship when the future was looking so bright.

Occasionally, Lilleshall would host conferences for the FA bigwigs, which would sometimes attract a few well-known football managers. Seeing these fellas walking around the place used to hurt like crazy. They might have been talking about you if it hadn't been for this stupid f***in' injury, I remember thinking as I spied Bobby Robson and Terry Venables in deep conversation.

Graham Taylor stopped by the rehab gym one morning. I was going hell-for-leather on the rowing machine when he wandered across.

'Keep up the good work, Paul,' he said, placing a fatherly arm round my shoulder. 'We need you fit, son.' Hearing this, John Barnes sidled over.

'You won't find anyone who grafts harder than him, Gaffer,' said John, nodding in my direction.

Mr Taylor meant well, of course – and it came as some comfort to know that I hadn't fallen off the England radar – but his remarks only served to rekindle my feelings of frustration.

That evening I whiled away a couple of hours in the launderette block, sitting in my boxers with my feet against the machine and my back against the stone wall as I watched my smalls tumble around. I picked up a battered newspaper that someone had left behind and idly leafed through the sports pages. LIVERPOOL EYE DERBY DUO.

SIR JACK TO TARGET KING KENNY. BLUES AIMING FOR HATTERS VICTORY.

The clock on the wall confirmed that City's match against Luton Town at Maine Road was already in full swing. And there was I, sitting on my tod doing my washing, more than 100 miles from Moss Side. Unable to see the floodlights. Unable to hear the roar of the Kippax. Unable to run onto the pitch. Unable to kick a football. It just seemed so wrong, so unfair.

I couldn't sleep that night. I somehow found myself walking aimlessly up and down the long Lilleshall driveway, muttering to myself as frightened rabbits fled into the dark woods. I counted them as they scampered past, seriously wondering how cathartic it would be to boot a bunny high over the fence.

These irrational thoughts scared me. My injury was clearly starting to mess with my head. It suddenly dawned on me that I was fast becoming a different person, a far cry from that carefree, happy-go-lucky lad from Denton.

I'd perked up slightly by the spring of 1991, as I seemed to be making decent headway. I was undertaking simple jogs and cone exercises, and my progression to the next level was looking ever more likely. The Lilleshall physios, however, having never dealt with a player who'd undergone my pioneering operation, were reluctant to give me the go-ahead to move forward until I'd been assessed by a surgeon. So back up north I traipsed, returning with the good news that I'd been given the nod to push on with pitch exercises and light ball work.

I was brimming with excitement the next day, my boots draped over my shoulder as I skipped past the gym and headed towards the practice pitch. After months of humdrum confinement, it was wonderful finally to have the chance to feel the morning sun on my back, breathe in the spring air and step onto the spongy turf.

My knee felt pretty good as I warmed up with a light jog around the perimeter. For the next 20 minutes I did some simple side-to-side work, followed by a session of short-distance passing. Then the time came for some more directional and rotational work. The combination of running sideways while passing a ball to a partner 15 yards away shouldn't have been a problem. It was, though, a bridge too far. As I controlled the moving ball, my knee joint rocked back, a stabbing pain shot through my leg and my whole body crumpled. The physios ran onto the pitch, scraped me up and carried me to the gym.

As I limped in, the whirr of the exercise machines stopped and the entire room fell silent, the lads watching anxiously as senior physio Grant Downey bandaged up my knee. I was then put back on crutches before hobbling over to my crappy little room where I lay face-down on the bed for the remainder of the afternoon, sobbing into my pillow, pummelling the mattress, gutted beyond belief at this latest setback. *This wasn't supposed to happen*, I wailed to myself. Something was seriously, desperately wrong.

Another night of fitful sleep followed, and I awoke the next morning in a very sorry state, all puffy-eyed and still wearing the same clothes as the day before. I picked up the phone and rang down to reception.

'Could someone come and help me down the stairs in half an hour or so, please?' I asked, feeling like some decrepit old-age pensioner.

I spent the next few months back and forth between Manchester and Shropshire for more medical assessments and more exhaustive rehab. My knee, however, felt way below par and deep down I knew that something wasn't right. It seemed obvious to me that my cruciate ligament was still damaged in some way, yet my advisers continued to assure me that it remained intact and that I could therefore crack on.

I carried on as directed, albeit tentatively, and in June 1991 was given the go-ahead to rejoin the fold at Manchester City. Returning to Maine Road felt really weird, not least because Peter Reid – who'd always been affectionately known as Fred, after Fred Flintstone – was now officially 'Gaffer'. On the first day of pre-season training he called me into his Maine Road den, reaffirming his excitement at the prospect of my return, and assuring me that he wouldn't be laying down any unfeasible deadlines. I could take my time, he said, adding that he was more than willing to wait until I was ready. Reidy had suffered a debilitating knee injury himself and understood better than most what I'd been through.

A few minutes later I was out on the training pitch, taking

part in an 11 v 11 practice match. The game was only about 15 minutes old when Gary Megson ran down the channel and squared a ball into the box. As I blocked the cross, my heel followed through into the turf and my knee suddenly locked. I felt something tear deep inside the joint. The pain was sickeningly familiar.

'I don't f***in' believe it,' I screamed, writhing on the ground in agony. 'It's gone again.'

A couple of hours later, in the hospital, I was informed that I'd need another arthroscopy to ascertain the damage. Great, I thought, just what I need. Another hole to be drilled into a knee that was already looking like the last Eccles cake in Asda. I was told not to worry too much, since I'd probably only tweaked the ligament. It doesn't feel like a f***in' tweak, I thought as I rubbed my tender, inflamed knee and geared myself up for yet more scalpel action.

The results, as I'd suspected, showed that my ACL had indeed re-ruptured. I was given the bad tidings that I'd have to undergo a second knee reconstruction, followed by another lengthy lay-off. I was too distraught to speak. I felt like throwing up. Whilst I had little medical knowledge, even I knew that the first procedure had clearly failed, and that somewhere down the line my injury was being badly managed. Piling on the agony was the fact that I had absolutely no control over what was going on.

Everyone could see that my head had totally gone, and I was told to go on holiday, get some rest, and give myself some time to come to terms with the forthcoming surgery. My knee was so swollen that I couldn't have the operation straight away, anyhow. So, in the words of Peter Kay, I booked it, packed it and f***ed off, jetting over to sunny Tenerife for a week with my good mate John Clarkson.

We took things easy – it's hard to trip the light fantastic when your knee's bollocksed – although I made a point of drinking myself into a stupor every night, necking down vodka and tonics like they were going out of fashion. Anything to take my mind off the trauma that I knew lay ahead.

The aftermath of the second op was horrendous; much, much worse than I'd ever anticipated. As well as being as sick as a dog from the anaesthetic, I had to contend with pain in my right knee (clamped in that horrible CPM machine) as well as a sore left joint, from which a second piece of tissue had been taken. My discomfort wasn't improved by the lip-service paid by the conveyor belt of doctors, physios and consultants who flitted past my bedside, some of them barely able to look me in the eye.

'Your knee will feel better than ever, trust me . . .'

'You'll be given all the time you need, Paul . . .'

'No stone will be left unturned, I can assure you . . .'

Save your breath, I felt like saying as these empty sound-bites went in one ear and out the other. Don't treat me like some kind of pea-brained lab rat. You know as well as I that, deep down, no one truly knows what's in store for me now.

I was confined for nearly a fortnight, staring blankly at

white-coated doctors as they bored me with their jargon, rolling over impassively as the nurses injected me with painkillers, and smiling wanly as the tea-ladies ladled out Knorr's soup of the day.

Although I appreciated visits from family and friends armed with fruit and magazines, in truth I'd never felt so alone and isolated. The prospect of ever playing for my club and country again seemed a million miles away, and it continually preyed on my mind. My thoughts, becoming ever bleaker by the day, drifted to some lucky sod in a sky blue home strip, a big number 11 stitched on to his back, rubbing his hands in glee and thinking 'less competition now that Lakey's out again.'

I contemplated the upcoming Euro '92 tournament, visualising Graham Taylor Tippex-ing my name from the squad list, blowing it dry, and scrawling some other jammy bastard's name in its place. I don't doubt that mine was a skewed version of reality but, as far as I was concerned someone else was wearing *my* shirt, and it was hard to stomach.

So, my morale crushed, I was never going to be the most sociable person on the ward, and kept myself very much to myself. My fellow patients, however, assumed that all I wanted to talk about was football. They weren't to know that I'd have rather discussed Russell Grant's star signs than Brian Clough's star signing. The bloke in the next bed would routinely pop his head around the curtain to inform me that the football was on the box, probably thinking that he was doing me a huge favour. I'd always nod politely, before pulling the covers up tightly, burying my head under the pillow and willing myself to sleep.

From autumn 1991 to spring 1992, I embarked yet again on the rehab trail, doing my usual two weeks out of three in Shropshire.

'D'you want your usual room, Paul?' the girl at reception smiled as I checked in for another stay. I was like a football version of Alan Partridge, for the Linton Travel Tavern read Lilleshall, for Norwich read Telford. I'd later learn that no other player in the centre's history spent as much time there as me.

It was at this stage of my rehab that I really started to notice the chasm widening between the quality of my treatment at Shropshire and in Manchester. The meticulous care and attention from the FA physios contrasted sharply with the understaffed and time-starved medical team at City. I think I was somewhat of a conundrum to them. Being the only long-term injured player at the club for whom return wasn't imminent, meant that I wasn't high on their list of priorities.

I'd undergone a unique surgical procedure which should have been followed up with specific rehabilitation techniques and defined timescales. But it didn't happen that way. Instead, I was met with 'ums' and 'aahs' and puzzled expressions from people whose expertise lay largely on the training pitch. Maintaining a fit first team squad was time consuming – I fully appreciated that – but being at the bottom of the pile was incredibly dispiriting.

Coming up against this wall of apathy did nothing to fill my confidence vacuum. I quickly came to the conclusion that the only way to progress during my week-long spells in Manchester was to devise my own gym-based rehabilitation. Using a local health club as my base, I replicated what I did at Lilleshall to the letter, training alone for hours on end. The medical team at City, probably relieved to get me out of their hair, had no misgivings about this unsupervised DIY rehab.

It remained that way for a couple of months, until the time came for me to be welcomed back into the first team squad for pre-season training. I felt like Doctor Who as I arrived at the club that bright June morning. Like the Time Lord, I felt I'd undergone some kind of personality change, morphing from an optimistic young captain to a confidence-sapped nearly-man.

Helping me readjust to life at City were long-standing team-mates like David White and Bob Brightwell, plus a smattering of new faces including Tony Coton and Adrian Heath. Being able to join in with all the gossipy banter and gallows humour in the dressing room gave me an enormous lift, and really brought home to me how desperately lonely the last 18 months had been.

'Welcome back, Sicknote.'

'Hey Lakey, how much disability benefit did you get, you f***in' scrounger?'

I also remember the squad's elder statesman, Gary Megson, taking me aside for a little pow-wow.

'Great to have you back, mate,' said Meggo, 'but if I can

give you one piece of advice, it's this. You've got to give it your all now. You can't be cautious, you can't hold back. If it ain't gonna happen, it ain't gonna happen, but at least you'll know that you gave it your best shot.'

My training at Wythenshawe went well – I could feel my fitness levels rising by the day – but I still had plenty of psychological hurdles to overcome and regaining the normal mindset of a carefree footballer was proving to be my biggest struggle. With my self-confidence in recovery, I was light-years away from being able to wake up in the morning, have a yawn and a stretch, throw open the curtains and think positively about that day's training session.

My first waking thought wasn't how's the weather? but how's my knee? Then I'd roll out of bed, cautiously place my foot on the floor and consider whether I should ice my knee before or after the training session. As I brushed my teeth, I'd wonder if my joint was going to stand up to 90 minutes of football. In the bath, I'd compare left knee with right, debating whether I felt better or worse than the previous day. The uncertainty was ever-present, the insecurity all-consuming.

We were lunching in a quaint little pizzeria when the gaffer announced the line-up for the opening game of our pre-season tour to Italy.

'And, last but not least, wearing the number 11 shirt against Brescia tomorrow will be Mr Paaaaaul Laaaaake,' said Reidy, hamming it up like a boxing promoter. The lads all jumped to their feet, clapping and cheering, as I tried to swallow the huge lump in my throat.

Being named in the side was a major achievement for me, of course, but I didn't want to get carried away. This was going to be the first time I'd kicked a ball in earnest for nearly two years, and I was keen to manage expectations, both my own and other people's.

Sensing this reticence, the gaffer gently eased me into the action. I played half of the game versus Brescia and even managed to nick a goal, scoring from close range. Second only to the goal itself was my delight at the nutmegging of Romanian maestro Gheorghe Hagi, who laughed, wagged his finger and clamped his legs shut when I had the cheek to try it a second time.

Against Cremonese, I managed three-quarters of the match and played a blinder, looping a chipped shot over the Italian goalie to score my second of the tournament. And I featured in the entire game against Verona, operating well alongside Quinny and Mike Sheron, the latter banging in a brace.

While I was encouraged by the flashes of the 'old me' – my pace, touch and timing seemed to be intact – there was still plenty of the 'new me' to contend with. A nagging hesitancy continued to bother me, as did the fact that my movement around the pitch seemed more mechanical than natural. But what was most perturbing was the length of time that it took for my knee to recover after a game. In Italy, while the rest of the lads were enjoying a post-match drink in the bar, I was holed up in my hotel room, icing my swollen knee for the thousandth time.

The British press were full of praise for my continental comeback, however.

'I'm just delighted to have Paul back. It's like being handed a new £3 million player,' Reidy was widely quoted as saying. I really appreciated this unstinting support, but it didn't make the burden of expectation any easier. As the new season loomed, the pressure for me to be fully fit and back to my best was mounting by the day.

8

Half the World Away

City's opening fixture of the 1992-93 campaign, on the evening of Monday 17 August, saw us lining up against Queen's Park Rangers at Maine Road. It was an occasion thick with significance. As well as being our first game in the newly formed English Premier League, it was to be the first match ever to be broadcast live via satellite by BSkyB. And, with any luck, it was going to be the night that I jump-started my football career.

I arrived at the ground nice and early, parking up in the players' car park, signing autographs for well-wishers and shaking hands with a couple of stewards who waved me through the gate into the stadium. I took a deep breath and stepped inside. The Platt Lane Stand, midway through a redevelopment project, was an empty shell. But the pitch, smooth like a bowling green, looked as immaculate as ever.

'If you can't play on that you don't deserve to be a professional footballer,' my old coach Glyn Pardoe had once said to me while staring wistfully at the glossy surface. Too right, Glyn, I thought as I walked alongside the Main Stand to the changing rooms, just hours away from making my comeback on this hallowed turf. I turned into the tunnel, made my way towards the hubbub of players' voices, and timidly pushed open the dressing-room door.

Like a kid on his first day at secondary school, I was gripped with first-day nerves, worried that I'd find it hard to fit into the new set-up. There had, after all, been a seismic shift in personnel since my last league match in 1990; old muckers like Steve Redmond and Jason Beckford had left for pastures new, with players such as Rick Holden and Keith Curle arriving in the opposite direction. This change in group dynamics was something that I'd just have to get used to, not least the appointment of Curle – a £2.5 million signing from Wimbledon – as team captain. He was a good lad and a useful defender, but this still didn't stop me feeling a pang of envy when I watched him slip on the black armband.

Give them their due, though, my team-mates couldn't have been more encouraging that day, patting me on the back, wishing me luck and breaking into chants of '*Lakey is back, Lakey is back hello, hello . . .*'

I tried my damndest to look cool and composed when the time came to pull on my kit, but in truth my heart was in my mouth. Slowly on went the white shorts, the shin pads, the navy socks, the tie-ups and the sky blue short-sleeved shirt with LAKE 8 on the back. My hands trembled as I put on my Adidas boots and tied the laces. These pre-match jitters must have caught the attention of David White, who came over and sat down beside me.

'Shall we go out onto the pitch, mate, get a feel for it?' he asked quietly. 'We can have a butcher's at the cheerleaders, eh . . .'

This was Whitey to a tee. It was a big night for us all, but his primary concern was to calm his old mate's nerves. You don't forget things like that.

The BSkyB bandwagon was in full swing when we ambled out of the tunnel for our warm-up. Helping to usher in this new dawn of sports broadcasting – 'A Whole New Ball Game', proclaimed the adverts – was a circus of reporters, cameramen, musicians, skydivers and dancing girls. Hoisted in the corner of the Main and North Stands was a makeshift studio that housed the TV pundits and buzzed with technicians. On the touchline, blokes in headphones carried out sound checks and the cheerleaders practised jiggling their pompoms. In the centre circle, a troupe of roadies rigged up a podium in preparation for the on-pitch 'entertainment', which amounted to a fireworks display, the assassination of Gerry Rafferty's 'Baker Street' by some tribute band, and the delivery of the match ball by parachute.

I felt like a stranger in my own backyard. It was as if the traditions of Maine Road, and football in general, were quite literally being trampled on ('it's like bloody Disneyland out here,' I remember whispering to Whitey). Being cut off from the club for two years was hard enough to cope with, but all this American-style razzmatazz only added to my feelings of disorientation. I tried my best to shake off the distractions, though, concentrating on some leg stretches and stride-outs.

Back in the dressing room, Reidy hollered out his instructions. I was going to be deployed up front behind Quinny, my remit being to play off the big man at every opportunity and to try to make things happen. It wasn't my instinctive role by any stretch, but I didn't care. I just wanted to get out there and play. The gaffer, it seemed, was prepared to give me some leeway for my first few outings; I'd need a handful of games before I properly found my feet, he reckoned, and I'd be wise to take things step by step.

'No pressure, Lakey. Try and relax, play your natural game, and remember that the lads are there to help you. Just take it easy and things will come right, I'm sure of it.'

Cheers pealed around the stadium as I ran onto the floodlit pitch, with 'Alive and Kicking', the Simple Minds anthem, booming out of the sound-system. I trotted over to acknowledge the fans in the Kippax. As I got closer, their emotion was palpable. Keep it together, Lakey, you're on telly, I remember thinking as a BSkyB cameraman shadowed my every move.

The game itself turned out to be something of a damp squib. Both sides cancelled each other out with their similarly cagey approaches, creating a party-pooping atmosphere that made all the pre-match hype look a bit daft. From a personal perspective, though, I was delighted to feel my confidence soar with each touch of the ball. And, better still, in the 37th minute I was involved in the game's first goal. The move had started with Niall Quinn, who'd neatly put Rick Holden into the channel. I'd met Rick's first-time cross and, after my strike at goal was parried by Jan Skejskal, the rebound was finally smashed in by David White. As I legged over to join the communal mauling of Whitey, the roar from the stands was phenomenal. A lot of things had changed at Maine Road, but that familiar wall of sound from the fans was as stirring as ever.

So was I heading for a dream comeback? Was I f***. This was Paul Lake, not Roy Race. Just before half-time, an incident near the halfway-line put the mockers on everything. I'd thwarted an advancing Alan McDonald with a block tackle – something that had always been an intrinsic part of my defensive play – and, as I lunged towards him, my kneecap juddered violently, almost giving way beneath me. Yet again, the frailty and instability of the joint had been exposed, causing my head to drop immediately and the alarm bells to ring louder than ever. I managed to make it through to half-time but to my relief was substituted 15 minutes after the restart.

'Well done, Lakey,' said Peter Reid as I walked past the dugout, trying my utmost not to limp. 'At least that's 60 minutes under your belt, lad. Onwards and upwards.'

Masking my grimace with a grin, I gave him a half-hearted thumbs-up and headed straight to the dressing room where a pair of ice bags awaited me.

After the game, which finished 1–1, I took part in my first ever formal press conference for the national media. Standing before a roomful of TV, radio and newspaper reporters, I fibbed my way through a five-minute Q&A session. Yes, I was extremely happy with how my first game had gone. Yes, the plan had always been to bring me off after an hour. Yes, I could indeed confirm that I'd had little reaction to the injury. And yes, I was sure that I'd be able to cope with a gruelling schedule of three games in seven days, including the match on Wednesday at Middlesbrough.

I hated spinning them a yarn but, since I couldn't face revealing the truth, the only other option was to lie through my teeth.

The squad travelled to Teeside the next day, staying overnight in a luxurious olde-worlde hotel. After a hearty breakfast we ventured outside for a few stretches, followed by a quick game of head tennis on the lawn. My knee felt terrible, like a stone in a beer can. I hovered around the sidelines, limiting my involvement as best I could, before sloping back to my hotel room, flopping down on the bed, flicking on MTV and phoning down to room service for a bucket of ice.

My head wasn't in a good place when we arrived at Ayresome Park. It was a favourite ground of mine – its traditional, earthy atmosphere was similar to Maine Road's – but as the coach swung onto the forecourt that evening, a feeling of dread took over. My knee clearly hadn't recovered from Monday's game, and playing two fixtures in three days was just plain ridiculous. Instead of listening to my conscience and declaring myself unfit, I turned a blind eye and clung on to the words of my medical advisers.

'You're going to have good days and bad days, Paul . . .'

'You've just got to bite the bullet and battle through it . . .'

With half an hour to go before kick-off, I warmed up near the centre circle, practising some short and long passing with Steve McMahon. The City fans chanted my name incessantly but, consumed with guilt, I couldn't bring myself to face the away end, purposely training with my back to it to avoid any eye contact. I knew I wasn't fit for purpose that night, and I shouldn't have been on the pitch pretending that I was. Not only was I deluding myself, I was conning all those Blues who'd put their faith in me. I felt like a fraudster.

Overcome by a sense of foreboding, I barely took in any of Peter Reid's pre-match team talk. I just sat there, nodding and saying 'yes, Gaffer' in the right places, while slathering Deep Heat on my blasted, bloated knee. I even swerved my usual massage, not wanting the physio Eamonn Salmon to suss out the full extent of my pain before shaking his head and banishing me to the bench. Eamonn hadn't long taken over from Roy Bailey, who'd parted company with the club in the close season. He seemed a nice enough bloke and I just couldn't face compromising him so close to kick-off.

I had to muster up all my courage to start the game, hoping that a late surge of adrenalin would anaesthetise the pain. I became more angst-ridden with each stride and, ten minutes into the action, all my worst fears were realised. A simple pass to McMahon followed by a sharp turn to follow the play was enough for my suspect ligament to snap for the third time in my career.

Once again, I found myself at the familiar vantage point, lying spread-eagled on the deck with a scrum of concerned faces looking down at me. As I was carried off by Skip and Eamonn, shielding my face in the crook of my elbow, I'm sure I heard a collective sigh from the away end.

You're not the only ones to feel let down, I felt like screaming.

In the post-match dressing room Quinny shared my devastation, admitting that seeing me flat out on the pitch had contributed to his sending-off three minutes later, after an anger-fuelled late challenge.

The coach trip back home was the lowest point of my lonely struggle. Sitting alone at the front with my leg strapped up, I feigned sleep all the way from Middlesbrough to Manchester. My dad was waiting to meet me off the coach when it arrived back at the depot in the early hours. We didn't need to speak – my stricken expression said it all – and we drove home in silence. Whenever we stopped at traffic lights, Dad would glance over at me, his eyes full of sorrow.

You're only ever as happy as your saddest child, I think the saying goes.

Six weeks later I found myself preparing for a trip to the United States in what was to be a last-ditch attempt to rescue my career. I was off to Los Angeles to have my knee assessed by Dr Domenick Sisto, a world-renowned expert in the field of cruciate ligament repairs who'd successfully operated on Ian Durrant and John Salako (the former, my old Lilleshall pal, was back in the Scotland squad, and the latter was continuing to shine for Crystal Palace).

Following the Middlesbrough nightmare I'd spent a few weeks undergoing exploratory treatment in Manchester, feeling lower than a snake's belly. I was laid up in hospital when Salako phoned me, having been urged to do so by Peter Reid.

'Take my advice, Paul,' he said. 'Get a flight over to LA pronto, and go and see Dr Sisto. He gave me a lifeline. I can't speak highly enough of the guy.'

Chairman Swales wasn't exactly cock-a-hoop about my trip to America. Loath to foot the bill, and reluctant to admit any culpability for my predicament, he sanctioned the surgery only after Peter Reid had convinced him that we'd exhausted all options in England, and that an op in the States was my last chance. I think Swales also felt under pressure from certain sections of the media, as well as some vocal supporters, who'd started to ask pointed questions as to why I hadn't received the same treatment as Salako and Durrant in the first place.

I believe Swales saw my injury as both an irritant and an embarrassment. He gave the distinct impression that *I* was the failure, and that my ongoing knee problem was somehow my fault, and nobody else's. He'd never shown any sympathy for what I was going through, hadn't once picked up the phone to check how I was, and habitually swanned past me at Maine Road without saying a word. I grew to despise the man, my hackles rising every time I caught sight of his Brillo-pad hairdo or his Bri-nylon suit. Many a time I'd felt like grabbing him by the throat and dragging him to Lilleshall to see exactly what I'd had to endure.

My simmering resentment finally reached boiling point one Monday morning just prior to my trip to LA, when we clashed dramatically in the club's reception area. Triggering our row was a no-holds-barred interview that I'd given to the *Sunday People*, in which I'd claimed that the club were treating me like a piece of meat left to hang in an abattoir. Strong words, I admit, but they'd accurately expressed my feelings at that time.

The chairman wasn't a happy bunny. The next day he confronted me on the stairs in the main reception, apoplectic with rage and accusing me of disrespecting the football club.

'I can't believe you've slagged us off like this, Paul,' he shouted, 'after all we've done for you and that knee of yours . . .'

It was a proper red-rag-to-a-bull moment. In a split second, all the despair, anger and anxiety that I'd harboured over the years rose to the surface. The usually mild-mannered Manc suddenly morphed into Mad Max, and Mr Swales found himself being blasted with both barrels.

'How *dare* you?' I yelled, as he recoiled in shock. 'In the last two years, you haven't once picked up the phone to see how I am. Not f***ing once. And I've lost count of the times that you've walked past me without even a good morning or kiss my arse. You give a very good impression of somebody who doesn't give a shit, Mr Swales, so don't start talking to me about disrespect . . .'

My rant carried on in a similar vein, as I reminded him how I'd had to read about other top players resuming their careers thanks to immediate, specialist consultation. How I'd had to spend the equivalent of a year of my life at Lilleshall, watching other players' knee injuries getting fully rehabilitated. Lads from all over the place whose medical teams had obtained the right advice for their players from the off, rather than just going for the convenient option.

A flustered Swales, caught on the back foot, had no response. But I didn't stop there. Everything spilled out.

'And what about Tony Adams?' I demanded, mounting a couple of steps and squaring up to him. 'Drink driving, smashing his car up, getting sent to prison and bringing shame on football. Yet *his* club still paid him his appearance money and bonuses, even when he was inside. It's called looking after your players, Mr Swales. Showing them a bit of respect. Repaying their loyalty.'

'I don't think you're being very fair, Paul . . .'

'Not being fair? What's fair about a player who strives for years to get fit, whose income is halved overnight, and whose chairman treats him like an outcast? That's not very f***ing fair, is it?'

Swales dismissively waved his hand in my face before storming off, probably regretting ever having opened his mouth. Had Libby the receptionist not brought me a calming cup of tea, I'd have punched the nearest wall.

*

In September 1992 Eamonn Salmon and I flew business class to the States, touching down on a hot, humid afternoon. The taxi ride to the hotel was unbelievable, a half-hour procession past countless LA images that I'd only ever seen in the movies. Light-reflecting skyscrapers. Six-lane freeways. Huge, gleaming Cadillacs. WALK/DON'T WALK neon signs. Beige-suited cops weaving their way through the traffic on their monster motorcycles, evoking memories of Saturdays in Haughton Green when I used to watch *CHiPs* on the telly, glued to Jon and Ponch's mobile crimebusting.

Our cab driver spent the entire journey lazily flicking through the many radio stations on the dial, and I remember being struck by the fact that most of the songs pulsing through the speakers were by British artists. From the Beatles to Bananarama and the Cult to Kajagoogoo, Britannia certainly seemed to rule the LA airwaves. It made me feel all proud and sentimental (I'm a sucker for a homespun tune), never more so than when my favourite Beatles track came on.

Here comes the sun, sang Paul McCartney as we cruised through the San Fernando Valley, my destiny awaiting a few miles down the highway.

> *Here comes the sun*
> *And I say, it's alright.*

We set up camp in a fabulous marble-floored, glass-panelled hotel on Ventura Boulevard. After freshening up, we headed straight over to the Blazina Clinic in nearby Sherman Oaks for formal introductions to the medical team. Dr Sisto, the lead surgeon, had made his name repairing the limbs of American soldiers wounded in the Vietnam War, pioneering a revolutionary cruciate ligament repair technique which involved the grafting of an Achilles tendon taken from a dead person. Gruesome as it sounded, I was prepared to give anything a go if it meant being able to kick a ball again.

Tall, dark and with a look of *M*A*S*H*'s Alan Alda, Dr Sisto cut a very impressive figure, with an air of honesty and self-belief that reassured me no end. He put me through a vigorous assessment that included a succession of x-rays and scans, followed by a bizarre 'distraction therapy' procedure that tested the strength of my knee. I'll never forget his response.

'Whoa there, Paul, this is a loose 'un,' he drawled. 'Boy, have I got my work cut out here . . .'

He went on to explain that, while my knee was salvageable, he'd seen quarterbacks smashed into by huge linebackers who had more stable joints than mine. He told me that I'd definitely need a double transplantation, one for my inside medial ligament and another for the cruciate, using grafts from separate donors. But what he couldn't fathom out was why I was seeing him so late in the day.

'If I'd seen you straight away you'd have been back playing soccer by now,' he said. His words cut me like a knife. Had City's physio not been standing there, I'd have probably responded by spouting chapter and verse about the club's various failings, but I didn't think it was the time or the place. I also thought it vital to maintain a positive mindset.

'I'll do the best that I can for you, Paul,' smiled Dr Sisto, 'and we'll see where that takes us.'

The operation wasn't scheduled for another 48 hours, which allowed Eamonn and I a full day's sightseeing. After supersizing ourselves with burgers the size of dustbin lids, we hired a Chevrolet, donned our Ray-Bans and drove over to the legendary Muscle Beach. A haven for models and bodybuilders, this open-air gym swarmed with Arnold Schwarzenegger and Brigitte Nielsen lookalikes, all honing and preening their beautiful bodies in the California sunshine. If I felt inadequate standing there, poor Eamonn – all 10 stone of him – no doubt felt worse. He looked like Supersonic Syd Little next to all these pumped-up poseurs, and his decision to keep his T-shirt on was a wise one.

We arrived back at the hotel in time for a light supper, and I spent the rest of the evening sitting alone on my balcony, sipping weak American tea and watching Ventura Boulevard by night. Something about this technicolour union of buildings, cars and neon lights had me transfixed for hours. There was a real feeling of activity and optimism about the place. Maybe it would rub off on me, I persuaded myself, as I started the countdown to the third major operation of my life.

I came round from the three-hour procedure to see Eamonn sitting at my bedside, poised to film my groggy awakening on his camcorder. He'd been keeping a video diary of our trip, at my behest, but on this occasion I was in no mood to face the lens.

'I just want to sleep, mate, if you don't mind . . .'

He didn't mind. Eamonn was a tolerant soul who understood my predicament, and whose post-op support I really appreciated. As things stood, however, he was only able to stay a couple more days and, conscious that someone would need to care for me after my discharge, he rang the club to ask if they could fly out my then-girlfriend, Lisa, for the remainder of my stay. The club, however, refused point blank to cough up for her flight and, since I didn't have the money to spare, I had to resign myself to the prospect of recuperating alone, half the world away.

My team-mates, however, were incensed when they heard about this and, mobilised by Niall Quinn and Peter Reid, promptly organised a whip-round to pay for the air fare. While I was extremely grateful for this unexpected act of generosity, it didn't stop me from feeling like some kind of charity case.

City's cold-hearted attitude perplexed me. I couldn't fathom why they were being so unhelpful, and why they seemed quite happy to let me fend for myself in a faraway country. After two years of misdiagnosis, failed operations, exhaustive rehabilitation, a diet of anti-inflammatories and enough anaesthetic to kill an elephant, I'd have thought that the club would have at least pretended to give a monkey's. The board of directors obviously deemed it acceptable for me to ask porters, taxi drivers and chambermaids to be my legs for three days, and didn't give any thought to any complications that could arise. From where I was standing – or limping – it seemed like I was doing my damndest to revive my career at a club that didn't appear to give two hoots.

Once Lisa had turned up, I was allowed to leave hospital and return to my hotel. According to Dr Sisto, the operation had gone 'as well as it could have', although he didn't elaborate further. What he did do, however was state categorically that he wasn't prepared to let me fly back to the UK until I could achieve a 90 degree bend in my knee. I was desperate to get home to Manchester, so for three days solid I worked my arse off with the physios to achieve the required range of movement, spending hours in the hospital gym before seeing out the day with ice, painkillers and bed rest.

During one such day I received a phone call informing me that Paul Hince, *Manchester Evening News'* chief City reporter, was on his way to LA to conduct an exclusive interview with me over breakfast. I can't say I jumped for joy at the prospect of having to explain the operation and discuss my feelings, and it took all my effort to drag myself from my room and go downstairs to do the honours.

Hincey was his usual bright and breezy self when he greeted me, although an hour spent in the company of a sullen and subdued 23-year-old soon put paid to that. Whilst I'm sure he wasn't expecting a Q&A with one of the Chuckle Brothers, I still don't think he'd truly foreseen the extent of my despair. Sat slumped in a sofa, my thumping knee shackled in a brace after days of rigorous physio, I couldn't have been more antisocial if I'd tried. For all I cared, he might as well have been a local reporter who had made a five-minute cab journey, because that day, and in that mood, I didn't give a flying fig that he'd undertaken a 10,000 mile round-trip to check on my progress. I was curt and crabby throughout the entire interview, giving terse responses to perfectly reasonable questions.

PH: (*cheerily*) So, what d'you think of the hotel, Paul?
PL: (*wearily*) It's the closest one to the hospital.
PH: (*happily*) You don't get breakfasts like this in Manchester, do you, eh?
PL: (*snappily*) I need fuel for my rehab, don't I?

After some regulation 'I'll be back' chestnuts I limply shook his hand and shuffled back to my sixth-floor sanctuary.

I wouldn't have blamed Hincey for cursing me under his breath as he flew back to Manchester; all this bloody way for that monosyllabic, uncooperative so-and-so. My behaviour that morning is something I still regret to this day. But, as someone who played a bit himself, I'd like to think that he understood the mindset of a footballer bereft of football and, I hope, made allowances for my petulance.

Six days after the operation, I was queuing at check-in awaiting my own transatlantic flight back home. Unfortunately it seemed that there was a problem with my booking, as I'd inexplicably been allocated a seat in economy class. That can't be right, I thought, knowing that Eamonn the physio had flown back in business class only a few days earlier. Presuming that the airport staff had made a mistake, I explained that I'd just had a serious operation on my knee, and that my employers would have made the necessary arrangements to ensure that I had an extra-spacious seat.

'I'm sure it's a simple oversight,' I said to the check-in girl, 'so if you could sort it out I'd be really grateful . . .'

'I'm so sorry, Mr Lake,' she said as she scanned through the passenger list on her computer, 'but I've checked the bookings and it says here that you're definitely down for economy.'

'Any chance of an upgrade?' I asked, beginning to panic. 'Unfortunately, all the business class seats are taken today, sir, so there's nothing I can do, I'm afraid . . .'

I was crestfallen. No, I hadn't been mistaken and, not for the first time, I'd been left distinctly underwhelmed by my club's idea of aftercare. Whoever had booked the ticket – the physio, the office staff or the chairman himself – had messed up big time, as it shouldn't have taken a rocket scientist to question the wisdom of shoving a 6′ 1 guy on crutches, recovering from major surgery, into such a confined space. It made me realise just how low in status I'd sunk – the powers-that-be were clearly more concerned about the physio's legroom than mine – and made me ask myself again why I was being put through such physical and mental torture.

I was in agony throughout the flight. My leg was folded up like a concertina as it was forced against the seat in front and, as the aisles were constantly busy with trolleys and passengers, I couldn't even extend my knee out to the side for fear of it being knocked out of kilter. The only way to ease my crippling discomfort, I discovered, was by intermittently walking up and down the plane, having to divert to the loo on numerous occasions due to all the water tablets I was taking.

I had to request a wheelchair after touching down at Manchester airport. The eight-hour flight had inevitably taken its toll, and my knee was now so contorted that I could hardly walk. The flexible bend that I'd tirelessly striven towards in LA had been undone in a matter of hours, and I shed tears of frustration as I was wheeled through customs. It's a good job that no one at the club could be bothered to meet me off the plane; the mindset I was in, they'd have been chewing on one of my crutches for a week.

Waiting instead outside Terminal 1 was my sister, Tracey, with a photographer from the *Manchester Evening News* lurking close behind.

'How are you, Paul?' she asked softly as the snapper grabbed some pictures of me looking suitably morose.

'Just get me home, Trace. We can talk in the car.'

Once I'd slept off the jetlag, I reported back to a Maine Road medical team still adhering to their hot-potato brand of injury management. There was some work going on in the Maine Road gym so I was promptly exiled to a tiny storeroom in the depths of the North Stand that housed a rusty exercise bike (a relic from the Bell, Lee and Summerbee era) and a multigym-cum-Spinning Jenny that would tip up due to the uneven floor after the slightest of exertions. Needless to say, I only put up with it for one training session. When I refused point blank to continue my rehab in a broom cupboard, I was handed a list of local gyms in the south Manchester area that I could go to instead.

Each morning, I'd routinely show my face in the Platt Lane physio room to inform the staff which venue I'd be training at that day – usually the Galleon in Cheadle – and what exercise regime I'd be following.

'Sounds fine that, Lakey. Might drop by later if I get the chance . . .' they'd say, but they rarely did. At first I'd get riled by all these empty promises, but I soon learned to take everything they said with a large pinch of salt. I conditioned myself not to expect any *ad hoc* visits and, after a while, stopped bothering to look up when the gym doors swung open. Intentionally or not, the medical team made me feel like I was a nuisance, and that any time they spent with me was time wasted.

I adopted a kind of siege mentality, shoving City's ambivalence to the back of my mind and throwing myself into my workouts. Determined to get as fit and as powerful as possible, I began to pump iron obsessively, hitting the gym all day, every day. I also started exercising in the evenings with my mate Kevin Cowap, either driving up to the Wythenshawe Forum to train alongside Commonwealth weightlifters, or hammering the life out of his garage-based multigym. I couldn't have wished for a better motivator than Kev. Convinced that I was on my way back to full fitness, he'd never talk about 'if' I was going to get back playing but 'when'.

I soon found myself in the best shape of my life, achieving a physique that wouldn't have looked out of place at Muscle Beach, back in LA. The gym became like a second home, a place of respite, somewhere that I could just focus on my fitness, shut out my thoughts and close down emotionally. Sweaty weights rooms and busy swimming pools were perfect venues for me, as there was always far too much activity going on for any interaction and small-talk. I took comfort from all the repetition and the monotony and became physically and psychologically dependent on the powerful rush of endorphins. Working out was the only thing in life that made me feel remotely good about myself.

I used to hate chucking-out time at 9 p.m., because that was the cue for me to stop my exertions and pack up my kitbag. I'd often be the last one out, helping the gym staff to switch off the TV screens and flick off the lights; anything to delay being home alone.

By that time, I was back living in my Heaton Mersey townhouse after my short spell at Mum and Dad's. My mortgage had soared to nearly £1,500 per month and, unsurprisingly, I was no longer able to find a tenant willing to stump up such an exorbitant amount for an ordinary gaff in suburbia. Despite the burdensome repayments I decided to move back in, with a view to sticking the property on the market and getting rid of it as soon as possible.

My heart would sink each time I turned my key in the lock, because it was a cold house in every sense of the word. I could hardly afford to heat the place and, with its unadorned magnolia walls and sparse furnishings, it wasn't exactly what you'd call homely. To Lawrence Llewellyn Bowen it would be minimalist; to me it was just miserable. It was a complete contrast to my parents' house, which was always a focal point for tea, talk and toddling grandchildren.

'It's like a bleedin' crèche in here,' my dad would often laugh when he came back from work, before scooping up one of my nieces or nephews and throwing them to the ceiling in that grandaddy way of his.

My post-gym week nights at the Bates Motel would usually pan out in one of three ways. The first one would see me falling asleep in the lounge in front of *Inspector Morse*, having weird nightmares about me and John Thaw lifting up the FA Cup before waking up at 2 a.m. and trudging upstairs to my bedroom. The second one would entail going to bed with a mug of milky coffee and escaping with a couple of videos until the early hours, my mind so gripped with worry that I'd awake the next morning unable to recall huge chunks of the films. The third one would come into play whenever insomnia took hold, and meant wrapping myself in a quilt and curling up in an old cane chair in the spare room. A small, square skylight was built into the ceiling, through which I'd spend hours staring blankly at the twinkly stars and moonlit clouds before finally surrendering to sleep.

With my career on the slide it was inevitable that the lease on my sponsored car – my beloved Astra GTE – was not going to be renewed. The club, however, was contractually obliged to provide me with another vehicle, particularly since I still had to travel regularly to and from Lilleshall as part of my rehab. While a replacement was being organised, the club asked one of its directors to source me a temporary hire car. He put me in touch with a dealership owned by a pal of his, who promised to find me a decent motor.

The garage, located along a desolate side street in North Manchester, comprised six shabby-looking cars and a Portakabin. As I walked across the tiny forecourt a beefy security guard came out, dangling a set of keys between his thumb and forefinger.

'Paul Blake, is it?'

'It's Lake, actually, but—'

'Your car's parked round the back, mate.'

'Oh, thank God for that,' I said, 'only I thought it was one of these old crates, and I've got to drive to Shropshire on Mond—'

My voice trailed off as he directed me to a white Nissan Sunny, spattered with mud and missing a couple of wheel trims.

'So when did it get back from the Paris–Dakar rally, then?' I asked, a question which elicited a menacing stare from the big lummox and a growl from a pit bull manacled to the Portakabin. It was time for a sharp exit. I climbed into the car, turned the key in the ignition and bunny-hopped off the forecourt.

As I began to pick up speed on the inside lane of the M61 (0–60 in five minutes if I pedalled hard enough), I heard the exhaust spluttering ominously. Near the Worsley turn-off it decided to backfire, giving me no option but to drift slowly onto the hard shoulder towards an emergency phone box.

I managed to get the AA to tow me back to Heaton Mersey, hoping and praying that the mechanic wasn't a City fan (he wasn't, thank the Lord). There was no way I was having that tin can parked up on my drive, so I made him abandon it round the corner, away from any curtain-twitching neighbours.

With a couple of line changes and the inevitable delays, the rail trip to Lilleshall the following Monday took nearly four hours. As the train rattled through the rolling hills of Cheshire and Shropshire I sat back and gazed out of the window, reflecting on recent events. A clapped-out old relic. An embarrassing breakdown. A once-gleaming specimen now on its last legs, destined for the scrap yard.

And the Nissan Sunny hadn't been much cop either. Boom boom, tish.

Mercifully, I shortly took delivery of a Ford Mondeo fleet car, and the following Saturday joined the match-day traffic to Maine Road. Attending every home game still remained a part of my contract, although I'd rather have impaled myself on a corner flag than endure this ritual torture. Being forced to watch other players running out in their sky blue shirts was never going to do wonders for my wellbeing, and the very prospect filled me with dread.

It would take hours just to get out of bed on those alternate Saturdays, and I'd have to draw upon all my energy reserves to psych myself up for the day ahead. I'd often pray for a phone call telling me that the game was postponed.

I'd always feel as flat as a pancake as I drove over to the ground. At exactly the same point in the journey (the junction of Lloyd Street and Ebberstone Street) I'd begin to take deep breaths to suppress the stomach lurches that gripped me whenever the stadium loomed into view. After taking a shaky right turn into the Maine Road car park I'd climb out of my car, wishing that I could just curl up on the back seat and go to sleep for the afternoon.

As I walked across the forecourt, painting on a phoney smile, many City fans would cheerily let on to me and ask for autographs, some of them with young boys or girls in tow.

'Who was he, Dad?' they'd say as I went on my way, their use of the past tense depressing my mood even further. Like it or not, I had to come to terms with the fact that to City's younger supporters I was just a vaguely familiar guy who once played a bit.

After saying a quick hello to the girls on reception, I'd head off to the executive suites in the Kippax and Platt Lane Stands to carry out the usual meeting and greeting that was expected of me. I'd frequently pass club directors who would out of duty ask how I was, my answer of 'yeah, not bad' lingering in the air like a bad smell as they breezed past without stopping.

I'd always try to avoid the dressing room like the plague. Any long-term injured player will tell you that it's the last place on earth you want to be on a Saturday afternoon. The fact that you have zero team involvement and that you're more familiar with the physio room than the boot room makes you feel like an outsider, an intruder even. Hearing the distant strains of a team talk, or the whoops of a post-match celebration, can be an unbearably painful experience for a sidelined player.

On the rare occasion that I found myself in the dressing room – usually to see the club doctor about something – I'd be warmly greeted by former team-mates like Quinny and Garry Flitcroft. That said, I could always sense their awkwardness as they asked me how things were going.

'How are you doing, Lakey? Still working your knackers off?'

'Yeah, Flitty, same old, same old . . .'

I'd notice some of the newer recruits, however, looking at me quizzically. Maybe unaware of my plight, and perhaps unacquainted with City's recent history, they no doubt wondered who this 'Lakey' character was, and what he was doing hanging around the inner sanctum. They probably had a point, come to think of it. I didn't really belong. I was a player in name only, a ghost from seasons past.

Watching the match was also pretty hard to stomach, since

every ounce of my body ached to be out there with the lads. Such deep yearnings often rendered me physically unable to look at the pitch – it was just too painful – and I'd find myself resorting to anything to distract myself from the field of play. I'd try to memorise the telephone numbers on the advertising hoardings, for example, or spot famous faces in the crowd. Sometimes I'd fix my gaze upon the directors' box, staring intently at Peter Swales's bonce, just like I did when I was a kid.

While I'd like to think that most of our players felt proud to pull on that sky blue shirt, there were a few who quite obviously didn't. It wasn't hard to pinpoint the mercenaries who were playing for money, not love, whose on-pitch demeanour suggested they cared more for lolly than loyalties. And although I could hardly blame these lads for agreeing lucrative contracts and accepting huge salaries, it was still pretty galling to discover that their pay packets were substantially heavier than mine.

My situation might have been easier to bear had my successors been up to much. If a young, gifted all-rounder had burst onto the scene and set Maine Road alight, I'd like to think that I'd have been the first to bow down to his superior talent. Not only that, I'd gladly have held my hands up and admitted that this super-starlet clearly had the ability to knock me off my perch and edge me out of the team, injury or no injury. Seeing somebody take on my mantle might have even come as a relief, at least enabling me to seek some kind of closure, to let go, to move on. In my mind, though, no one at that time fitted the bill.

My match day duties included performing the half-time draw in the Millennium Suite, which was by and large a soul-destroying experience. I'd stand there like a tailor's dummy, pulling out raffle tickets for the assembled corporate crowd, creating an illusion of composure and competence when in reality I was the most insecure person in the room.

Many of these supporters, often three sheets to the wind, would engage me in conversation. The majority were pleasant enough, but as soon as they brought up the subject of my health or my rehab I'd clam up and go into autopilot. To deflect probing questions and deter further discussion, I'd trot out my trusty, oft-used 'back in six weeks' reply, even though I had no idea when – or if – I was ever going to play again.

'So, everything going to plan, Lakey? When will we be seeing you in that blue shirt?'

'Should be back in six weeks, mate, all being well . . .'

Other fans wouldn't be as upfront though and, bristling with unease, never knew what to say for the best. It was all very *Fawlty Towers*-esque – *don't mention the knee* – and on those occasions I'd usually make some lame joke to ease their discomfort, my heart sinking as I resorted to taking the piss out of myself.

For all the decent, sympathetic fans, however, there were a few dunderheads who displayed the diplomacy of a charging rhinoceros.

'Wouldn't mind your job, Lakey, being paid to do f*** all . . .' was one memorable comment.

'You're here so often you'll be serving behind the bloody bar soon,' was another gem, only trumped by the subtle-as-a-brick 'here he comes, Hopalong Cassidy.'

Their remarks were sometimes tagged with a conciliatory 'only jokin' mate', but the damage to my fragile ego had already been done. All these little sideswipes hurt like hell, and I'd mull over them for days.

Following the final whistle I'd have to go and show myself in a few executive boxes, only to be greeted by a sea of disappointed faces. It wasn't hard to get the punters' drift; they wanted, quite understandably, to schmooze and booze with an in-form first-teamer, not a conked-out part-timer. I vividly remember one guy in a box calling me David, mistakenly thinking that I was David White, and having to correct him through gritted teeth.

'Ah,' he proclaimed, 'the injured fella. I can't see you ever playing again, mate, but can you sign this ball for me anyway?'

I signed it 'David White' in capital letters, just to spite him.

As I floated around on a match day it almost felt as if I was goading the City fans, haunting them with my presence. It wasn't an easy time to be a Blue in the early- to mid-1990s; the football wasn't always pretty, the club's financial state was perilous and the trophy cabinet continued to gather dust. My failure, I felt, reflected both that on the pitch and behind the scenes.

Moreover, I hated not being there for the fans. They'd supported me through thick and thin, yet here I was, still out of action, and unable to repay them. So much had been expected of me as a player and, as far as I was concerned, I was letting everyone down. By continuing to show my face at Maine Road I felt like I was rubbing the fans' noses in it, taunting them with their loss, a bit like Jim Bowen used to do to contestants on *Bullseye*.

'Look at what you would have won . . .' he'd say to a downcast couple from Dewsbury going home with a bendy Bully instead of a flash new motorboat.

After the game I'd get home and flop down onto the sofa, often so energy-sapped that I'd have to swerve the Saturday-night pub crawl. After one particularly demoralising afternoon, I remember sitting at my kitchen table, a beer in one hand and a biro in the other, and violently defacing that day's match programme. Turning to the squad list on the back page, I furiously scrubbed out all those names that I didn't think deserved to wear a City shirt (about five survived the cull) before ripping it to shreds like a tantrumming toddler.

I was full of remorse when I saw the remnants of that tattered programme in the bin the next morning. I knew I was better than that, and that stooping to such levels wasn't going to help anybody.

The repercussions of my waning star were many and far felt. Certain friends faded into the background once I could no longer get hold of free tickets or players' lounge passes. Embarrassed by my lack of kudos, I also stopped claiming discounts at a clutch of exclusive clothes shops. And, other than the occasional get well card, my fan mail dried up, the majority of my post coming from either Lilleshall, the PFA or a groupie from Birmingham who used to send me photos of herself in various states of undress.

As my career remained on hold, certain people at Maine Road made great efforts to get their money's-worth from me and claw back their pound of flesh.

You're not earning your corn on the pitch, so we're going to make you graft off it, seemed to be their thought process as they pulled me out of rehab sessions to perform lottery draws, attend school presentations or hand OAPs their keys to a new Motability scooter. Often, no attempts were made to hide the fact that I was the last resort, the booby prize, the club's resident Z-list celebrity.

'Michael Vonk and Terry Phelan can't make that charity Dart-a-thon because their training schedule's been changed,' I'd be informed with all the tact of a sledgehammer, 'so I've told the organisers that we'll send you instead . . .'

So off I'd trot to a suburban pub to do the usual shaking of hands, signing of beer mats and smiling for photos, before facing a barrage of well-intentioned questions about my knee, my operation, my hopes, my fears, my future. As was my wont, I'd try to make light of my shipwreck of a career.

'So, Paul, where d'you see yourself in ten years' time?'

'Dunno, mate. Maybe I'll be back at City as a car-park attendant.' (Cue laughter.) 'One of those grumpy old fellas hobbling around in an orthopaedic shoe and yelling at drivers, that'll be me . . .' (Cue more laughter.)

Sometimes the chat would turn to City's on-field inconsistencies.

'Losing at home to Sheffield Wednesday? What's that all about?' a fan would moan.

'We need someone to sort that back four out, Lakey,' another would pipe up. 'When are you gonna be fit, mate?'

'Should be back in six weeks, pal, all being well . . .'

Sometimes all the pretence would get too much and I'd find myself escaping to the toilet for five minutes' respite. There I'd sit on the loo, holding my head in my hands, wishing I could pull a chain and flush it all away.

It was on a spring morning in 1994 that I realised my life was coming apart at the seams. I remember waking up, rolling out of bed and, for the first time in years, not whacking a CD into my hi-fi to jump-start my morning. An hour later, on my way to the ground, I broke with my usual routine of switching on the car radio, opting instead to drive to Moss Side in total silence.

It was almost as though a fuse had blown inside my head. Without warning, I suddenly found myself unable to listen to my beloved music. I could no longer cope with lyrics and tunes that served only to drain my emotions. Sad songs blackened my mood by reflecting my misery, and sunny songs made me feel like crap as I couldn't relate to them in any way. By depriving myself of music, I was spurning something that I'd used throughout my injury troubles both as a comfort and an escape. It was like severing ties with an old friend.

I'd come to understand that this state of lockdown, this avoidance mechanism, was symptomatic of a serious medical disorder. It was a common trait of a complex mental illness that I'd shortly learn didn't discriminate between rich or poor, male or female, young or old, footballer or non-footballer.

Depression had finally taken hold.

9

Sky Starts Falling

My long love affair with music began somewhere in between Elton John's first hit and Elvis Presley's last burger. One of my earliest childhood memories is of punching the air in delight when Showaddywaddy reached the top of the 'hit parade', as it was still called in the mid-1970s.

Listening to Radio 1's chart rundown was a Sunday-night ritual in the Lake household. When it was announced that 'Under the Moon of Love' had hit the top spot I remember turning up the volume on the music centre and doing a celebratory Teddy Boy-style march around the house, with Mike, Tracey and Susan following closely behind. My parents loved the song too; Dad getting into the spirit with a spot of knee-drumming in the lounge using two fags as drumsticks, and Mum shimmying in the kitchen as she cleared up after the roast dinner, drying the dishes and closing the drawers in time with the music, just like that famous Morecambe and

Wise sketch. The only person not to join in the frivolity was my brother David who sat at the dining-room table, cringing with embarrassment. Haughton Green's resident indie kid was way too cool for Showaddywaddy.

My taste in music was heavily influenced by David. Four years my senior, he was well into guitar bands like Orange Juice, Joy Division and Aztec Camera and, when he wasn't in the classroom or on the football pitch, he would loll around his bedroom listening to his vast record collection. Mike and I loved earwigging the heavenly sounds coming through the wall, from the mesmerising vocals of the Associates' 'Party Fears Two' to the melancholic lyrics of 'Tinseltown in the Rain' by the Blue Nile.

Sometimes when David was out of the house, we'd craftily pick his bedroom lock with a screwdriver (our older brother fiercely guarded his privacy), home in on his record player and rifle through his neat pile of 45s and 33s. I remember us once having a sneaky listen to his brand-new Roxy Music album, *Country Life*. Its cover, featuring a pair of greased-up models in see-through underwear, still gives me happy flashbacks.

Our house was always filled with music, whether it was the *Jimmy Young Show* on the kitchen wireless or a medley of hits coming from the dining-room hi-fi. I liked playing at being the DJ, stacking the singles underneath the arm of the record player, flicking the fluff off the stylus with my fingertip and carefully lowering the needle onto the revolving vinyl. Mum liked listening to all the 50s and 60s crooners – Jim Reeves,

Perry Como, Dean Martin – and would harmonise along to them while doing her household chores. I can still picture her hoovering the lounge carpet to the rhythm of 'That's Amore'.

'When the moon hits the sky like a big pizza pie – legs up Paul, love, while I vac underneath – *that's amore . . .'*

Dad was a keen country and western fan, favouring stuff by Glen Campbell and Boxcar Willie. Later in life, however (and influenced by my mate Jason), he gravitated towards reggae music – mispronouncing it 'raggy', bless him – and used to tap his feet to the lilting rhythms of Bob Marley and Peter Tosh while he did his odd jobs in the garden shed. I suppose it wasn't the norm for a 60-year-old bloke with a polyester shirt 'n' slacks combo and a Bobby Charlton comb-over to be into Rastafari music but Dad developed a real fondness for it, something that I'm always reminded of whenever I hear the strains of 'Buffalo Soldier' or 'No Woman, No Cry'.

I've always had a knack of linking memories to melodies. I'm rubbish at matching faces to names, and am forever forgetting family birthdays, but I can effortlessly cross-reference incidents and milestones of the past with specific songs. This is particularly the case when it comes to my playing days.

I can, for example, remember exactly which Pet Shop Boys hit was playing on the coach journey to Ipswich in 1987 ('West End Girls'), what was thumping out of the ghetto blaster when Reddo, Whitey and I lay on an Ibizan beach the year later (Narada's 'Divine Emotions'), and which Stone Roses track pulsed through my headphones when I jogged along Hyde Canal on a blazing hot day in 1990, just before the start of pre-season training ('Fools Gold'). Not so long ago I heard OMD's 'Messages' on the radio and was instantly transported back to a late spring day in June 1980. It was that three-minute burst of synth-pop that had been blaring out of my dad's car as he dropped me off at Stockport station on the eve of our Smiths Crisps Trophy final at Wembley.

The older I got, the more into music I became, never missing an issue of *Melody Maker* or my weekly dose of *The Tube* on Channel 4. As I progressed through the ranks at City, I started to attend lots of gigs in and around Manchester, going to see the Pale Fountains at the International on Anson Road, Primal Scream at the International 2 in Plymouth Grove, and the Bible at Manchester University. I became friendly with a few members of the city's buzzing music scene, notably those of a Blue leaning like the Cult's Billy Duffy and M People's Mike Pickering, two great guys who were as keen to discuss our latest match as I was to discuss their latest album.

I ran into Manchester's most famous musical brothers, Oasis' Noel and Liam Gallagher, on a fair few occasions. In fact, one of the band's earliest Manchester gigs, just before they hit the big time, remains one of my musical high spots. A friend of mine had given me one of their demo tapes, and the following day turned up with a coveted ticket for their upcoming date at the Haçienda.

The place was packed to the rafters, crammed full of punters checking out this up-and-coming band from Burnage. Liam was in fine form, snarling at the microphone, beating the crap out of a tambourine and theatrically goading the crowd, while Noel pointedly ignored his brother's antics and concentrated solely on his guitar and vocals. The other three lads – Bonehead, Guigsy and Tony – seemed quite happy to do their own thing and remain in the shadows.

The highly charged atmosphere, combined with a terrific set list (imagine 'Supersonic' and 'Shakermaker' in your face at 100 decibels) made for a memorable night. The whole gig bristled with energy and attitude, the band's blend of humour, swagger, grit and defiance embodying the spirit of Manchester.

Their fame soared after the release of their debut album, the brilliant *Definitely Maybe*. The band were more than generous when it came to doling out concert tickets and backstage passes to us City players, including their famous homecoming concert at Maine Road in 1996. Even at the height of their notoriety the Gallagher brothers came across as pretty grounded; they seemed as much in awe of the players as we were of them, often sporting their replica shirts with pride and asking us to sign bits and bobs of memorabilia.

Noel, sharp, witty and incredibly switched on, was always the more relaxed and approachable of the two. He'd be the first to come over, asking us if we'd enjoyed the show before discussing the goings-on at City. Liam was less chatty and more guarded than his older sibling, but seemed a decent lad to me, his dry wit and laid-back manner totally at odds with the wild man of pop image often peddled in the media.

Helping me to keep tabs with all the new music releases was a good pal of mine, Howard Johnson, a City-supporting journalist who penned reviews for magazines like *Q* and *NME*. The nature of his work meant that he'd get deluged with promotional CDs which, once they'd been listened to, would be carefully parcelled up and posted to me. I used to love receiving my box of musical freebies – I remember being completely blown away by Ocean Colour Scene's 'Moseley Shoals' – and would return the favour by sorting him out with City tickets when I could.

One morning, in the midst of my injury woes, a small beige packet that I assumed to be from Howard hit the doormat. Inside, though, was an envelope containing a blank cassette and a letter that had been redirected to me by the club. A well-wishing City fan had enclosed one of his favourite songs for me to listen to, believing that its lyrics might lift my spirits and inspire my fight back.

I slotted it into my tape deck and pressed Play.

'Hey now, hey now, don't dream it's over,' sang Crowded House, filling my lounge with mournful vocals. *'Hey now, hey now, when the world comes in . . .'*

Unsurprisingly it didn't have the desired effect. After a minute or so I pressed Stop, then Eject, and broke down.

*

In August 1993, despite steering City to two consecutive top-five placings, Peter Reid became the latest managerial casualty at Maine Road. Replacing him in the hot seat was the ex-Hull City and Oxford United boss, Brian Horton. Though Horton's relatively low-key managerial pedigree didn't seem to instil the City fans with much enthusiasm, I was quite happy to give him and his staff the benefit of the doubt.

However, without my big ally at the helm, and with a new backroom team to get accustomed to, my day-to-day life at Maine Road quickly deteriorated. The first few weeks of the new regime saw the odd pleasantry being trotted out as I ploughed my usual furrow.

'Chin up, Lakey, we're all rooting for you, son,' said coach David Moss. After a few more weeks, my daily diversions to the physio room sparked thinly veiled irritation, with 'you off for another pamper session?' being a regular dig from Mossy. I'm sure he never meant any harm – Dave was renowned for his banter – but somehow I never saw the funny side.

It took the intervention of Robbie Brightwell, former Olympic silver medallist and father of City players Ian and David, to stop the rot. In 1994 Horton had enlisted Robbie's services in order to boost the team's fitness levels and to bring some fresh ideas into the camp. Known affectionately as Bullet, he was a brilliant athletics coach whose no-nonsense manner and wealth of experience commanded everyone's respect. He worked us tirelessly, laying on intermittently paced runs (known much to our amusement as 'fartleks'), alongside punishing 100-metre dashes, 300-metre sprints, and the occasional relay race.

I found Bullet's structured schedule and scientific approach both interesting and innovative. But what I loved most about his training was its focus on straight-line running, with none of the twists and turns that habitually gave me problems. This meant that I could confidently train with the rest of the lads for once and escape my usual solitary confinement.

'I can't believe how strong you're looking, Lakey,' panted David Brightwell seconds after I'd trounced them all in a sprint across the pitch. 'Seems my old man's done the trick, eh?'

While Robbie's input had certainly revitalised me – I always felt like I had an extra lung whenever he was around – I was under no illusions. In spite of all my efforts, my knee was only ever going to be properly tested in a match situation, something of which I was only too aware.

Sadly, for whatever reason, his stint at City was short-lived. Having thrived under Bullet's tutelage, I was desperately keen to carry on our good work and luckily the club gave me the green light to travel to Congleton for thrice-weekly training sessions. We continued apace with the jogs, sprints and fartleks, and I loved every single minute. Not in a million years would I have thought that working with an Olympic athlete in the middle of nowhere would have brought me such contentment and renewed vigour.

It wasn't just my physical conditioning that Robbie helped me with. He proved to be a huge emotional prop, too, becoming a close confidant and sounding board for many years. With his acute understanding of the mental burden of long-term rehab, Bullet could sense when I was having an off day and did his utmost to rev me up.

'Come on, Lakey, if we're going to increase that blardy lung capacity, you need to get your head up, man,' he would say in his clipped sergeant-major tones whenever I turned up looking glum.

'Drop your shoulders, and get those blardy arms moving. Faint heart never won fair maiden, young man . . .'

It was following a chilly sprint session in a snow-bound quarry that I experienced my first ever alfresco ice bath. Guiding me to a semi-frozen lake, Bullet told me to whip off my trainers and tracksuit bottoms before ordering me to wade in.

'Trust me, Lakey, it'll cool the knee and calm it down . . .' he said.

'Are you having a laugh?' I whinged, convinced that he was off his rocker. As I immersed myself in the icy cold water, my body shuddering in shock, Bullet calmly explained the method to his madness, telling me how this type of therapy was the done thing in Sweden.

'Oh, w-well that's all right, th-then,' I hissed through chattering teeth. 'What's g-good enough f-for f***in' Bjorn and Benny is g-good enough for me . . .'

After the longest 20 minutes of my life I was eventually

allowed to stagger back out, my face gurning in pain, watched with bemusement by a trio of woolly hatted ramblers.

I couldn't believe how great I felt afterwards, though, and from that day onwards ice baths (albeit indoors) became an integral part of my recovery sessions. Within a few years they'd become commonplace at Premier League football clubs, with most players worth their salt taking a regular post-match dip.

Bullet, I now realise, knew best.

The thing I most dreaded during my time on the sidelines was the team photograph. This annual ritual was usually arranged for late July, just prior to the start of the new season, and it became more toe-curling as each year went by. Having to don a crisp new Umbro kit, not even knowing if I was actually going to get to wear it that season, was pure torture. And seeing my shirt squad number dropping lower and lower down the list each year, sliding from a coveted number 11 to a token number 32, didn't do wonders for my self-esteem, either. Most demoralising of all was lining up next to 20 or so team-mates who were buzzing with excitement about the season ahead, and rightly so. I, on the other hand, felt like a spare part, like I was gate-crashing a private function.

'Right, lads, eyes front and centre, let's see your pearlies,' shouted the photographer, as Steve Lomas, Peter Beagrie, Nicky Summerbee and the rest of the class of '95 joked around and jostled for position. I stood on the pitch, stiff and awkward, summoning yet another plastic smile as the snapper clicked away.

It suddenly struck me that I'd rather have been anywhere else on earth at that moment than on that pitch. The photographer must have noticed my expression glazing over as my thoughts drifted to happier times.

'Over here please, Mr Lake. Are you with us or what?'

No, I felt like saying to him. *I'm not really here.*

Despite feeling like the club's misfit, I continued to be surprised at the level of media interest that I still managed to attract. I can't say that every newspaper article filled me with joy, however, especially those riddled with inaccuracies. I once read somewhere that one of my donor ligaments had come from a gunned-down LA drug dealer, for goodness sake.

But much worse were those headlines that referred to INJURY-RAVAGED PAUL LAKE or JINXED CITY STAR. I'd see such attention-grabbing back-page banners and shake my head, wondering whether these reporters truly realised the bruising impact that a clunky turn of phrase could have on a soul as over-sensitive as mine, or how a badly chosen word could affect my whole day. The worst example of this, by some distance, was the ubiquitous 'crocked', as in CITY WON'T GIVE UP ON CROCKED LAKE, or CROCK LAKE'S FITNESS BID. It is a word only used by tabloid journalists, and I found it both callous and insulting. Even now, my hackles still rise whenever this flippant, throwaway remark is used to describe an injured sportsperson who is doubtless hurting in more ways than one.

It was often the case that newspapers would set up photo-shoots to accompany their articles and interviews, hence a succession of snapshots featuring me scowling in a rehab pool, wincing as I attempted some keepy-uppy at Platt Lane, or slumped on a seat in the Kippax Stand, staring broodingly into the distance. One particular portrait, printed next to a piece by Patrick Barclay in the *Observer*, still spooks me to this day. An atmospheric, black-and-white close-up of my face, it perfectly captures my deep sense of desolation. My eyes – supposedly the windows to the soul, they say – look dead.

When full-blown depression finally hit me – in my mid-20s, when I was at my most vulnerable – the impact was devastating. With my confidence shot and my career in tatters, I found myself trapped in a world of pain where, in the words of that old Sad Café song, every day hurt.

Problems rained in from every direction. The smallest of daily chores became a huge effort. Every thought, deed and action weighed me down. All the elements of my personality that had previously given me strength – my drive, my optimism, my humour – were suddenly snatched away, leaving behind a dreadful sense of emptiness. I felt like one of those snakeskin exhibits often found in natural history museums: a hollow, fragile shell, the life and soul having slithered out and departed.

Getting the better of Manchester United's Viv Anderson.

Showing Tony Cascarino and Dwight Yorke a clean pair of heels at Villa Park, April 1990. Five months later, I would rupture my cruciate ligament during the match against Aston Villa at Maine Road.

This portrait of me was taken for *The Observer* in 1992. The dark clouds were gathering.

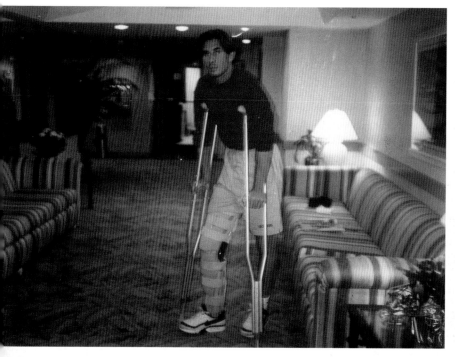

On crutches in a Los Angeles hotel after yet another major operation to rescue my career. I think my demeanour says it all.

Embarking on my rehab programme at Lilleshall alongside physio Grant Downey, cricketer Neale Foster, and tennis player Chris Bailey.

Painting on a smile as I prepare for a hydrotherapy session with physio Eamonn Salmon and three City colleagues.

A 1996 X-ray of my right knee, taken after surgery to straighten it. You can clearly see the metalwork keeping the joint together.

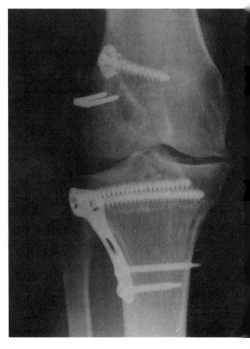

My emotionally charged testimonial game, October 1997. I still find it extremely difficult to look at this photograph.

The hardest goodbye. My sad farewell to the Maine Road faithful.

Jo and I on our wedding day,
September 2001.

Saluting the fans before the
last ever match at Maine Road,
May 2003. It was a very
poignant day. The old stadium
meant the world to me.

Adopting a new role as a physio. Here I'm consoling Macclesfield Town goalie Tommy Lee after his sending off at Stamford Bridge in 2007.

Lakey, Skip and Bob too, 2010.

Fame at last. Gracing the front cover of the Manchester City programme in order to promote the club's community scheme.

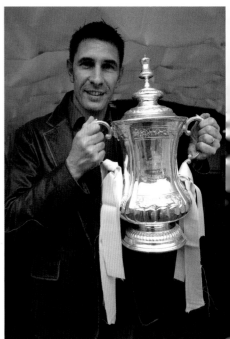

You beauty..!
Getting my hands on the FA Cup,
won by Manchester City in May 2011.

Jo and I at the City of Manchester Stadium. I'm incredibly honoured to be among a select group of players whose names are emblazoned around the ground.

I was tormented by the triple-whammy of insomnia, inertia and amnesia. I'd lie awake until dawn, equally fearful of the day as I was of the night. I'd use up all my strength just getting washed, dressed and out of the house each morning. I'd forget to phone friends, to pay bills and to keep appointments. Sometimes I'd even bypass food and drink, going through a whole day totally oblivious to my rumbling stomach and sandpaper mouth. My hopelessness ran so deep that nothing, and nobody, could make any difference to the way I felt. I could have scooped the Vernon's Pools jackpot, or spent the night with Pamela Anderson, and would have still felt depressed the following morning.

But, while my head was all over the place, the world still turned, and I had to continue fulfilling my role as an upstanding employee of Manchester City Football Club. Like some kind of remote-controlled robot, I'd troop from gym to pitch and from executive box to supporters' club, feeling like I was everywhere and nowhere at the same time.

By far my worst nightmare was being in company. The willpower required to bottle up my emotions, conceal my symptoms and feign normality ('I'm fine, honest!') left me utterly exhausted, and would only sink me further into despair. As a consequence, I'd find myself withdrawing from social gatherings, wriggling out of meals with my family and avoiding drinks with my friends. I could just about manage a trip to the cinema, only because it was dark and diverting, a place where I could binge on Coke and popcorn and not have to speak to another human being for a couple of hours.

Crippled with paranoia, I'd steer clear of my local pub and off licence, worried that people would think I'd plumbed the depths and hit the bottle. I'd even go to the lengths of visiting supermarkets and petrol stations late at night, in order to avoid bumping into anyone I knew and having to conduct the same old conversation.

To relieve the pressure in my head and the sickness in my stomach, I'd go for lengthy evening walks, obsessively counting the number of steps I took as I pounded the pavements to the video shop in Didsbury or the Kansas Fried Chicken in Burnage. Often, following my usual Friday night in the gym, I'd wander aimlessly for hours on end. With my hood up and my head down, I'd pass pub terraces teeming with weekend revellers, groups of students chatting at bus stops, and weary nurses clocking off their shifts at the Alexandra Hospital.

One particular summer's night, I found myself standing on a motorway bridge in Cheadle. I leant over the rails and peered down at the grey tarmac and white lines, watching the afterglow of the headlights and tail-lights as the traffic rumbled beneath me. Despite my sombre frame of mind, I didn't contemplate jumping off; I just remember drawing comfort from watching this vibrant slice of life below, idly wondering about the drivers and the passengers, trying to guess their destinations and imagine their conversations.

I noticed a police car driving past me on the bridge and, half an hour later, after passing me again in the opposite direction, it stopped. Two uniformed bobbies got out. They crossed the road and came over to ask if I was okay (they didn't recognise me, thankfully) no doubt concerned that I was about to leap into the path of an oncoming juggernaut.

'Could be better, I s'pose,' I replied, before assuring them that I wasn't planning death by Eddie Stobart, that I was just having some thinking time, and that I'd got a lot on my mind at the moment. I told them I was grateful for their solicitude, but that they needn't worry because I was just about to go home for a few cans in front of the telly. They looked at each other, nodded and headed back to their car. I took a deep breath, turned on my heels, and started the long walk back to Heaton Mersey, counting the steps as I went.

Not long afterwards, I decided to seek professional help. Never before had I felt so physically strong, yet so mentally weak, and after an emotional chat with the physios at Lilleshall, I took a deep breath, picked up the phone and made an appointment to see my GP. As is typical with many blokes, I'd put my problems on the backburner, thinking that if I left them alone they'd go away, that things would naturally remedy themselves. I was also petrified at the prospect of finally owning up to my frailties, visualising the scenario of being certified doolally and being carted off in a van by the men in white coats.

Even in the 1990s, admitting to a mental illness came with a great deal of stigma attached. In those days it was still something of a taboo, and was virtually unheard of within the masculine sporting fraternity, where bravado was flaunted and emotions were hidden. To many, the concept of a rich and famous professional footballer suffering with depression was impossible to grasp. Paul Gascoigne wasn't seen as a troubled, vulnerable young man exhibiting signs of obsessive compulsion; Gazza was just mad as a hatter, off his head, daft as a brush. When Stan Collymore was diagnosed with depression while at Aston Villa, his manager, John Gregory, reacted with cynicism, reportedly asking 'what's he got to be depressed about?'

Driving to my GP's surgery that morning, knowing that I was about to come clean about my sad little secret, was one of the hardest things I've ever done. In saying that, I felt a profound sense of relief when I knocked on the doctor's door. Stepping into his consulting room, I could feel the pressure deflating in my head as I crossed the threshold between denial and disclosure.

All it took was a simple 'so tell me how you're feeling, Paul?' for the floodgates to open. I told him everything. How football had been my birthright, how I'd been born with the game woven into my DNA. How I'd grown up on local pitches and playing fields, and how happy, secure and free I'd felt in this natural environment. How football had been my sole calling in life, and how it had become ingrained in my personality, like writing is to authors, like painting is to artists.

I then described how my career had collapsed around me, leaving all my hopes and aspirations in ruins. How the people that I'd entrusted with my health and welfare had let me down. How the game that I'd loved with all my heart had become the bane of my existence.

The GP was incredibly sympathetic, listening intently to my story and nudging over a box of Kleenex when I lost my composure. It came as no surprise to me to be told at the end of my appointment that I was suffering from severe depression. The doctor wrote out a prescription for a long-term dose of antidepressants.

'I also think you'd benefit from some therapy, Paul,' he added, 'so I'll be referring you to the Priory.'

The Manchester Priory was situated in Altrincham, a well-heeled town on the border of Cheshire and Greater Manchester. I started to attend the clinic once or twice a week, undergoing hour-long sessions with a psychotherapist. Other than my close family, not a single soul knew about these regular visits, and I took great pains to keep things from the club, worried that I'd be seen as some kind of basket case.

Not only that, I was scared to death of bumping into a City fan, worried sick that news would leak out that Paul Lake was seeing a shrink. I'd cover this particular base by always going to the Priory with a spare cheque in my pocket that I'd scrawled on. If waylaid by someone in a sky blue shirt, my plan was always to wave the cheque quickly around before claiming that I was en route to present it to some mental health charity based at the centre. Whether anyone would have actually believed this pitiful ruse was debatable.

In an airy, white-walled room my therapist explained how

our sessions would help to pinpoint my issues and develop some coping strategies. Part of this process, she said, would involve analysis of my recent and distant past to identify what had sparked off my depression. She spent ages grilling me about my childhood, my relationships and my career, paying particular attention to my trip to the States to see Dr Sisto, and more specifically the return journey.

'I reckon it was that flight home from LA that did the most damage,' she said, pacing slowly around the room.

'Being shoved into that cramped seat made you feel worthless and neglected and ever since then these tensions have built up to create a kind of breakdown,' she explained. 'What's happened is that you've closed yourself off from the world, Paul, battened down the hatches, built walls around yourself.'

She then told me how depression was often linked with feelings of deep loss or sudden change, and how the unexpected halt to my career had ticked both boxes and contributed to my despair.

'Your injury's been like a bereavement, in a way,' she said gently. 'You're in shock. You're in mourning. You feel like a huge chunk of your life is missing.'

I sat there in my comfy *Mastermind* chair, amazed at how this woman was able to pin down my mindset and dissect my illness with such accuracy. Everything she said rang true; it all made sense.

'You've almost been living a lie, haven't you?' she continued, as I bit hard into my trembling lip. 'Pretending that everything's all right when it's clearly not, and having to put on a brave face, day in, day out. That must have been so hard for you to cope with.'

I nodded. 'It was. It is.'

And then she sat back down, peered at me over her specs, and told me that, if I was to give myself the best chance of recovery, I had to realise that my depression was a chemical imbalance, not an emotional weakness; that it was an illness, not an attitude.

'It's not your fault, Paul,' she repeated in order to emphasise the point.

Life on antidepressants felt different. Not better, necessarily, just different. My GP had warned me not to view my supply of Seroxat as a cure ('they treat the symptoms of depression, not the root cause,' he'd said), and I was told not to expect any sudden urges to break into song or frolic through cornfields.

What these blue torpedo-shaped pills did do, however, was regulate my mood swings and reduce my stress levels, thus taking the edge off my anxiety and allowing me to get through my day a little more easily. The flip side of this sedative effect, however, was a persistent numbness that blunted my senses and blurred my judgement. It seemed like everything was in soft focus, as if every thought and impulse was on a five-second time delay. This chemically induced fug meant that the most banal decision became a major dilemma, and I'd find myself hovering at newspaper stands, unable to decide between a *GQ* or an *FHM*. I felt like I'd gone from being under a cloud to having my head in one.

Though the aches in my head had subsided, my knee joint was as troublesome as ever. I remember hobbling across the Maine Road forecourt one morning and being collared by a City fan who appeared to be holding what looked like a urine sample.

'Lakey, this is for you,' he said in a heavy Dublin accent, pressing the vial into my palm. 'It's holy water, all the way from Ireland. Hope it helps.'

Despite not being particularly religious, I was really touched by this man's kind sentiments. I took the magic potion back home and, each morning for a whole week, gently dabbed it on my operation scars. The fact that it had no discernible effect came as no massive surprise, but it got me thinking about giving some complementary therapies a go. So-called 'Western' medicine hadn't worked, so why not try some alternatives? I'd nothing to lose, other than the contents of my moth-eaten wallet. I was prepared to give anything a go if it meant me making the greatest comeback since Lazarus (© Sid Waddell).

First up was a course of faith healing. I had found the practitioner's details on a leaflet, and had been attracted by the glowing testimonials from people whose lives and fortunes had apparently been transformed for ever.

Driving to her treatment room in Yorkshire, I remember pulling over at a service station and sitting in the car park thinking, what the bloody hell am I doing? Had it not been for another voice in my head telling me to *gwan, gwan, gwan* like Mrs Doyle in *Father Ted*, I'd probably have cut my losses and done a U-turn there and then.

After relieving me of £50, the faith healer, a slight woman in her 40s, gestured to a bed in the middle of the room.

'Lie down, close your eyes and try to relax,' she whispered, and proceeded to waffle on about inner energy and magnetic fields. Bloody get on with it, I felt like saying as I totted up the pence-per-minute rate. She then held her hands out and hovered them over my knee for what seemed like an eternity.

'I sense lots of negative energy on the right side of your body,' she said. 'Come back next week, and let's see if we can sort it out.'

On the M62 back home I tried to convince myself that my spiritual healing experience had had a positive effect, that miracles could indeed happen, and that it was money well spent. However, after two disappointingly uneventful follow-up visits, my optimism turned to scepticism. I'm sure Madame Faith meant well, and had doubtless given many patients comfort and hope, but I came to the conclusion that I was just clutching at straws.

I also gave Chinese acupuncture a go, attending a clinic in central Manchester, but again came out feeling disappointed. While the minuscule needles helped to reduce my discomfort and ease my insomnia, they didn't take away the need for my daily dose of painkillers, and for that reason I knocked it on the head. Knowing what I do now about acupuncture (I went on a course a few years back) I was kidding myself if I thought an ancient therapeutic remedy was going to compensate for a ravaged knee that was missing a ligament. But desperate times called for desperate measures.

The most effective therapy, I discovered, often came from sources much closer to home. One morning, beset with aches and pains, I turned up at Maine Road with a face like a dropped pie. My old pal Niall Quinn – who was himself sidelined through injury – must have sensed I was having a bad day of it.

'Lakey, you're coming with me. I'm taking you for a proper Irish breakfast.'

'Nah, you're all right, Quinny . . .'

'I'm not asking you, big fella, I'm telling you.'

'What about the gaffer . . . ?'

'Ah, don't you be worrying about him, I'll sort it.'

And with that he frogmarched me across the forecourt and bundled me into his car, driving me to a city-centre café nestled beneath the Mancunian Way flyover.

A few months before, Quinny had suffered a cruciate ligament rupture similar to mine. Unlike me, though, he was recovering nicely, his operation having been performed by a suitably experienced surgeon in the south of England with a reputation comparable to Dr Sisto's. Ironically enough, I'd helped Niall to secure the best treatment possible. Not wanting my team-mate to relive my nightmare, I'd advised him to bypass any advice from the club and consult the experts at Lilleshall instead, who subsequently pointed him in the direction of a tried-and-tested knee specialist. (Peter

Swales's tacit approval of this course of action spoke volumes; in my opinion, it was tantamount to an admittance of failure regarding my own treatment.)

Quinny and I walked into the café to be greeted by a smiling waitress, clearly pleased to see one of her most famous customers.

'Howya, Niall – what can I get you?'

'Two full Irish and a big pot of tea, please,' he grinned.

Ten minutes later a colossal plate of eggs and bacon with all the trimmings arrived. You could keep your sodding Seroxat; that morning, it was a good old-fashioned fry-up that dragged me out of the doldrums. My friend, bless his heart, did his best to take my mind off the doom and the gloom, regaling me with his latest family news and chatting about anything but football. So there was no 'can't wait for you to be back playing alongside me, pal,' or 'I wish you'd had the same surgeon as me, Lakey.' Instead, it was 'can you shovel any more in that feckin' big gob of yours?' as he watched me hungrily tuck in.

The internal politics of Maine Road were never usually at the forefront of dressing-room discussions. The average player didn't give a chuff about AGMs and behind-the-scenes power struggles, and was far more bothered about the tasty secretary in the clingy top.

In the autumn of 1993, however, it had been a totally different story. The whole club, from the boardroom to the boot room, buzzed with rumours that Francis Lee, City legend-turned-millionaire-businessman, was about to oust our unpopular chairman by mounting a takeover bid for the club. Fed up with Peter Swales' dictatorship, most fans threw their support behind the former Blues' hero, most notably the vocal 'Forward with Franny' pressure group which organised countless anti-Swales demonstrations, leaflet drops and candlelit vigils.

The whole thing, in classic City style, was one long soap opera with, if you ask me, definite shades of *Coronation Street*'s classic Ken, Mike and Deirdre love triangle. In one camp you had the crusty old stick-in-the-mud, entrenched in his ways, desperate to cling on to his one-and-only (even though she was a bit dowdy and in need of a good makeover). And in the opposing corner was the dapper, dynamic entrepreneur, trying his hardest to snatch his bitter rival's true love with promises of money, glamour and a brand-new start.

Unlike Barlow versus Baldwin, though, the Swales versus Lee saga didn't end in fisticuffs. Instead, they did their sparring via the press. Not a day went by without a provocative tabloid headline or a mud-slinging allegation, often coming courtesy of shadowy 'sources close to the chairman' or secretive 'friends of Francis Lee'.

I remember the media going into overdrive when, at the height of the hostilities Lee unexpectedly turned up in the directors' box for the match against Queen's Park Rangers, the first time he'd been seen there for years. From my vantage point in one of the executive suites, I watched him brazenly take his seat only yards away from Swales, prompting a scrum of photographers to leg it over to the Main Stand to get their shot of the main protagonists. As they did so, deafening chants of 'Swales Out, Swales Out,' rang around the ground.

Had he not treated me so abysmally in the wake of my injury, I might have felt a modicum of sympathy for City's beleaguered chairman – it can't have been easy for him, and there were worrying reports of intimidation of his family – but all I felt was a cold indifference. Maybe *now* he knows what it's like to be ostracised and hung out to dry, I remember thinking as I watched him sink lower and lower into his seat.

By December 1993, Swales had more or less given up the ghost and he stood down as chairman, but it wasn't until the following February that 'St Francis of Moss Side' (as the fans dubbed him) finally wrested full control. The majority of fans, of course, were delighted to see the expulsion of the old guard and the heralding in of the new.

Since Brian Horton had been a Peter Swales appointment, many assumed that he would be sacked immediately by the new chairman. He wasn't, as it happened, and was instead given the chance to prove his worth. To his credit, an uncomplaining Horton orchestrated what was probably the most entertaining season at Maine Road for years, fielding a side of go-getting crowd-pleasers like Uwe Rösler, Paul Walsh and Peter Beagrie. Their characteristic free flowing, attack-minded football, however, was tempered by an inconsistency which, for example, saw us trounce Spurs 5–2 but, four games later, suffer a crushing 5–0 defeat at Old Trafford. This haphazard form led to us finishing a mediocre 17th in the division and Horton, harshly but predictably, was given the chop at the end of the season.

Speculation was rife as to his replacement, and for a few days the talk among the players and my City-supporting pals was of nothing else. Who would the new manager be? Graeme Souness, maybe? Or what about Dave Bassett, eh? He might fancy it. And don't rule out George Graham, either . . .

None of the above, as it happened. In the summer of 1995, into the breach stepped the flat-capped figure of Alan Ball, hero of 1966, erstwhile manager of Portsmouth, Stoke City, Exeter City and Southampton, and former England colleague of the chairman.

'The ego has landed,' announced one of my team-mates as the news broke.

'I think I'd have a bit of a swagger if I'd won a World Cup winner's medal,' I replied.

In reality, though, even I was surprised at the extent of the little fella's confidence. From day one he left the playing and coaching staff in no doubt as to what he'd achieved in his career and what, in comparison, they hadn't. Don't get me wrong, I've a deep respect for any player who's won major honours, but I don't think Ball, as a manager, totally grasped the difference between uplifting a squad and undermining it.

Over the next few months I witnessed at close quarters a

rapid demolition of team spirit as the new gaffer set to in his, erm, unique style. Player morale slumped even lower following the arrival of Georgi Kinkladze in July 1995. 'Kinky' was the closest thing we'd ever seen to Diego Maradona in a City shirt (borne out by his spectacular mazy goal against Southampton) but Ball severely overstated his role. By putting the Georgian on a pedestal around which everyone else had to revolve, the manager succeeded in alienating and humiliating many first-teamers.

'I feel like a f***ing afterthought,' one player complained to me after a game. 'It's like being an extra in the Georgi Kinkladze Show . . .'

The spine of the team predictably crumbled as a result, even more so when the decision was made to offload such solid players as Tony Coton, Garry Flitcroft and Paul Walsh in the space of a few months. In spite of Kinky's flashes of genius, and Rösler's nose for goal, I knew I was watching a side doomed to fail and, as the season progressed, the spectre of relegation loomed ominously.

While Francis Lee was building his Maine Road empire off the pitch, I was having another stab at rebuilding my career on it. I'd made great strides with Robbie Brightwell – he'd got me as athletically fit as I could possibly be – and I knew it was high time to test out my knee in a proper match situation. It was agreed that I could have a few run-outs with City's 'B' team, a side of 16- and 17-year-olds managed by my old pal and former team-mate Neil McNab.

In March 1994 I travelled over to the Melwood training ground to play Liverpool's youth side. The game was only 12 minutes old when one of the full-backs inadvertently headed the ball skywards to the far side of the six-yard box. Aware that nobody seemed to be claiming ownership, I shouted 'Lakey's ball!' and went up for a header with my Liverpool opponent. Unluckily for me, the numpty mistimed his jump and my face smashed into the top of his head with all the force of a Glasgow kiss.

I was unconscious for nearly five minutes. When I eventually came round I found myself in an ambulance, my mouth dripping with blood and throbbing like hell. I retched when I caught sight of my reflection in the window. All I could see were my front teeth protruding through a flapping top lip which had been split into a V-shape by the force of the collision. I looked like the monster from *Predator*. It was horrific.

I felt mortified as I sat in Bootle Hospital's A&E department, waiting for a nurse to stitch me up. My comeback attempt was turning into a farce. I was a joke, a hapless, accident-prone fool, football's very own Frank Spencer.

'Maine Road's Unluckiest Player', the *Manchester Evening News* dubbed me the following day.

I recovered in time for a 'B' team game against Preston North End a few weeks later. Things seemed to be going okay until, halfway through the match, I gave away the lamest penalty of my career. What I'd intended to do was sprint across to the corner of the 18-yard box, time a tackle, win the ball cleanly, and bring the ball out of danger. Taking the play from defence to attack like this had always been a forte of mine, and I'd done it a thousand times before.

But I got nowhere near the ball, clumsily barging into the fray and taking out some poor kid at knee height. My gammy leg couldn't keep up with the rest of my body, it seemed, and was refusing to listen to the commands from my brain that were saying 'time it, control it, tackle him . . .' As another Preston player converted the spot-kick, I stood in the centre circle, hands on hips, dazed by my own ineptitude.

Later that spring, I returned to the Blazina Clinic in LA to see Dr Sisto for a check-up. I might have had the red carpet treatment a couple of years earlier, but that certainly wasn't the case this time. A routine exploration of the knee was followed by a debrief that took all of two minutes.

'I'm sorry, Paul, but I've done all I possibly can,' said the surgeon. 'What you're left with is a knee that works, but not a knee that's necessarily going to function in professional football. How you play it from here is entirely up to you. I wish you lots of luck.'

I slung my overnight bag over my shoulder, calmly walked out of the hospital, hailed a taxi to the hotel, took my pain-killers, went downstairs to the bar and drank myself stupid.

I put Dr Sisto's sobering assessment to the back of my mind when I returned home. Helping to lift my spirits was my wedding to Lisa, at St Mary's church in Denton in May 1995, which we followed with a relaxing honeymoon in sunny Portugal.

Back in the UK, I stubbornly carried on with my rehab as normal. For the next few months I continued apace with my daytime gym visits and evening weights sessions but overdid it one night like a fool and badly wrenched my back. I was in agony by the time I got home – I'd never known pain like it – and ended up having to drive to the Beaumont Hospital in Bolton, where an emergency operation was performed to remove a bulging disc from my lower back.

The Beaumont was one of the best rehab hospitals in the north-west. I'd started to spend a lot of time there and got to know the staff well, particularly Tony Banks – a renowned orthopaedic surgeon and sports injury specialist – and Philippa Hopkins and Mandy Johnson, two hotshot physios.

Once I'd recovered from my back injury, I was able to resume my rehab. However, on the advice of Mr Banks, I was only allowed to train wearing a cumbersome knee brace. He'd also advised me to shelve the 'B' team matches for the time being and instead concentrate on non-contact, low-impact exercise. Firstly, because my body wasn't up to any rough and tumble and, secondly, because my brace would have lacerated any player colliding with it. This unwieldy contraption weighed me down in more ways than one. Pacing up and down the pitch like Robocop, I felt I was a burden to myself and a danger to other players. I was sick and tired of the lads having to pussyfoot around me, and I think they felt the same.

In my heart of hearts I knew I couldn't put up with this sham existence for much longer and, as Christmas 1995 approached, I made the decision to go to see Tony Banks for a do-or-die reality check. I needed to know, once and for all, whether I was fighting a losing battle, deluding myself and merely prolonging the agony. Lacking the mental strength to make the decision on my own, I needed someone with the bollocks and the backbone to grip me by the shoulders, look me in the eye and give it to me straight.

Perhaps no one at City had the heart to put me out of my misery, but breaking bad news to a player, no matter how hard it can be, should be a club's duty and responsibility. Stringing players along and stoking their delusions is the easiest option of all, yet it can also be the most destructive. As someone once wisely said, 'it's not the disappointment that kills you, it's the hope.'

I sat on the treatment bed in Mr Banks's room, staring up at an illuminated x-ray. Even my non-medical eye could see that it didn't look good. The glowing white areas clearly showed that the bones in both my legs were starting to bend and warp as they tried to compensate for my injuries.

Mr Banks cut to the quick, explaining that my right knee was collapsing and that in order to save the joint I'd have to undergo surgery to re-straighten my leg. Part of my shinbone would have to be sliced off, and titanium screws would then be hammered into my bone. It was a body blow in more ways than one. While I hadn't expected to be showered with good news, I hadn't envisaged yet another major operation.

'The thing is, Paul, your knee can't take much more of all this pounding,' Tony said, shaking his head. He paused for thought and took a long deep breath.

'I know this will be hard for you to take, but I think there's a real danger of you being crippled for life if you carry on trying to play football.'

And then, as my mind whirred and my stomach churned, he spoke the words that so many before him had feared to utter.

'I'm so sorry to have to tell you this, Paul, but it's time to call it a day.'

I drove straight to Mum and Dad's in Haughton Green, weaving my usual way through Belle Vue and Longsight, reflecting on the many ambitions that I'd harboured over the years. Since boyhood I'd dreamed of surpassing Alan Oakes's awesome record of 676 appearances for the Blues. Added to that was a burning desire to win some kind of silverware with City – FA Cup, League Cup, I wasn't fussy – followed by a nice little foray into Europe; Milan, Madrid, maybe. Last but not least, I'd always fantasised that I would one day become one of the finest England players of my generation, perhaps emulating Colin Bell's tally of 48 international caps.

Time to stop dreaming, I thought as I pulled up outside the house, yanked the handbrake and jolted myself back to reality.

Mum answered the knock on the door. The look on my face told her that all was not well.

'What on earth's the matter, love?'

'It's over, Mum.'

My parents were, of course, devastated for me. They'd never contemplated a worst-case scenario, always remaining upbeat and clinging on to the hope that their youngest son's efforts would come to something, that our Paul's injury would never defeat him. As my tearful mum put on the kettle, my stoical dad put on a brave face.

'You couldn't have tried any harder, son, and we couldn't be any prouder of you,' he said, hugging me and ruffling my hair, just like he used to do when I was a kid.

10

One Day Like This

I finally laid my career to rest on Thursday 4 January 1996. After half a decade of setbacks and letdowns, the day had come for me to join the rank and file of ex-professional footballers.

I'd spent most of December trying to come to terms with my imminent retirement. Christmas in the Lake household had been anything but merry, with me in no mood for any cracker-pulling or cork-popping as the cold reality of my situation began to bite. New Year's Eve – never a good time for your average clinical depressive with a ruined career and a mangled knee – was spent sitting in front of Jools Holland's *Hootenanny* on BBC2. As the Britpop brigade raised their glasses to the chimes of Big Ben, I downed a glass of Southern Comfort and reflected on my predicament, trying to console myself with some 'New Year: New Start' positive thinking. At least now I could wave goodbye to those torturous match days and training sessions, and finally rid myself of all that false hope and fake optimism.

'To 1996,' I slurred, anaesthetising myself with another swig of bourbon as Jools & Co rang out the old and rang in the new.

Just before the festive break I'd met up with City's general secretary, Bernard Halford, to inform him of my decision to retire. I liked Bernard a lot. One of Maine Road's most loyal servants, he'd been at the club since the 1970s and had followed my development from shy rookie to proud captain. He seemed genuinely upset to hear my news, although I'm sure it didn't come as a major shock to him.

'I'm so sorry it all has to end like this, Paul, I really am.'

'So am I, Bernard, but enough's enough. Maybe it just wasn't to be.'

Over tea and biscuits we discussed the media game plan – a press conference would need to be arranged – and also addressed a few pertinent financial issues. I was keener than ever to secure my future, especially now that my final player's wage packet had dropped onto the doormat. There was talk of an insurance payout – Peter Swales had taken out a policy on all the youth team lads in the 1980s, apparently – and I also wanted to test the waters as regards the possibility of City granting me a testimonial year. Bernard promised to look into my queries.

'And if there's anything else I can do to help, you know where I am,' he said, with typical kind-heartedness.

After our meeting, I nipped over to the nearby administration offices. I'd been told by a solicitor friend that I was legally entitled to access my medical notes, so I decided to request a copy. Now that I'd quit, it was as good a time as any to examine my case history and gain a better understanding of why things went so wrong. It might even be a cathartic experience, I told myself.

However, when I went to see the relevant member of staff I was breezily informed that the entire contents of my medical file had been shredded because – and I quote – 'they didn't make any sense.'

Words failed me then, and still do to this day.

It was with a strange sense of calm that I drove up to Platt Lane to announce my retirement to the media. Thanks in part to my morning cocktail of Seroxat and Nurofen, it was numbness, not sadness that I felt as I swung into the car park. I just needed to get this day over and done with as quickly and painlessly as possible.

All the City players had left Platt Lane by the time I arrived. A good job, really, because I don't think I could have faced being confronted by a troupe of fighting-fit, smiley-faced lads on this day of all days. I trudged up to the main entrance, eyes downcast, trying to avoid catching sight of my old training pitch, the scene of so many achingly happy memories. Coming at me from the opposite direction was Alan Ball.

'Hello, Paul.'

'All right, Alan.'

'Listen, I'm sorry you've had to give up, son. It's a real shame, that.'

'Thanks.'

'But life goes on, doesn't it?' he grinned, patting me on the back. 'There's no point looking backwards and dwelling on the past, eh. Time to start afresh and move on . . .'

I gritted my teeth. He probably thought he was saying the right things, and I'm sure he hadn't meant to appear patronising, but the last thing I needed on a day like this was a mini-lecture from someone I barely knew. Had these words been uttered by my dad, or Tony Book, or Ken Barnes, it might have been a different matter, but coming from him they sounded a bit shallow. Ball hadn't the first idea of what Manchester City Football Club meant to me, or the devastating impact of five years spent stagnating on the sidelines, and it grated.

'Thanks for the advice,' I said tartly.

Mercifully, his platitudes were cut short by the intervention of a *Manchester Evening News* photographer requesting a snap of us together. We posed beneath the illuminated Platt Lane sign, Ball standing there in his tracksuit and a woolly hat, and me next to him wearing a long dark coat and an even longer, darker expression.

'Paul, could I get a shot of you hanging your boots up in the dressing room?' the pressman asked casually as he changed his camera film.

'Good idea,' said Ball, 'you can borrow a pair from—'

303

'Not a chance,' I snapped. 'I'm not hanging any boots up for anyone, Alan. It's the biggest cliché in the book, for God's sake. This is the worst f***ing day of my life, and I'm damned if I'm posing for some cheesy photo just to please some bloody newspaper.'

Ball just stared at me blankly, shook his head and walked off, no doubt thinking I was a complete tool. The photographer reluctantly had to settle for a far less mawkish image of me signing an autograph for a random City fan ('try to seem really, really upset,' I heard him say to her). After that I reeled off a couple of interviews to local TV crews, who then filmed me walking out of Platt Lane looking sad-eyed and weary.

When I returned to my car, I paused and took stock for a moment. It was at this precise spot in the middle of the car park that my dad had dropped me off for my first training session with Tony Book. On a wet and windy Thursday evening in 1982 he'd wished me luck, waved me off and driven away in his Hillman van, leaving me standing there alone, eyes wide and knees knocking, not quite knowing which way to turn or what lay ahead. Nearly 15 years later, that same doubt and uncertainty prevailed.

Over the next fortnight I was inundated with hundreds of kind messages. My letterbox overflowed with cards, letters and gifts from City fans and rival supporters, postmarked from Manchester and beyond. I took a steady stream of consoling phone calls from ex-City team-mates, and was also contacted by many former opponents. Robbie Earle – a long-time City fan – sent me an enormous card signed by all the Wimbledon lads, saying how much they'd respected me as a player and acknowledging how hard I'd fought to save my career. I also received a very moving letter from my Crystal Palace rival, Mark Bright, that intimated 'there but for the grace of God go I.'

Old acquaintances like Billy McNeill passed on their good wishes, my former boss sending me a heartfelt letter saying how sorry he was that I'd had to quit, and how much potential I'd shown. He wrote something along the lines of 'if you use half the determination that you showed as a player, you'll do brilliantly in life,' which was a nice thing to say and I appreciated a lot.

Most touching, perhaps, was a tribute that Howard Kendall gave to the *Pink Final*, Manchester's weekly sports paper.

'It's a tragedy not just for Manchester City, but for England as well,' said my former manager. 'I haven't the slightest doubt in my mind that, but for the injury, Paul would have been capped for the England seniors that season, and would by now be a vital part of the international team. I've seen a lot of brilliant young players in my career, with many of them going on to become household names. But believe me, Paul Lake was as good as anything I've ever seen.'

Once everything had died down, my search for a new career began in earnest. At that time, in the mid-1990s, only a small minority of big-earners, usually those who'd had several money-spinning moves, were able to exit the game virtually set up for life. The vast majority weren't so well-off, and had no choice but to find another job once our playing days were over.

It was my physio friends at the Beaumont Hospital who steered me in the right direction. I'd had to undergo the dreaded leg-straightening procedure shortly after my retirement – without doubt the most traumatic, blood-curdling operation I've ever had in my life – and Mandy and Philippa had spent hours with me as I recuperated, sitting at my bedside, trying valiantly to lift my spirits and distract me from the pain.

'So, c'mon Paul, what are you going to do with your life?' asked Mandy one afternoon. 'Don't tell me you're going to open a flippin' pub . . .'

'To tell you the truth,' I replied, 'I've got absolutely no idea. Football's been my life since I was a kid. It's the only thing I know about.'

'No it's not,' she said.

'Yes, it is,' I replied.

'Er, no it's not,' she countered, our exchange taking on shades of pantomime. 'You know all about injuries. You know all about rehab. You've been there, done it, worn the T-shirt. No other player knows more about life on the sidelines than you.'

'Maybe not,' I said.

'Only we've been talking,' said Philippa, nodding con-spiratorially at Mandy, 'and we both reckon you'd make a great football physio.'

'Ah, you're just saying that to cheer me up.'

'Not at all. We've been saying it for a while now. You've got the right grounding, the right attitude.'

'Yeah, but I'd need a degree if I was going to do physiotherapy, wouldn't I?'

'Well get off your backside and get on a course, then,' barked Mandy.

Mandy and Philippa had lit the blue touch paper and, following a week or so weighing up the pros and cons, I made up my mind to look at the physio option. My pals at the Beaumont had stated a pretty good case; I had indeed developed a keen interest in sports medicine over the years – the only positive aspect of undergoing endless surgery, I suppose – and I knew that, by drawing on my own experiences, I'd be better placed than most to help other injured footballers get back on track. Having gone through the mill myself, I'd be able to both empathise and sympathise with players trying to salvage their careers.

Moreover, carving my own niche as a physiotherapist would, perhaps, help to rebuild the pride, dignity and self-worth that had been demolished in my wilderness years. Watching my football career gurgling down the plughole had been an extremely painful experience, and a fresh challenge might just be the perfect antidote. Not only that, it would also keep some much-needed structure and direction in my life. Like most footballers, I'd been bred into a creature of habit, adhering to set training times, rigid fixture lists and regimented rehab sessions. A new vocation, I hoped, would maintain a similar sense of order and daily routine, shielding me from a life of comfy sofas, Pot Noodles and daytime television.

The last thing I wanted was to end up bored and unfulfilled, like a former opponent of mine who found it hard to acclimatise to Civvy Street, and had gone from being household name to house-husband in a matter of months.

'The only run I do now is the bloody school run,' he said glumly when I bumped into him in the Trafford Centre one afternoon. 'How the mighty fall, eh.'

I was also very conscious of the fact that physiotherapy might in the long term provide me with a route back into the game I loved. Having been institutionalised within football since my youth, I had neither the self-confidence nor the social skills to function in any other walk of life. Football was my safety net, my comfort blanket, the only profession in which I was known and respected, and in which I felt I truly belonged.

Helping me to navigate my way through this new world of opportunity was the PFA which, I discovered, attached as much importance to the welfare of former players as those still in action. Its education officer, Mickey Burns, gave me some great advice about my study options. He explained that, if I wanted a place on the PFA-funded physio degree course at Salford University, I'd have to prove my aptitude and commitment. First I'd need to get an FA Sports Therapy diploma course under my belt, followed by an 'A' level in human biology.

'But we'll pay for all your course fees, Paul,' said Mickey. 'We see it as money well spent if it means that ex-players can stay in the game.'

So, in September 1996, clutching my shiny new leather case, I went back to school, attending my first 'A' level evening class at South Trafford College. Despite my relief that I wasn't the only mature student in the class (another old goat looked like he was pushing 30), I was still beset with nerves. Having not set foot in a classroom for 12 years, I was way out of my comfort zone, a proper fish out of water.

Luckily it didn't take me long to get into the swing of things. I found human biology a fascinating subject, and the relaxed teaching style was light-years away from the raps on the knuckles and the flying board rubbers of old. Though my brain can't have known what hit it, going from a decade of virtual dormancy to a sudden bombardment of facts, figures and diagrams. I threw myself into my studies, burying my head in textbooks during my spare time and burning the midnight oil in order slowly but surely to finish my homework. And when I say slowly, I mean slowly. I was a computer novice, with virtually non-existent keyboard skills, so I had no option but to write everything in longhand. This was a pretty tall order for someone who'd spent half his life using pens just for scribbling autographs, signing contracts or tackling the *NME* crossword.

After submitting a particularly difficult assignment, I received an urgent message to report to one of the senior course tutors. Damn, I thought, I've messed up my essay.

Either he thinks it's rubbish, or he can't read my child-like scrawl. Or both, maybe. I should have known I wasn't up to this studying lark, I berated myself as I trudged along the corridor after class. Maybe I should've gone and opened a pub after all.

I knocked on his office door and gingerly walked in.

'Hi, Paul. Thanks for coming over so quickly.'

'No problem,' I replied, steeling myself for a pep-talk.

'I hope you don't mind, but it's my grandson's birthday tomorrow,' he said, pulling out a familiar sky blue shirt from his drawer and passing me a marker pen. 'He's a huge City fan and it'd make his day if you could sign this . . .'

'Course I will,' I said, smiling to myself as I signed.

'Oh, and while you're here you can have your essay back. Pretty impressive, considering you're new to all this. I've given it a B. Well done.'

After a long, hard slog which culminated in two terrifying written exams, I managed to scrape a C grade at 'A' level in May 1997. A bog-standard result to some, but the Holy Grail as far as I was concerned; a mini-victory after years of disappointment and underachievement.

Earlier that year I'd also commenced the sports therapy diploma, which, in one of those twists of fate, had its hub at Lilleshall. This time round, though, the circumstances couldn't have been more different. I approached the rambling old abbey with a spring in my step, rather than a knot in my stomach. For the first time in ages I felt in control of my life; for once, my destiny wasn't in the lap of the gods.

The morning drive from Manchester to Shropshire had given me the chance to reflect on a recent chat that I'd had with Roy Bailey. Over a coffee at Platt Lane, I'd told him all about the career path that I intended to take, explaining how keen I was to utilise my past experiences and how, ideally, I wanted to stay working in football. I didn't go as far as a Yosser Hughes-style 'gizza job', but it wasn't far off.

My overtures must have had the desired effect, though, because, having listened to what I'd had to say, Roy went on to speak with Francis Lee, who agreed, subject to me obtaining my sports therapy diploma, that I could join the medical team as an academy physio. The club was in desperate need of another pair of hands to treat its fledgling players, and the chairman was more than happy for me to step into the breach.

So, with a role at City resting solely on my exam results, I got my head down and worked my knackers off. I became, as Rik from *The Young Ones* might have said, a girly swot, sidestepping the legendary Telford pub crawls and opting instead to hole myself up in my poky room and study through the night. Previous stays had seen me bemoaning Lilleshall's gloomy campus accommodation, but this time around I really embraced my drab surroundings. What hadn't been conducive for a dejected footballer was ideal for a diligent student, the bare brick walls and the faulty telly providing the perfect climate for undisturbed study.

My reclusive lifestyle paid dividends, thankfully, and I ended up passing the diploma with flying colours. As he presented me with my certificate, the FA's Head of Sports

Medicine, Alan Hodson, told me that, by finishing in the top half of the group, I'd done myself proud.

'You've got enough skills and experience to become a decent physio, Paul,' he said. 'I know that nothing will ever match your playing days, but you never know, this might come close.'

I travelled back to Manchester feeling thrilled at my achievements and flush with optimism. But, while my hard-earned diploma marked an upturn in my fortunes, I knew it was only a small step on a long journey towards my reinvention. The Seroxat in my toilet bag, the Priory appointment card in my wallet and the unplayed CDs in my glovebox told me I still had some distance to go.

I officially joined forces with City's medical team in the 1997 close season. I'd had to take a massive drop in salary, but far more important to me was the opportunity to forge a second career at Maine Road.

By rights, there should have been plenty of reasons to turn my back on City and seek pastures new, but I just couldn't bring myself to sever the ties. For the past 20 years, my life had revolved around that old stadium – it had been my home, my sanctuary, my social hub – and cutting loose seemed unthinkable. The emotional attachment to my mother-club was as strong as ever, the gravitational pull still as powerful, and I couldn't envisage my daily commute being anything other than up Didsbury Road, down Kingsway and along Wilbraham Road towards my Moss Side mecca.

The Manchester City Academy – my new workplace – was based at the Platt Lane complex. One of Francis Lee's success stories, the Academy was among the best of its kind in the country, offering our fledgling players expert coaching and hi-tech facilities. I was tasked with looking after a 20-strong group of 14- to-16-year-old protégés, my general remit being the treatment of injuries and first aid cover during matches. I also devoted a couple of evenings to the under-12s and under-14s, advising them about their health and fitness, although the kids' tender ages – allied with some Kevin the Teenager-style apathy – meant that I'd often spend as much time briefing their parents in order to get certain messages across.

Most of the mums and dads were very cooperative, but there were always a few exceptions to the rule. I remember one fella collaring me after a training session, keen to discuss his 12-year-old lad who was going through an adolescent growth spurt. This bloke – who wasn't the sharpest tool in the box – proceeded to voice his concerns about his son's size seven feet, which were apparently growing far too fast for his liking. According to this football genius, not only were smaller feet better for striking a ball ('look at Scholesy!'), but those players with bigger feet tended to be injury-prone ('like yourself, Lakey, if you don't mind me saying').

'What's your point, pal?' I said, feeling my hackles rising.

'Well, I just can't see City taking on my lad if his feet get any bigger, and I need to know if there's anything you can do to keep them at a size seven. Special boots, maybe, or an operation or something.'

'So let me get this right. You're asking me to stunt the growth of your son's feet.'

'Yeah, I s'pose so. I need him to make the grade, see,' he replied, deadpan, nodding in his son's direction. 'He's got one chance of getting it right, and it's down to me to make that happen.'

My attempts to explain the importance of allowing his son's body to develop naturally, avoiding terrible problems both now and in later life, fell on deaf ears. Mr Know-It-All wasn't having any of it; he was the lad's dad, and he knew best. As far as he was concerned, he told me, his next pair of boots would be a size smaller, and that was that.

'You know what they say, no pain, no gain,' he smirked, as his son timidly followed him out of the door. My heart bled for the poor boy.

It came as no massive surprise when he was released by the club a few months later. It transpired that he'd been regularly breaking down during matches, complaining of – well, whaddya know – agonising cramps in his lower limbs.

Unfortunately, this wasn't to be the only case of parental pressure I'd witness. Occasionally I'd come across a Mr X or a Mrs Y who'd gaze at their golden boy with pound signs in their eyes, viewing him as more of a going concern than a growing kid. Thankfully, however, these money-obsessed parents were few.

One of the first Academy games I oversaw was a routine friendly against an open-age Stoke City XI. Immediately catching my eye was a blue-shirted young striker called Shaun

Wright-Phillips. Although he was on the lower rungs of the football ladder, the kid was head and shoulders above the rest (metaphorically speaking of course; he was the smallest player on the pitch) and displayed the same blend of sharpness and instinct as his father, Ian. Equally impressive was the opposing left-sided midfielder, an Australian lad called Danny Tiatto who displayed remarkable power and aggression. Further down the line, of course, both Shaun and Danny would find themselves gracing Manchester City's first team.

As most of my academy work took place in the afternoons and evenings, I often had a couple of hours to spare earlier on in the day. Cottoning on to this, my colleagues in the medical team – as short-staffed and time-starved as ever – asked me if I could lay on some post-op fitness sessions for my former team-mate Richard Edghill. Edgy had undergone a success-ful cruciate ligament reconstruction by the same surgeon who'd operated on Niall Quinn, and was halfway through his rehab. I agreed without a second thought. I got on well with Richard – I'd trained with him in the latter stages of my own rehab – and I was more than happy to lend a hand.

Or so I thought at the time. Had I perhaps given the request a little more consideration, and had I had more of my wits about me, I might have foreseen the negative ramifications. Here was I, just months after my traumatic retirement, agreeing to help out a player who'd suffered the very same injury that had defeated me. A player who, as the result of expert, immediate treatment, had an excellent prognosis and a retrievable career.

Unsurprisingly, my psychotherapist at the Priory tried her best to dissuade me.

'It's far too soon after your own injury, Paul,' she said during one of our weekly sessions. 'Trust me, you're not ready for this yet. You'll only be reopening old wounds.'

She was spot on, of course, but I carried on regardless. Without wanting to sound like some kind of martyr, I felt almost compelled to come to Richard's aid. After all, I was probably the only person at Maine Road who could truly understand the fear and panic going through the head of a player with a career hanging in the balance. And I was damned if my pal was going to suffer mentally and physically like I had; I couldn't just stand there and watch him fight the same solitary battle and face the same wall of indifference. 'Do unto others as you would have them do unto you,' as my old school priest used to say.

Over the next three months, I helped to ensure that Richard received the duty of care that I'd never experienced and, after hour upon hour of painstaking rehab, he finally achieved full fitness. I was sitting in the Main Stand when he made his City comeback against Nottingham Forest in September 1997, my feelings a fusion of elation and envy as he lasted the entire 90 minutes, returning to the dressing room relatively unscathed, and giving me a thumbs-up as he trotted past. While delighted that such a good lad had resurrected his career – and happy that I'd played my part – I watched on, green-eyed, as he passed a point that I'd never been beyond myself.

*

Like every other City fan, I'd been left broken-hearted when Alan Ball's side was relegated to Division One in May 1996, following a fraught 2–2 draw with Liverpool. More than a year after the event, however, the aftershock of demotion still seemed to be rumbling on. The subsequent slump in fortunes, both on and off the pitch, had been hard to stomach for many of my colleagues, and I noticed a fair few dampened spirits around the place. You couldn't blame them, really. Preparing for home games against Port Vale and Bury, with all due respect, didn't have quite the same kudos as previous visits by Chelsea and Arsenal.

Masterminding City's football affairs at that juncture was Frank Clark. The former Nottingham Forest boss had been handed football's poisoned chalice towards the tail-end of 1996, his arrival at the club capping a tumultuous period of managerial mayhem that had seen Alan Ball coming to his senses and throwing in the towel, followed by Steve Coppell going mysteriously AWOL after just 33 days in the job. Interim caretaker stints from Asa Hartford and Phil Neal meant that City had gone through five managers in 18 months.

The football fault-lines at Maine Road were so deep that I don't think any manager could have waltzed in, banged his fist on the desk and immediately changed City's fortunes. Clark and his staff tried their best to revitalise the side (there was much rhetoric about 'turning things around' and 'regaining our focus') but it was always going to be an uphill struggle to remedy the ills of his predecessors. Alan Ball's legacy amounted to a 40-strong unit with, in my opinion, only Rösler and Kinkladze for the fans to get truly excited about. There were some decent lads in the ranks who cared for the club and gave it their all (Kit Symons, Michael Brown and Steve Lomas spring to mind) but I personally didn't feel that there were enough characters, or warriors, to rally the troops and carry us forward.

As far as I was concerned, the club was crying out for a firm managerial hand to bring everything into line; a hard-nosed tough-guy to filter out the dead-wood and draft in some class. I'm not knocking Frank Clark's ability or integrity – his track record was decent enough – but I don't think he was necessarily the right person to deal with that particular squad at that particular time. Indeed, City would fail to gain promotion during his 14-month reign, and it would take another manager – a certain Joe Royle – to steady the ship eventually and restore our pride.

Also becoming increasingly apparent in 1997 – judging by the whispers in the corridors and the chants on the terraces – was the feeling that Francis Lee's honeymoon period as chairman was over. Despite overseeing many behind-the-scenes improvements – the renovation of the Kippax Stand, the redevelopment of executive suites, the revamp of the club shop, and the unveiling of a new 'laser blue' Kappa strip, for example – to some fans it was all a bit 'fur coat and no knickers'. Fancy lounges, flashy merchandise and trendy kits were all well and good, but most supporters would have traded it all in for a decent side and some top-flight football, neither of which looked very likely at that time.

The fact that a certain team from Old Trafford was storing up trophies left, right and centre only served to rub salt into the wound. I remember a lad once approaching me in my local Tesco as I did some late-night shopping.

'Oi, Paul, how many City fans does it take to change a light bulb?'

'Don't know, mate,' I said, looking past him and quickly steering my trolley towards another aisle.

'None,' he yelled after me. 'They're all happy living in United's shadow.'

'Our day will come,' I whispered under my breath.

Despite all the mickey-taking from other fans, the City faithful held their heads high and kept up their famously robust support. Home attendances continued to hit the 30,000 mark during the 1996–97 and 1997–98 seasons, and the travelling away support was as ardent as ever. According to my City-mad mates, the Division One years of the mid-1990s were, oddly enough, among the most entertaining in which to be a Blue. They still talk about the fun-filled, beer-fuelled day trips to Southend and Grimsby that compensated for some of the dross they had to witness on the pitch.

Being a member of the medical team meant that I was now privy to a lot of behind-the-scenes shenanigans. I regularly had to attend coaching staff meetings, many of which encroached on first team affairs and were about as enjoyable in those uncertain times as bubonic plague. There were slanging matches aplenty; if it wasn't someone condemning the sacking of City coaches Tony Book and Colin Bell (a decision that had saddened me, too), it was another staff member slamming a string of half-baked managers and lazy-arsed players for contriving the club's fall from grace.

Witnessing these short tempers and long faces was horrendous, both in my capacity as a fan and as a former player. I hated the club's dirty laundry being aired, and far too often heard and saw things that just made me want to close my eyes, insert my fingers into my ears and shout 'la la la la, not listening, not listening . . .'

Coming as a welcome distraction from all this turmoil was some good news from Bernard Halford. In recognition of my loyal service at City, the club had finally agreed to grant me a testimonial. Comprising a year-long programme of fundraising events, it was to culminate in a benefit game at Maine Road against a team yet to be decided.

A testimonial committee was promptly set up spearheaded by Tudor Thomas, a Stockport-based businessman who was also one of City's honorary presidents. Tudor – a well-connected and highly respected figure in Mancunian football circles – was a staunch Blue who over the years had become a good friend of mine. So esteemed was Tudor at City that he'd even been allocated his own hospitality area at Maine Road which, with its array of fascinating photos and memorabilia, was more like a museum than a lounge. On the day of a game, 'Tudor's Room' would swarm with celebrities and former players, all enjoying the Thomas family's famously warm welcome. It also doubled up as a pre- and post-match meeting point for the match officials, and I'll never forget an enraged Ken Barnes standing at the bar and calling Uriah Rennie a 'f***in' clown' following a controversial penalty dismissal against Newcastle.

The testimonial committee, comprising a broad spectrum of City devotees, quickly formalised a calendar of events. A Paul Lake Golf Classic, a barbecue at a Cheadle hotel, an all-star cricket match, a 70s Night in Manchester, a soirée at a London sports bar and a race night in Rochdale were just some of the dates in the diary.

One suggestion that didn't make the cut, however, was an offer from Bernard Manning to host a night in my honour at his famous Embassy Club in Harpurhey. Despite the fact that his love for City was legendary, his risqué (and that's putting it mildly) humour was something that didn't rest easy with many of the committee. I'd been to Manning's club just once before and though I'd enjoyed some of his more general, observational gags, I'd felt really uncomfortable when he'd started on all the 'black fella' stuff. I was well aware that some of my pals saw him as an out-and-out bigot – and the last thing I wanted to do was to cause offence just for the sake of a few quid – so his offer was politely declined.

The committee faced another comedian conundrum when the time came to decide which star entertainer should be booked for the Paul Lake Gala Dinner, a glittering occasion to take place at Manchester's Palace Hotel. Some wanted bald-headed funnyman Mick Miller in the spotlight. Others preferred Stan 'Geeermans' Boardman. Paul 'Hi-de-Hi' Shane's name was also thrown into the ring, similarly Jimmy 'There's More' Cricket. As the discussions descended into bickering, somebody suggested Roger de Courcey and Nookie Bear.

'Roger de Courcey?' I asked, half-laughing. 'Are you serious?'

'Straight up,' one of the committee replied. 'I saw him at a sportsman's evening a few months ago and he was fantastic. He got Nookie to tell dirty jokes and sing daft songs. Had the audience in stitches, he did.'

'Yeah, but are people really going to want to pay good money to see a bloke and a puppet?' somebody else pointed out.

'Well, it'd make a nice change from the usual run-of-the-mill comedians, wouldn't it?' he countered, as many of the committee stroked their chins and nodded in agreement. 'People get bored with hearing the same old gags from the same old faces. Why not go for something different, eh?'

I can't say I was convinced that a ventriloquist whom I'd last seen on *Seaside Special* in 1978 was going to be our best bet, but the majority ruled, and Nookie was booked.

Fast-forward to a swanky banqueting hall one night in May where over 300 VIP guests, having enjoyed their five-course meal, were eagerly awaiting the star turn.

Cometh the hour, cometh the dummy. Roger de Courcey

walked on with his freaky little bear, sat on a stool, glared at the audience, and proceeded to bomb like I've never seen anyone bomb before. Narky and irritable, he was obviously in a foul mood and made no attempt to hide the fact that he didn't want to be on a Manchester stage with his hand stuffed up a teddy, entertaining the guests of some has-been footballer he'd never heard of.

The act comprised feeding Nookie a string of lame jokes about getting pissed and shagging birds, although unfortunately de Courcey's garbled brand of voice-throwing meant that most of the punchlines fell flat. As the tumbleweed floated past, I squirmed in my seat, wishing that a trap-door would swallow up this rambling, shambling 'entertainer'.

Nervous titters soon turned into noisy jeers as our star attraction (whom we'd paid a fortune, incidentally) continued to die a death. It was excruciating. Ten minutes into his set, realising that he was going down like a lead balloon, de Courcey put us all out of our misery by calling it quits, muttering some expletives and gesturing angrily as he dismounted his stool. Then – in what turned out to be the funniest part of the act – Nookie Bear, that cuddly puppet beloved of children everywhere, told us all to f*** off. De Courcey stormed off stage and fled into the night, presumably to drown his sorrows with a few gottles of geer.

Thankfully, the rest of the night made up for this unmitigated disaster. Master of ceremonies and former referee Neil Midgley did a grand job, filling the humour vacuum with some choice gags and anecdotes. Then, after fortifying myself with a vat of wine, I took to the stage to say a few words, thanking everyone who'd helped me through my many ups and downs.

Once I'd got that particular ordeal out of the way (public speaking wasn't my forte) I drank the hotel bar dry, partying until breakfast with many old friends, colleagues and supporters, loving the fact that this special occasion had been about celebrating my career, not mourning its demise.

Our schedule of events continued to motor nicely until just before the start of pre-season we were floored by some bad news regarding my showpiece benefit match.

A few weeks earlier, the club had confirmed a date for the game, Sunday 5 October at Maine Road, prompting Tudor to contact Glasgow Rangers about the possibility of fielding a side to play against a Manchester City XI. They'd kindly agreed, and the arrangements had begun in earnest. Before long, however, our meticulous plans fell through. During a meeting with Greater Manchester Police, it had become clear that the cost of patrolling thousands of Scottish fans (supervising them on trains, marshalling them to hotels and escorting them to Maine Road, for starters) would be way beyond our budget. Therefore, the committee was left with no other option but to scrap the plans and go back to the drawing board.

I went into panic mode (we only had a few months to go before the big day, after all) but a tireless Tudor pledged to use his contacts to come up with a more local and less costly alternative. A couple of days later he asked me to meet him at Maine Road, since he had something important to discuss.

'Good news, Paul,' he said over lunch in his private lounge. 'I think we might have rescued the game. A team you might know quite well, in fact.'

'Go on?'

'Well, let's just say they're not a million miles from here . . .'

'Bolton? That's great, Tudor . . .'

'Not Bolton. Much closer than that.'

He smiled broadly, and the penny dropped.

'You don't mean United . . .'

'I spoke to Alex Ferguson this morning. He's more than happy to help out. Says it's the least he could do.'

It turned out that Keith Pinner, a member of the committee and a long-time friend of the United manager, had floated the idea past Ferguson, who'd countered by questioning why he hadn't been asked in the first place. Keith explained that we'd assumed that, since the Reds were scheduled to play a league game the day before, and since half the team were due to leave for midweek internationals 24 hours later, it was bound to be a no-can-do. How wrong we were.

'I'd be delighted to help out, and so would my players,' Ferguson said when Tudor contacted him at Old Trafford. They chatted for a short while, the United boss revealing that he'd been in the stands watching me during that fateful game against Aston Villa in 1990.

'Paul was a special player, there's no doubting that,' he said to Tudor, 'and if there's anyone who deserves a decent send-off, it's him.'

I nearly shook Ferguson's hand off when I met him at Maine Road, prior to the press conference announcing the news of this impromptu derby match. By stepping in at the 11th hour, he had done me an enormous favour. I couldn't have hoped for a more prestigious, crowd-pleasing spectacle to mark the end of my career.

On the first Sunday of October 1997, wearing a full City kit, my old-faithful football boots and a leg brace to stop my knee from falling apart, I jogged onto the Maine Road pitch for my last hurrah.

The day had already had its fair share of drama and emotion. At 6 a.m. I'd become a father for the first time, my son Zac having decided to make his appearance a little later than expected. Cradling his tiny warm body in my arms gave me a huge surge of paternal pride, as well as a massive lump in my throat that stayed with me for the rest of the day.

Once I'd spent a precious couple of hours with my newborn, I had to head back home. I had a quick shower and shave, chucked my kitbag into the boot, and set off for my big event. As I made tracks to Moss Side, I contemplated the day ahead, crossing my fingers that things were going to go to plan.

I hope a few people turn up, I remember thinking to myself as I conjured up nightmarish visions of deserted turnstiles and half-empty stands. The testimonial treasurer had estimated that we needed only 10,000 bums on seats to make the day financially viable, but he was keen for me to manage my expectations.

'You've got to bear in mind that City and United are both playing the day before,' he'd pointed out to me after a committee meeting. 'Some fans won't have the time or the money to attend two matches in one weekend, so let's not assume anything.'

Just before three o'clock, I emerged nervously from the tunnel to be greeted by a crowd of nearly 25,000 fans. Looking up to see the stadium almost three-quarters full, with row upon row of blue-shirted fans cheering and chanting my name, was truly humbling. Even the United supporters, housed in the North Stand, gave me a standing ovation. As I walked slowly onto the Maine Road turf, both sets of players formed a guard of honour for me, which I can categorically say was one of the most moving moments of my life.

In a break with the norm, Frank Clark and Alex Ferguson opted to field full-strength sides initially, which meant that Georgi Kinkladze, Uwe Rösler, David Beckham and Peter Schmeichel were all present in the line-ups. Testimonial games traditionally feature a large quota of reserve teamers (the result of clubs understandably preferring to rest their top players and shield them from injury), but on this occasion they both threw caution to the wind and went for the full complement. It was a magnificent gesture.

I was taken aback to see Paul Scholes, Nicky Butt and both the Neville brothers, as well as Beckham, limbering up on the pitch. Not only had they played 24 hours earlier, this international quintet were due to be reporting for England duty later that afternoon, with a vital World Cup clash with Italy just six days away. But here they were, turning up to show their respect and, by all accounts, getting up the nose of the FA by delaying their trip to Bisham Abbey.

Once I'd made my entrance, the plan was for me to stand in the centre circle with a microphone and thank everyone. I chickened out, however. So highly strung was I that day – my head was still spinning after my son's birth – that I feared I'd become a gibbering wreck. So, after the referee blew his whistle, I instead commenced proceedings with a wave, a smile and a side-foot pass to Kinky. I turned around to face the Kippax Stand for one last time and raised my arm to acknowledge the applauding faithful. I hoped to God that this wondrous image would never, ever fade from my memory.

Trudging towards the tunnel, I was able to see the crowd at much closer quarters, and was shocked to see a few fans shedding tears.

'Thanks for the memories, Lakey,' shouted a voice from the stands.

'You'll always be a legend to me, son,' yelled another.

I'd been aware that my swansong would be a poignant occasion for many, but nothing had quite prepared me for this. I decided to hurry to the dressing rooms as fast as my knee brace could take me. While I was deeply touched, this was a day on which I needed to be strong, and I knew that if I hung around the pitch any longer my emotions would spill over.

For the rest of the afternoon, I managed to maintain my composure. I was so busy circulating with staff and sponsors, and checking up on family and friends, that I didn't get to see the whole match. Though it was not as fiercely contested as your average Manchester derby (other than a few reckless tackles from City's Michael Brown, which got Alex Ferguson hot under the collar), by all accounts it was a pretty entertaining game that ended fair and square at 2–2. United's England contingent managed the first 20 minutes – boss Glenn Hoddle had imposed a strict time limit, apparently – and, after they jogged off, Tudor and I made a point of going down to the dressing room to thank them for their efforts.

'It's a pleasure, Paul,' said Phil Neville. 'Me and the lads all really wanted to play. Just sorry it wasn't for longer, that's all.'

Also leaving early for international duty was Peter Schmeichel, who gave me a pat on the back with a huge, gloved hand. 'I just hope everything goes well for you, Paul. It's about time you had a bit of good luck.'

Back out on the pitch, Ryan Giggs, a player whom I admired a great deal (despite being the nemesis of many a Blue) paid me the ultimate compliment by insisting on seeing out the entire 90 minutes, something that he needn't have done. He too was a Manchester lad, a player living the dream with his local team.

After the game I presented both teams with some cufflinks as a small token of my appreciation. Then, after toasting my hard-working committee with a glass or two of bubbly, the time came for me to gather my belongings and head out of Maine Road. This time, of course, I didn't need to put my muddy Adidas World Cups back in the skip destined for the boot room. So, instead, I carefully wrapped them in a plastic bag, tucked them under my arm and walked out of the club towards the car park. I drove back home with my boots on the passenger seat, my thoughts see-sawing between my final farewell and my newborn son.

The true significance of the occasion hit home a few days later. I'd been waiting to collect a takeaway from an Indian restaurant in Cheadle, when a couple in their 40s walked in and headed for their table for two. The bloke – obviously a City fan – saw me, did a double-take and came over.

'Good to see you, Paul,' he said, firmly gripping my hand. 'How are you doing?'

'Not so bad, mate, bearing up, y'know.'

'This is just weird,' he said, shaking his head. 'Me and the missus were only talking about you this morning. I was telling her how I'd once had a bet on you to become the next England captain . . .'

'Oh, right . . .'

'You ask any City fan, I said to her, and they'll tell you that

Paul Lake would have skippered his country for ten years had he not been injured. Didn't I, love?'

His wife smiled at me and nodded.

'You know what, I can't tell you how much pleasure I used to get from watching you play,' the fella continued. 'You and Colin Bell were my all-time heroes. Such a shame things didn't work out for either of you. And so sad that you had to retire without being able to prove how good you were.'

As I was about to thank him for his kind words, he put his hand on my shoulder and told me that he owed me an apology.

'I didn't go to your testimonial game the other day, y'see, and I just want to say sorry for not being there.'

'It's all right, mate, I understand,' I shrugged. 'Lots of people couldn't make it, what with it being on a Sunday and all . . .'

'It wasn't that,' he said, his voice starting to crack with emotion. 'I stayed away for a reason, Paul. I just couldn't bear the thought of saying goodbye to you.'

'Takeaway for Lake,' called a waiter from the serving hatch. I collected my curry, bid them farewell, walked to my car, rested my head on the steering wheel and dissolved into tears.

11

All Possibilities

It was on the morning of 17 February 1998, en route to a physio course at Lilleshall, that I saw my brother's name flash up on the carphone.

'Hi Mike, how are things . . .?'

'It's Dad,' he said, the tremor in his voice suggesting that something was badly wrong. 'He's collapsed in hospital. It's not looking good. You'd better come back.'

I bombed up the motorway to Manchester, frantic with worry. Dad hadn't been very well over the winter – he was recuperating in hospital after a chest infection brought on by his emphysema – but he seemed to be picking up, and there'd been nothing to indicate that anything serious was afoot. He'll get through this, I convinced myself as I screeched into the hospital car park. My dad's as tough as teak.

I arrived at the main reception and breathlessly rattled out his details. A few moments later a nurse appeared, her expression grave.

'I'm so sorry, Mr Lake, but your father passed away a few minutes ago.'

My blood ran cold.

'Where is he?'

'Um, I'm afraid I'm not quite sure . . . I think he may have been taken away from the ward, but then again he might be, er, I can check on the system if you want to take a seat . . .'

In no mood to wait, I roamed around the hospital, asking anyone in a blue uniform or a white coat if they knew the whereabouts of my dad, Ted Lake. Corridor after corridor, I was met with a succession of blank looks and head shakes. It was the longest five minutes of my life. I was about to head back to the main reception when I suddenly caught sight of my twin sister, Tracey, descending a flight of steps. I rushed towards her.

'Where is he, Trace?'

Gulping down sobs, she gestured to a side ward.

My twin and I clung tightly to each other as we walked in. Behind a pastel green curtain, lying on the bed, was Dad. Around him sat Mum, Mike, Dave and Sue, their pale faces stained with tears and etched in pain. Mike looked up at me.

'He didn't suffer, kid. The doctor said his heart just gave up.'

We spent the next hour taking it in turns to squeeze Dad's hand and stroke his forehead, as if our collective warmth would somehow stoke him up and fire him back to life.

Dad had started smoking at the age of 12, at a time when it

was deemed the epitome of cool to spark up a cigarette. In the early 1940s – long before any whiff of health scares – the young Ted Lake would have been bombarded by positive images of smoking, from Humphrey Bogart puffing on a Marlboro to adverts proclaiming that 'More Doctors Smoke Camels'. What started as a crafty pre-school fag with his Ardwick mates soon developed into a full-blown habit, and for the next 50-odd years he'd routinely get through a packet a day. When I was a kid, he'd often slip a pound note in my pocket and ask me to nip to the newsagents.

'Twenty Embassy Number 6, please,' I'd chirp up to the man behind the counter. Back in the day, it was as acceptable to pick up your dad's fags as it was to buy your own 5p box of Barratt's Sweet Cigarettes.

Other than my dad, the Lake family were all strict non-smokers. I've only ever had one cigarette in my life, while tanked-up at Jason Beckford's wedding, and promptly puked down my best man's suit. We all tolerated Dad lighting up, though. He had no other vices in life – he wasn't a big drinker, only occasionally supping the odd bottle of Mackeson stout – and we didn't begrudge him relaxing in front of *Open All Hours* with a fag and a brew after a tough day at work, wheezing with laughter as he watched Arkwright lech after Nurse Gladys Emmanuel.

When he reached retirement age, Dad had opted to leave his job at Manchester Building College. This change in lifestyle hit him harder than he'd expected, though, and he dearly missed the craic, the company and the daily routine.

His health took a dive – he developed chronic emphysema – and after one particularly severe coughing fit a concerned Mum packed him off to the doctor's.

'If you want to get better, Mr Lake, you'll have to stop smoking,' was the GP's stark advice. 'You need to get rid of all that tar in your lungs.'

Dad did as he was told and gave up the fags overnight, trying valiantly to wean himself off his tobacco fix by using nicotine patches and gums. In spite of all his efforts, though, his blood pressure shot up – as did his weight – and his coughs and splutters increased. For the next few months he was in and out of Tameside Hospital, the family making regular trips armed with bottles of Lucozade and Cadbury's Chocolate Fingers, as well as his *Daily Mirror*.

I vividly remember going to visit him one frosty Saturday morning. Prompted by the sounds of a kids' football match floating through the window – his ward backed on to some playing fields – we spent an hour or so reminiscing about the games of my youth. As I sat on the end of his bed delving into his bag of boiled sweets, we talked about our trip to Warners Holiday Camp on the Isle of Wight, when Dad had accompanied me to the island's annual Junior Soccer Festival. Our side, Blue Star under-12s, had excelled that year, overcoming a number of feeder teams from top clubs and beating Benfleet Boys 7–0 in the final. And to cap it all, I'd ended up winning Player of the Tournament.

'You'd have thought it was my birthday in the pub that night,' said Dad, casting his mind back to Easter 1981.

'Everywhere I turned people were patting me on the back and buying me a Guinness. I think I had about twenty pints lined up at the bar.'

We chuckled together about how Dad had got uncharacteristically hammered that evening, as I slept soundly in our *Hi-de-Hi*-style chalet. By last orders he was so paralytic that he'd had to be carried to bed.

'You looked so awful the next morning,' I said, recalling how he'd clambered onto the Manchester-bound coach wearing a crumpled suit, his un-Brylcreemed hairdo looking more like a wilting Mohican than his usual comb-over.

'Happy days though, eh, son,' said Dad.

'Yeah, happy days,' I replied.

The day after Dad died, we visited the morgue at Tameside Hospital to say our goodbyes. As we sat silently in the waiting room, lost in our own thoughts, flashbacks of my old fella kept appearing before me. I felt as though I was looking through the lens of one of those red View-Master toys that I'd had as a kid, my mind clicking through happy, frozen-in-time snapshots. Dad handing me my new City kit one Christmas Day, with its red and black diagonal stripe; Dad winning our Friday-night game of blackjack, pocketing the midget gems we used for currency; Dad twirling Mum around to Hound Dog at a family wedding reception; Dad sitting in the garden shed, making miniature cricket bats for me and my mates.

As my family and I were slowly ushered forth, I realised

that there was so much I wanted to say to my father, so many good times I wanted to recall, so many thank-yous I wanted to express. But all I could manage was 'Bye, Dad,' as I kissed him for the last time.

Following my father's funeral I sat down and took stock of things, coming to the conclusion that it was now the right time for a clean break. My subconscious – and my therapist – had been telling me for months that Maine Road, with all its bittersweet memories and unfinished business, wasn't the healthiest of environments for me. It had become a psycho-logical battlefield and, despite giving it my best shot, I wasn't up to the fight. I needed a fresh start, and thus made the painful decision to leave the club that had shaped so much of my life.

Also prompting me to take flight was City's decision to renege on their promise of an insurance payout. The £10,000 that had been due to come my way (not a huge windfall for a player once valued at £3 million, but money I was entitled to, and money that I needed) was suddenly kyboshed by the club. No explanation was given – just a categorical 'no-can-do' – but it wasn't hard to read between the lines.

'You've got your bloody testimonial fund, haven't you?' they might as well have said. 'Surely you don't need any more . . .'

Against my better judgement, I just accepted it. I simply couldn't be bothered to argue the toss, aware that I'd only have been labelled mercenary had I kicked up a stink and pointed out that my testimonial monies had come from the pockets of thousands of generous fans, not the dusty coffers of the football club.

It wasn't the only parting of the ways I had to contend with, as by now my marriage was in its final throes. A miserable couple of years had sadly taken their toll with my father's death and my traumatic retirement marking the lowest points of a hellish time. According to the PFA, 70 per cent of players get divorced within three years of quitting the game; it's a grim statistic that doesn't surprise me at all.

My son, Zac, however – one of the few shining lights of a very dark period – remained a priority. I loved my brown-eyed boy with every fibre of my body, and vowed to play a hugely active part in his life.

I soon heard on the grapevine that there was a vacancy for an assistant first-team physio at Burnley FC. New boss Stan Ternent and coach Sam Ellis had recently jumped ship from Bury, and were seeking some fresh faces at Turf Moor. It would be the perfect opportunity for me, I reckoned. Burnley wasn't a million miles away – I was keen to remain in the north-west – and, like City, it was a club steeped in history that was striving to repeat past glories. I bit the bullet and rang Sam, whom I already knew from his days as Peter Reid's assistant at Maine Road.

'You'd love it here, Lakey,' he enthused. 'Burnley's a cracking little club with some big plans. I reckon you'd fit in really well. I'll have a chat with the gaffer and let you know what's what.'

'I'd appreciate that, Sam.'

A few days later, after a quick meeting with him and Stan, I was offered the job.

A farewell do was hastily arranged by my City colleagues once the news leaked out that I was leaving. We all traipsed into the Deansgate area of town for a night of dancing and drinking, interspersed with much bear-hugging and back-slapping. Sad though it was to bid my farewells, I felt sure I was doing the right thing.

In August 1998, following a drizzly journey up the M65 and through the narrow streets of Burnley, I arrived at Turf Moor for the first day of pre-season training. Stan Ternent met me at the ground and spent the morning giving me a guided tour of my new workplace. It was as typical of a traditional football club as you could imagine, from the varnished wooden benches and exposed brick walls in the changing rooms (glossed in claret and blue, of course) to the padded leather swivel chair and antique walnut desk in the manager's office.

I was then taken down to the bowels of the stadium to check out the boot room, with its array of metal vices, wire brushes and suede dusters, and its ingrained aroma of sweat and dubbin. Next door was the laundry, swirling with steam, its huge tumble-driers adding a drumbeat to the tunes blaring from the staff radio.

'Oh, and by the way, Lakey,' Stan said matter-of-factly as he led me up the tunnel towards the treatment room, 'there's something I forgot to tell you. The senior physio's buggered off, so the main job's all yours if you want it.'

'Erm, okay,' I replied, wiping my sweaty palms on my shell suit and trying to mask my sheer panic. While my sports therapy diploma carried plenty of weight in professional football circles, I was a relative novice when all was said and done. Football's best first-team physios boasted a physiotherapy degree, yet I was three years shy of achieving mine, having only recently embarked on my part-time course at Salford University.

Still reeling from Stan's bombshell, I was taken over to the training ground at nearby Gawthorpe to meet the players. The Clarets' squad, Stan explained, comprised a blend of youth and experience, with lower league warhorses such as Peter Swan and Ronnie Jepson lining up alongside young upstarts like Paul Smith and Glen Little. My first impression of a solid, close-knit unit boded well, seeing as I'd now be spending a lot more time with the lads than I'd originally thought.

My first impressions of the Gawthorpe gymnasium-cum-dungeon weren't as good, though. Catching my attention as we entered the musty room was a dead mouse that had probably been flattened by the mangy leather medicine ball resting a few inches away. Across the room, situated next to an ageing multigym, was an old 'anvil boot'. This medieval-looking steel contraption had probably been at the cutting edge of rehab when Burnley legend Jimmy Adamson had used it to strengthen his quads in the 1950s, but it had no place in the 1990s.

'So where's the ducking-stool, Stan?' I felt like asking as I cast my eye around this chamber of horrors.

I think he got the message. Within days he'd secured the use of a plush hotel gym, with facilities befitting a club that was intending to go places.

The relationship between a football manager and his physiotherapist is a bit like a marriage, I suppose. If it's going to work, it has to be based on the fundamentals of mutual trust, respect and understanding. There are bound to be tiffs along the way – one party standing their ground over a point of discipline, perhaps, or the other claiming they know how best to handle the youngsters – but a sound partnership will help them ride the storm. Too many rocky patches, however – maybe due to personality clashes or differing opinions – and it just won't last the distance.

The ideal gaffer, from a physio's point of view, is a model of patience and understanding. Likely to be at the helm of a successful club with a large squad at his disposal, he's less inclined to pressurise you to rush players back in unfeasible timescales. He's someone who gives you and your medical team total responsibility, deferring to your scientific judgement and allowing players to return in the safest possible time without risking further injury.

The boss from hell, on the other hand, is probably in charge of a struggling outfit with a threadbare squad, maybe with a chairman breathing down his neck and fans bashing his ear. Irrational and unreasonable, he treats the appliance of science with contempt and attempts to cheat nature by demanding that unfit players are returned in the shortest possible time, regardless of the ramifications.

Stan Ternent, like most managers I worked with, wavered between these two extremes. A taskmaster extraordinaire, he was one of the most committed and conscientious people I'd ever come across in football, yet he also happened to be one of the most volatile. From players to physios, anyone who failed to match his high standards would be subject to a monumental bollocking, screeched at high volume in his broad Geordie accent.

Stan and I generally worked well together – there was plenty of mutual respect – but from the outset he made it abundantly clear who was boss. This was certainly the case when we travelled to Bournemouth for the first away game of the new season.

Conscious of my elevated position as first-team physio – and having kittens at the prospect – I made titanic efforts to ensure that all the pre-match arrangements were in order. Packing the medical supplies: done. Loading the energy drinks onto the coach: done. Checking the first aid kit: done. My final chore was to fax our breakfast and pre-match meal requirements to the hotel. Having never arranged this before (I remembered Roy Bailey carrying out this onerous task at Maine Road) I spent hours familiarising myself with the FA's guidelines on diet and nutrition and picking the brains of my physio friends, Mandy and Philippa. So keen was I to demonstrate my highly professional approach that I even sought advice from a top sports scientist at a Premier League club.

'Breakfast is the most important meal of the day,' he'd stressed, 'so go heavy with the carbs and proteins. Lots of cereal, wholemeal toast, fresh fruit, that kind of thing.'

An hour or so before we set off for Dorset, I faxed over our super-healthy menus to our hotel, satisfied that all my hard work would gain me a few brownie points from my new gaffer.

Having been woken early the next morning by the cacophony of Bournemouth seagulls circling the hotel, I came down for breakfast slightly earlier than planned. However, as I walked into the restaurant area, all I could see was a large serving hatch groaning with bacon, sausages, fried eggs, baked beans, black pudding and mushrooms. Not a banana or a bran flake in sight.

I was just about to wipe the floor with the kitchen staff when I heard a familiar Geordie voice coming from the other side of the room. There, sitting alone at a corner table, was Stan, mopping up a pool of orange egg yolk with a slice of fried bread.

'Can I have a word, Lakey lad?'

'Sure . . .'

'Let's get one thing straight,' he said, his voice laced with menace. '*I* choose the f***in' food at this club.'

I just burst out laughing. This was one battle I knew I wasn't going to win.

'Pass us the HP will you, Stan . . .' I asked, once I'd helped myself to an egg and bacon doorstop and drawn up a seat opposite him.

At Dean Court that afternoon, with their stomachs lined with ketchup and bacon fat, the Burnley lads played out of their skins and beat Bournemouth 2–1.

'You know where you can stick your FA diet sheets, don't you?' snorted Stan as we filed into the dressing room, and I made a mental note to never get above my station at Burnley FC.

The manager and I only ever had one major run-in, but when it came it was a humdinger. And it involved the visit of Manchester City to Turf Moor in March 1999.

City had undergone a huge shift in personnel over the previous year or so, with Francis Lee being unseated by a new chairman, David Bernstein, and Frank Clark being replaced by Joe Royle. Unable to avoid relegation to Division Two in May 1998 – he'd arrived too late in the day to halt the decline – Big Joe set about reinforcing and revitalising the side, drafting in grafters like Andy Morrison and Danny Tiatto, the strategy being to get out of this purgatory as quickly as possible. By the following spring, his plans were well on track, and City remained unbeaten in the league throughout January and February.

In contrast, Burnley were having a dreadful start to the new year, the low point being a 5–0 thrashing at home by Gillingham. Stan, unsurprisingly, was like a bear with a sore head. Not only was there talk of his job being under threat, his next league opponents – my former club – had hit a rich vein of form.

On the morning of the game, once training had finished, he called me into his office.

'You know how important this match is tonight, don't you?' he said, drumming his fingers on his desk.

'Course I do.'

'My bloody job might be on the line if we lose this one.'

'I'm sure the boys will raise their game for you, Gaffer . . .'

'Now, the thing is, Lakey, I know you're a City fan. I know how much that club means to you. But you work for Burnley now. So just think on . . .'

'I get the message, Stan.'

'I hope you do, because if I see you acknowledging the City fans, I'll knock you out.'

There's no answer to that, as the great Eric Morecambe once said.

City came, scored and conquered. The irrepressible Shaun Goater ran rings around the Clarets, and the visitors found themselves 3–0 up after half an hour. It took all my self-control not to leap up when the Blues hit the back of the net but, mindful of Stan's eyes lasering into my head, and out of respect for the Burnley lads, I sat on my hands, bit my tongue and watched on impassively as the goals rained in.

It took some time for the City fans to twig that I was the opposing physio. I'd slipped away from Maine Road quietly and without fuss – few people knew that I'd left for Turf Moor – and it was only when I jogged onto the pitch to treat

Burnley centre half Neil Moore, who'd collapsed in front of the away end, that I was rumbled. Once one supporter recognised me, the news spread through the stand like a domino rally, and the banter came thick and fast.

'Look who it is! It's only f***in' Lakey!'

'Oi, what you doin' working for this bag of shite?'

'Get yer kit on, mate, we need a fourth . . .'

I tried hard to stay calm and collected, ignoring all the comments from the stands as I strapped up Neil's knee and beckoned for the stretcher. However, as I walked around the pitch perimeter, only yards away from a sea of sky blue shirts and scarves, my resolve crumbled.

'Lakey, Lakey give us a wave, Lakey, give us a wave,' the City faithful sang gleefully. How could I *not* acknowledge them, for chrissakes? I adored these fans. So I acquiesced to their request and gave them a wave – a little covert one, like Mr Bean – which was met with thunderous applause.

I realised my grave mistake within a millisecond of raising my hand. Over in the dugout I could see an enraged gaffer angrily gesturing towards me and bouncing off the Perspex canopy, like a bluebottle battering itself against a kitchen window.

'What did I f***in' say to you this morning?' he spat as I sheepishly returned to my seat.

The game ended in a 6–0 whitewash, with 'The Goat' grabbing a hat-trick as a chant of 'your best player is your physio' rose up from the away end.

Stan didn't utter a single word to me, or the rest of the

players, for an entire week. I couldn't blame him, to be honest. But he didn't lose his job, and I didn't get my lights punched out, so it could have been much worse.

The next time I watched Manchester City was on a pub TV screen. In May 1999, having missed out on automatic promotion to Fulham and Walsall, the Blues found themselves up against Gillingham in the Wembley final of the Division One play-offs. It was, by far, one of the most surreal games I'd ever seen.

With five minutes to go City were trailing 2–0 and, like the thousands of travelling supporters, I felt utterly dejected as I watched our promotion hopes go down the pan. Many Blues were so disconsolate that they left the stadium early, unable to stomach defeat by the Gills. I was in two minds whether to slide off myself, but a little masochistic voice in my head told me to stay the distance.

I'm so pleased I did, because the next hour saw Joe Royle's men stage one of the most amazing football fightbacks in the club's history. Kevin Horlock pulled a goal back in the dying seconds of the game, only for Paul Dickov to equalise four minutes into injury time, rifling the ball into the top corner. A fruitless period of extra time led to a torturous penalty shoot-out. The Blues held it together, thankfully, and emerged as 3–1 victors, my old pal Richard Edghill showing nerves of steel by calmly slotting his effort home. The scenes that followed – at Wembley, as well as my local pub – were of total delirium.

With my whoops of delight, however, came pangs of envy. Appearing at Wembley in a Manchester City shirt would have been the ultimate honour for a home-grown player like me, and this do-or-die final, packed with so much excitement and incident, would have been tailor-made for my game. Running out of the tunnel as a fit and healthy 30-year-old, I'd have probably been at my professional peak, in the prime of my career, playing the best football of my life.

Feeling sorry for myself, I opened a bag of Scampi Fries and downed another pint, wishing that I was on a pitch in north London, not a pub in south Manchester.

I felt similarly down-in-the-mouth six months later, not long after the turn of the Millennium, when I was asked to appear on ITV's *Tonight with Trevor McDonald* show. I took part in a football-themed edition titled 'The Arthritis XI', which focused on the physical after-effects suffered by such former players as Tommy Smith, Ian Hutchinson, Peter Osgood, Kevin Beattie and Allan Clarke. As I cast my eye around the TV studio I realised I was by far the youngest there, with most participants well into their 50s. Comparing creaking knees and dodgy backs with blokes who were two decades my senior wasn't the best feeling in the world.

Whilst all ex-footballers tend to experience some degree of wear-and-tear later in life, this group of old pros had found themselves suffering more than most. The programme alleged that some players had been the victims of slipshod medical practices, and had borne the brunt of poor surgery and shoddy rehabilitation, many having their careers curtailed as a result. It went on to examine the amateurish aftercare that had prevailed unchallenged at clubs through-out the years.

I did a piece to camera about the numerous medical procedures that I'd undergone at a relatively tender age, all to no avail. I outlined the hardships of being a 30-something arthritis-sufferer, and also raised concerns about the amount of pre-op anaesthetic that I'd had to consume (inhaling all those toxins can't have been good for me).

The other stories disclosed that day, some on-camera, some off-camera, were jaw-dropping. I heard accounts of non-medical staff injecting players with cortisone simply to get them onto the pitch anyhow; of lads being fed cocktails of painkillers to ensure that they made the team sheet on a Saturday afternoon; and of players with broken legs being roughly dragged onto stretchers as if they were carcasses. Anecdotes were swapped about the inexperienced (and occasionally reckless) bucket-and-sponge men who dealt with injuries in the 1960s and 70s. These fellas – usually members of the coaching staff who'd once been sent on a first aid course – were charged with match-day medical duties and tasked with caring for footballers worth hundreds of thousands of pounds. Back then, nobody bothered to question the fact that these designated 'trainers' probably knew more about tactics than tendons. It was scandalous, really.

Fortunately, such archaic practices were outlawed in the mid-1990s, when the FA and the PFA intervened to raise and regulate standards of medical treatment. As a result, it became mandatory for all Premier League physios to be Chartered (in possession of a physiotherapy degree) and obligatory for every club doctor to have a recognised sporting qualification. This influx of qualified practitioners coincided with huge scientific and medical advances that allowed professional footballers a much improved quality of care. It's just a shame that this breakthrough came too late in the day for Osgood, Clarke, Smith and the rest of the Arthritis Allstars.

It was with some reluctance that I left Burnley FC after just one season. I was finding it impossible to juggle my day job with my evening studies and, for the sake of my future career path, university had to take precedence. There were no hard feelings between Stan and I (he totally understood my predicament) and I was pleased that we were able to part on good terms. I'd thoroughly enjoyed my year at Turf Moor – the change of scenery had come at a good time – and I appreciated the opportunity that I'd been given. But the time had come to focus on my studies.

Founded and funded by the PFA, the Chartered Physiotherapy course at Salford University was geared towards training up retired footballers to become Premiership-level physios. The game's authorities, it seemed, were aware that some NHS-trained professionals were getting eaten alive in this most demanding of arenas, and that a new breed of physio with a solid football background was required if standards were to be upheld. They needed lads who knew what made this unique little industry tick, and who knew exactly what it took to make the grade.

The class of '98 included ex-pros such as Everton's Gary Stevens and Tranmere Rovers' Chris Malkin, as well as some lesser-known players, like Andy Barr and Matt Radcliffe (Altrincham and Bury respectively). There was even a former actor among us, a scouser called Neil Davies who, after leaving Lincoln City, had bagged the part of Robbie Moffat in Brookside. The camaraderie among this close-knit band of brothers was fantastic. Sitting in the campus coffee bar before a lecture was like sitting in the dressing rooms of old, as we'd share stories, swap banter and support each other through what was an extremely demanding degree course.

A large part of our curriculum comprised hands-on hospital placements. Since everyone on the PFA degree was planning a career in football, not the NHS, many tended to view the six-week blocks in respiratory or neurology wards as a bit of an inconvenience ('I want a job at Leeds United, not Leeds bloody General,' being the common consensus). Only the orthopaedic placements – the closest thing to being a sports physio – aroused much enthusiasm.

Though some elements of my NHS training were boringly repetitive (the amount of paperwork was ridiculous), I found other areas enriching. Treating so many brave patients – people who suffered severe head injuries or serious strokes – hammered it home to me how talented the NHS physios were, how trifling my own problems were in comparison, and how trivial the cosseted world of football could be. That said, having paced up and down hundreds of male wards in Manchester, I can vouch for the fact that the main topic of conversation was, nine times out of ten, City or United related.

Sometimes I'd get recognised by Blues' fans who, until my name badge gave the game away, would scrutinise me with a 'don't I know you from somewhere?' expression on their faces. The following day, these same patients would often produce an old match programme (or a leg plaster) for me to sign before their morning constitutional. I didn't mind, of course; it was nice to still be remembered.

As it happened, it wasn't too long before I found myself back working in football. This was due in part to a conversation I had with David Pleat at a sportsman's dinner. We harked back to the good old days – in the late 1980s, when managing Leicester, he'd been quoted as saying he'd have signed me up if he had a spare million – and also got chatting about my fledgling physio career. Having spent years at football's sharp end, he offered me some valuable advice.

'The best physios I've seen are those lads who've worked their way up the divisions,' he said. 'Gives you the best grounding. When you learn how to manage on a shoestring, you can cope with anything.'

With those wise words ringing in my ears, I decided to make a start with the football Conference and accepted a part-time job with Altrincham FC. Working at a cash-strapped semi-pro club, I learned how to budget and economise, snipping tubes of Deep Heat in half to extract every last globule, and buying re-usable bandages and ankle strappings.

The general manager, Graham Heathcote, was a multi-tasking workaholic who oversaw everything from PR to personnel, from scouting to accounting. Graham was supremely organised, especially when it came to the business of recruiting players on loan, a common practice among semi-pro clubs and often the only way for them to remain solvent. By forging fruitful relationships with lower league clubs like Stockport County and Wigan Athletic, Graham ensured that a steady stream of promising youth teamers or out-of-favour reserves passed through Moss Lane.

I spent a full season with Altrincham before climbing another rung of the career ladder. I got a job with Oldham Athletic, joining forces with head physio Paul Caton (younger brother of the late Tommy Caton, City's celebrated centre-half) and the newly installed boss, Iain Dowie. An astute tactician and a fantastic man-manager, Dowie impressed me greatly. He realised that the only way a hard-up club like Oldham could compete with the bigger, wealthier clubs was by fielding a side bristling with tenacity and team spirit. With this in mind, he set about breeding a culture of invincibility, convincing the players that they could beat anybody, especially on their home turf.

'Make Boundary Park a fortress,' he'd bark at his charges,

telling them to take full advantage of its inhospitable location. Perched atop the Pennines, this bleak, windswept stadium – one of the highest professional football grounds in the country – was the nemesis of many away teams, especially those travelling from balmier southern climes.

With the manager's plans and tactics coming to fruition, and with influential pros like Darren Sheridan and David Eyres buying into his philosophy, Dowie's team propelled themselves up the division. However, just as things were perking up on the pitch, Oldham hit financial problems. Being forced to flog the best players in his squad, and being prevented from buying any replacements was a bridge too far for this highly principled man and, much to the dismay of the Latics fans, he left Boundary Park in December 2003 to take the top job at Crystal Palace.

A few weeks beforehand, I'd also decided to head for the exit door. The club's cost-cutting measures were going into overdrive and, as the newest member of staff, I reckoned I was ripe for the chop. So I jumped before I was pushed, landing a more stable job as first-team physio at Macclesfield Town. Going for security, albeit in a lower league, was definitely the sensible option, especially since I'd recently got married again.

Jo and I had known each other for a while – she'd worked in Manchester City's commercial department – and over time our friendship had grown into something more serious. We were kindred spirits, the missus and I, and our wedding at a small Cheshire hotel, surrounded by our nearest and dearest, was a day I'll never forget.

Being in a happy, solid relationship did me the world of good. The cloud of depression that had suffocated me during the 1990s gradually began to lift, and before long I'd weaned myself off the anti-depressants and cancelled my Priory sessions. However, it was only when I ceremonially dusted off my treasured CD collection that I knew I was properly on the mend. I remember welcoming my beloved music back into my life by sliding Oasis' (*What's the Story*) *Morning Glory?* into my in-car CD player, each sublime track reminding me exactly what I'd been missing all these years. As I warbled tunelessly along to 'Champagne Supernova', tapping my fingers on the steering wheel, I felt my sparkle returning. My old self was back. I'd missed him.

My graduation day added further bounce to my step. In May 2003, following four years of hard graft, my fellow students and I gathered together at a conference hall at Salford University, dressed in our black gowns and mortar boards, to celebrate our achievements. As I went up to accept my degree, with Mum and Jo looking on, I felt all the weight and tension lifting off my shoulders. I'd done it. I'd stuck it out. I'd made the grade.

With its compact but ageing stadium, together with its tiny but loyal fan base, Macclesfield Town had the air of a non-league outfit rather than a Division Two side. Home attendances rarely exceeded 2,200; not surprising, perhaps, for a club that hadn't exactly been blessed with success, and that happened to be situated within 20 miles of both City and United. Trying to persuade the local townsfolk to choose Moss Rose instead of Maine Road was always going to be an uphill struggle.

The club's facilities were functional, to put it mildly. My physio room was a shrine to the 1970s, with its woodchip wallpaper, greying net curtains and cheap carpet tiles, together with the most ancient ultrasound-machine-cum-Enigma—code-cracker that I'd ever seen. But what the club lacked in flashiness, it more than made up for in friendliness. Macclesfield Town's greatest asset was its dedicated workforce, a cluster of tireless employees who wore more hats than the Queen Mother.

One such gem was Eric Campbell. Every lower league club has its own Mr Fixit – a man with a pencil behind his ear and a Swiss army knife in his pocket – and Eric, God rest his soul, was ours. He did everything. If the showers were knackered, he'd mend them. If a coach needed booking, he'd sort it. If the goalposts collapsed, he'd rebuild them. Put it this way, had your aeroplane crashed into the Amazon jungle, it's Eric you'd have wanted sitting next to you. He was a wonderful man who made coming into work a pleasure.

As the club's sole physio, I was the proverbial blue-arsed fly. I hardly stopped to catch my breath. If I wasn't treating the youth- and first-team lads – massaging backs, taping limbs, patching up blisters – then I'd be either shuttling the non-driving players to the training ground or stopping off at

Tesco to buy 30 ready meals for the weekend coach journey. In fact, I did everything for the lads other than spoon-feed them their lunch or wipe their backsides (and even Eric would have drawn the line at that).

As regards the playing staff, let's just say that Macclesfield struggled to attract the cream of the crop. Most new signings were either lower league specialists like Steve Payne, or 30-something journeymen, such as Tommy Widdrington and Clyde Wijnhard, in the twilight of their careers. Finally, there were the short-term loan signings from bigger clubs, namely Boaz Myhill and Colin Little, who came from Aston Villa and Crewe Alexandra respectively.

A constant presence amid all these comings and goings, however, was our player-coach, John Askey. Macclesfield born and bred, John had spent his entire professional career at the club, notching up over 700 appearances in the process. He was also a former team-mate of my brother Mike, who'd spent a couple of seasons with the Silkmen in the mid-1980s.

John was a revelation. I remember sitting in the dugout when, at the grand old age of 40, he scored a memorable goal against Rochdale on the last day of the 2002–03 season. He'd hardly featured in the team that year, concentrating mainly on his coaching duties, but an unprecedented glut of injuries had led to his name being added to the list of substitutes that day. John was so delighted to poke in the 88th-minute equaliser that he dived into the crowd of adoring home fans, badly injuring his calf in the process.

'It was worth every one of these bruises,' John said the next morning, as I patched him up in the physio room. 'You're a long time not playing, as you know yourself, Lakey. I've got to enjoy it while I can, haven't I?'

It was, as it happened, his final match for the Silkmen. But what a career, and what a fantastic servant.

It was at Macclesfield, probably more than any other club I worked at, that I bonded most with the players. My five-year stint at Moss Rose gave me the chance to get to know the squad well, particularly the injury-susceptible lads who'd spend more time on the treatment table than on the training ground. For many of them, I like to think that my physio room was an oasis of calm, a place where they could ditch all the macho dressing-room banter and chat freely and frankly.

Nothing of a personal nature ever went further than my four walls, and once players realised that they could trust me they'd frequently open up, discussing their problems and divulging their innermost secrets. Sometimes the subject matter would lean towards on-field matters – fear of losing their place in the team, for example, or anger at being played out of position – but more often than not the chat would involve affairs off the pitch. As I treated their injuries, I'd hear stories of marriage break-ups, financial meltdown and severe depression. I felt like Moss Rose's resident agony aunt: a psychologist, financial adviser and relationship counsellor rolled into one.

I remember trying to mask my shock when a self-confessed sex addict once poured his heart out, admitting to me that he'd seen 50 different prostitutes in the space of a year. Then there was the lad in his early 20s who was so plagued with worry about his heavy gambling debts that his game had gone into freefall overnight.

'How can I keep my mind on the pitch when I've got bailiffs knocking on my door, and heavies threatening to smash my face in?' I recall him once telling me.

Getting to know all the lads helped me from a professional perspective, too. I became an expert at determining each player's pain threshold, pinpointing which mard-arse players were more likely to hit the deck like a wet paper bag, and identifying those hard nuts who'd stay down only if they were in serious trouble. Throughout my physio career I usually found that players who theatrically writhed around following an injury, rolling about in seeming agony, often weren't badly hurt. It was those who remained completely still on the ground – a sure sign of the body going into shock – that aroused the most genuine concern. I'd had enough personal experience of this to know the score.

There was always a strong Manchester City contingent at Moss Rose. Many of the players, including Michael Welch and Danny Adams, were lifelong Blues' supporters, as were the kitmen, Paul and Frank. And, in the summer of 2004, joining a band of Maine Road ex-pats that included manager Brian Horton, was my old buddy Ian 'Bob' Brightwell. Bob's arrival as reserve team coach pleased me no end, as he and I had always got on famously. He possesses the most irritating sense of humour of anyone I know (his favourite prank being to stir your cup of tea and burn your hand with the spoon) and it was great to rekindle our old friendship. Richard Edghill came aboard a couple of seasons later, having decided to see out his playing career at Moss Rose.

This influx of City aficionados meant that the morning chatter in my physio room often had a distinct sky blue theme. Over mugs of tea and bacon butties, we discussed Joe Royle's replacement, Kevin Keegan who, together with new chairman John Wardle, had succeeded in bringing some stability to the club after a couple of yo-yo seasons. We discussed the merits of new signings like Peter Schmeichel and Robbie Fowler. And, in the spring of 2003, we mourned the end of an era, the decision having been taken to relocate Manchester City Football Club to a brand-new stadium at Eastlands, the venue of the 2002 Commonwealth Games.

On Sunday 11 May 2003, a bright, sunny day, Maine Road staged its final game. Along with a host of other former players, I'd been asked by the club to make a guest appearance on the pitch before kick-off to mark one of the most poignant occasions in City's history.

I took Zac along with me that day, purposely arriving nice and early so that I could give him a potted history of Dad's old stamping ground. Shepherding him from one side of the stadium to the other, I pointed out various Maine Road landmarks. Stan Gibson's house that adjoined the souvenir shop; the window of Ken Barnes's old office-cum-social-club; the turnstile that Albert the milkman and I used to walk through; the old fella weighed down by his 'Repent All Ye Sinners' sandwich board.

After letting Zac pat the nose of a friendly police horse, I walked him past the bustling main entrance, where we were grabbed for a radio interview by England rugby star (and City fanatic) Will Greenwood. And, as we passed the St John Ambulance meeting point, I decided to tell Zac all about my infamous tongue-swallowing story.

'And d'you know what?' I said to him after describing the gory drama that had unfolded, 'your daddy nearly died on the pitch that day.'

Zac paused and looked at me, his eyes widening.

'Can I have a hot dog, Dad?' came the reply from a six-year-old far more bothered about a sausage in a roll than my near-death experience.

I bought him his hot dog, and for nostalgia's sake grabbed myself one too. As we wolfed them down, leaning against the ticket office wall, I told Zac to savour all the sights, the sounds and the smells of Maine Road, because soon all this would be no more.

Then, with him clinging on to my coat, just like I'd done with Albert all those years ago, we wound our way to the Main Stand entrance. We mingled with hundreds of supporters as they emerged from the backstreets, trudged across the forecourt, and passed through the turnstiles, their faces riven with sadness. This lovely old stadium had been home to some wonderful memories, had been a haven to generations of Mancunians, and over its 80-year existence, had touched thousands of lives. For many fans, myself included, it hadn't properly sunk in that our temple, our shrine, would soon be reduced to rubble.

I hoisted Zac onto my shoulders and walked onto the Maine Road pitch for the last time, joining the throng of former players gathering round the centre circle. This roll-call of footballers spanned five decades, from Roy Clarke and Ken Barnes to Gary Owen and David White; from Tommy Booth and Dennis Tueart to Uwe Rösler and Georgi Kinkladze.

Each of us was handed the microphone for a couple of minutes, having been asked to address the sell-out crowd with our own Maine Road memories. I told everyone how grateful I was to have played in this wonderful stadium, in good times and bad, and thanked the fans for their unswerving support through the years. As my little speech came to a close, I felt a wave of emotion wash over me.

'No matter what happens, and wherever we go, one thing will never change,' I said, just about holding it together. 'Once a Blue, always a Blue.'

Zac and I returned to the Main Stand to watch a typically tragicomic City performance. On such a momentous occasion, in a stadium full to bursting with diehard fans and former footballers, the lads wilted under the pressure and were beaten 1–0 by Southampton. Compounding this was the fact that all the ex-players had been herded into seats located behind the biggest pillar in the stand. Occupying the worst position in the stadium meant that we could see only one half of the pitch.

'Are all City games like this?' asked a bemused Zac, unimpressed with the crappy view and the even crappier scoreline.

'No, son,' I replied. 'We'll probably play better than this next season, and still get beaten.' And I grinned at him, inwardly pleased that he was experiencing a day in the life of a City fan, with the usual dashing of expectation and shattering of illusions. His character would be built upon it.

Sitting elsewhere in the Main Stand that day was my wife. Despite being heavily pregnant, Jo, a life-long Blue, had insisted on attending this momentous match with her friend Adam, waddling through the back streets of Moss Side and up the concrete steps of C Block.

Exactly a month later, another Lake was welcomed into the world, a dark-haired, blue-eyed boy whom we named Edward, in memory of his grandad.

It was on a freezing-cold January night that I paid my first proper visit to our new ground, the City of Manchester Stadium, part of the Eastlands sporting complex. I was attending the club's inaugural Hall of Fame awards dinner, Blues' fans having given me the ultimate accolade by voting me into an elite that included Bert Trautmann, Colin Bell, Francis Lee, Mike Summerbee and Joe Corrigan.

I'd been concerned that City's new home would end up an ugly, soulless block of concrete like other grounds that I'd visited. My fears subsided, however, when I walked up Joe Mercer Way and was confronted by what I can only describe as a work of art. With its gleaming glass panels and blue uplighting, together with its spiky, space-age cables and spiral ramps, it took my breath away. I made my way to the main entrance and stared up in wonderment, marvelling at the symmetry and detail, hoping that the City squad realised how lucky they were to call this monument to perfection their workplace.

The stadium interior was equally impressive. While nothing would ever replicate the comfy homeliness of Maine Road, I was nonetheless blown away by the plush facilities, more in keeping with a five-star hotel than a sports venue. As I followed the guests into the hospitality lounge, I heard a familiar voice call out my name.

'Come here, Paul,' said my old friend and former testimonial committee chairman Tudor Thomas. 'Let me show you something before the ceremony starts.'

He proceeded to lead me through a door that opened out onto one of the most beautiful playing surfaces I'd ever seen. Flooded with light and framed by a swathe of 47,000 sky blue seats, it looked absolutely stunning.

'What d'you reckon?' asked Tudor.

'I think it'll grow on me,' I smiled.

An hour or so later I was officially welcomed into the Hall of Fame, proudly sharing a stage with some of City's most revered players. Niall Quinn accepted his award just before me, and brought a tear to my eye when he made a point of singling me out, describing me as the best footballer he'd ever played with.

The joy of the occasion, however, was tinged with sadness.

It was on this night, perhaps more than any other, that I found myself yearning for my father. I really wished he'd been there to share in such a huge honour, and I said so in my acceptance speech.

'This one's for you Dad,' I said, kissing my award and looking skywards.

12

There Is a Light That Never Goes Out

In a move that came as a surprise to many, Paul Ince was appointed player-manager of Macclesfield Town in October 2006. With the Silkmen propping up the Second Division, seven points adrift of their rivals, the Moss Rose board had sacked Brian Horton and taken a gamble on the former Manchester United midfielder, despite his complete lack of managerial experience.

'All right, Lakey,' chuckled Paul as he walked into my physio room on his first morning in charge. 'Been a long time, eh?'

Fifteen years, in fact, had passed since I'd last seen my old opponent. It had been on Christmas Eve 1991, waiting in the queue at HMV in Manchester city centre, that I'd felt a tap on my shoulder and had turned round to see Paul standing there with his wife, Claire.

'Lakey, how are you, mate? Good to see you,' he'd smiled.

'Likewise, mate, likewise . . .'

With Claire only weeks away from giving birth to their first child, we'd chatted for a while about their plans and preparations for the new arrival, Paul shaking his head as his other half described the amount of baby gear that was being stockpiled at their Bramhall home.

'I've spent a bloody fortune in Mothercare,' he'd said. 'Seriously, you wouldn't believe how much a pushchair costs these days. Nearly as much as a car . . .'

Despite his Red allegiances, over the years I'd got on very well with Paul, and football-wise we'd always had a lot in common. Until injury had ruined my best-laid plans, our careers had followed similar paths, both of us enjoying schoolboy and youth team success (his school team had won the National Six-a-Side championship the year before mine), followed by a swift progression to professional football and England honours. He and I had also been Adidas bedfellows, the pair of us having secured exclusive boot deals as our careers had ascended.

As we stood nattering away in that record store, however, it struck me that our circumstances couldn't have been more different. There was I, in the midst of my post-op rehabilitation, struggling physically, emotionally and financially. And there was Paul, fighting fit and entering the prime of his career, cementing his place in the England set-up and playing for a United side that was on the cusp of greatness. He was well off, happily married and with a kid on the way – life was obviously treating him well.

He told me to get fit soon ('I need payback for that 5–1 nightmare,' he grimaced) and we bid our farewells. I shook his hand, gave Claire a kiss, and wished them both a merry Christmas and a happy New Year.

'The same to you, too,' Paul smiled. 'Hope 1992's a good 'un for you, Lakey . . .'

Confounding the many critics who'd doubted that a former Manchester United, Liverpool and Inter Milan player would acclimatise to football's basement, Paul made an immediate impact at Macclesfield Town. He shook things up behind the scenes, ridding the dressing room and manager's office of hangers-on, and working closely with the commercial department to raise the club's profile and get more bums on seats. Neither too proud nor too blinkered to accept advice from the game's elder statesmen, he wisely drafted in lower league specialist Ray Matthias as his right-hand man.

As for matters on the pitch, Paul was confronted with a side completely lacking in leadership and morale. He set about reinstating self-belief and discipline within his young squad and signed loan players including Blackpool's John Murphy and Simon Wiles, to inject some much-needed experience. With the aim of improving the lads' physical condition and fitness, he also brought in a nutritionist, a sports scientist and a chiropractor, very much the norm in the higher divisions, but less so in the depths of Division Two. It was no coincidence that Macclesfield's fortunes soon began to change: they strung together a ten-match unbeaten run and the gap at the foot of the table started to close.

In January 2007 the Silkmen received a timely lift – and a financial windfall – when they were drawn against Chelsea in the third round of the FA Cup. The gaffer made the most of our trip down to the capital, organising a luxury coach and booking the squad into the swish Chelsea Village hotel that adjoined Stamford Bridge. On the eve of the match he invited the backroom staff out for a drink with a few of his old football pals, including Ian Wright, Mark Bright and Jamie Redknapp. I'd known Ian and Mark during my playing days, of course, but I'd never met Jamie before. It seems he knew me, though, revealing that his old man, Harry, had always spoken highly of me, and that he himself had once watched me play at White Hart Lane.

'You were different class that day,' he smiled. 'Head and shoulders above the rest.' It was a nice thing for him to say, particularly in such esteemed company.

Twenty-four hours later we were on the coach heading back to Cheshire, having been beaten 6–1 by Mourinho's boys. The scoreline flattered Chelsea, believe it or not, with the Macc minnows scoring an improbable early equaliser and playing the last 15 minutes with only nine men.

'Onwards and upwards, fellas,' yelled Incey as we made our way up the M6. 'Let's keep that team spirit up for the rest of the season . . .'

Macclesfield's survival hinged on the final game of the season against Notts County at Moss Rose. With just one point needed to ensure another year of league football, it was typically nail-biting stuff, especially when John Miles' early goal was snuffed out by County's Andy Parkinson just before the interval. Nerves continued to jangle in the second half, the bumper 4,000 crowd bellowing their support as the Silkmen did their damndest to peg back the opposition. The Macclesfield fans were probably as surprised as me when, with five minutes to go, our player-manager began peeling off his tracksuit.

'I need to try and calm things down a bit,' he said, before crossing the white line and chalking up his first appearance of the season. As the referee blew for full time, news filtered through that fellow strugglers, Boston United, had been beaten by Wrexham; final confirmation that Macclesfield were safe, and had escaped the dreaded drop.

'Fair play to you, mate,' I said to Paul amid the exultant scenes in the post-match dressing room. 'You've proved a few people wrong.'

He smiled, before taking a huge swig from the bottle of champagne he was clutching.

The following week Paul celebrated our great escape by bussing the players and the backroom staff (as well as their wives and girlfriends) to his Wirral mansion for an end-of-season party. He and Claire couldn't have been more hospitable – the food was top-notch, and the drink flowed all night – and I remember smiling to myself when I spotted the teenage Thomas Ince whacking a ball against a brick wall. How time had flown since he'd been the main topic of conversation in Manchester HMV.

*

Midway through the 2007–08 season I received a phone call from a friend of mine, Andy Barr, with whom I'd graduated at Salford University. Employed as head physio at Premier League club Bolton Wanderers, at that time managed by my old team-mate Gary Megson, Andy wanted me to come aboard as his assistant. I felt the time had come for a new challenge, so I accepted his invitation. By doing so, I finally fulfilled my ambition of working in every division of the league.

I was immediately impressed by the superb facilities and resources at the Reebok. From gyms packed with state-of-the-art rehab equipment, to the platoon of talented physios and masseurs, it was light-years ahead of anything I'd experienced before.

'Pretty impressive, eh, Lakey,' said Andy as he showed me around the space-age cryotherapy unit, explaining how this piece of kit aided post-match recovery by exposing the body to extreme cold temperatures in short blasts.

'Blimey,' I said, 'we only had crushed ice and witch-hazel at Macclesfield . . .'

The Bolton players were a good bunch of lads. I had a lot of time for players like Kevin Nolan, Andy O'Brien, Kevin Davies and Gavin McCann; their enthusiasm and easygoing nature made them a pleasure to work with.

I got to know Gavin particularly well, spending a week with him in Colorado where he underwent a knee operation. I remember us both getting a shock when we touched down at Denver airport, though. Having been told to expect warm weather in September, we'd packed our cases with summer clothes. However, unbeknown to us, a freak blizzard 24 hours earlier had blanketed the place with snow, and stepping off the plane felt like walking into that cryotherapy unit back in Bolton.

'Are you sure we haven't caught a flight to Alaska, Gav?' I moaned, before heading to a Duty Free ski shop to stock up on some winter gear.

Our hotel, based in the beautiful mountain resort of Vail, was first-rate. As it was the off-peak season for skiing, however, meant that the place was spookily empty, not unlike the hotel terrorised by Jack Nicholson in *The Shining*. I did toy with the idea of bursting into Gav's room armed with a coathanger ('Heeeeeere's Lakey!) but decided against it, figuring that a crazed knifeman act wouldn't be the best preparation for a player nervously awaiting surgery.

The entire resort was like a ghost town; wherever we went that week, from cafés to shops, from bars to restaurants, we seemed to double the population.

The Steadman Clinic, where Gavin was due to have his op, was based on the outskirts of town. It was headed by Dr Richard Steadman, a world-renowned knee specialist whose big-name clients included Tiger Woods, Martina Navratilova and Rod Stewart. His office, where we attended a pre-op consultation, was more like a museum, its walls plastered with thank-you cards and mementos sent by hundreds of celebrities.

Having the opportunity to chat with one of the top orthopaedic surgeons on the planet was thrilling enough, but I nearly died and went to heaven when he asked me if I wanted to watch him perform the operation.

'That'd be fantastic,' I replied.

'I'm assuming that you're not squeamish, after all the ops you've had . . .' said the doc, who was well aware of my back catalogue of knee surgery.

It turned out to be a truly fascinating experience, and I could only marvel at the precision and expertise involved. Afterwards, Dr Steadman even took the time to give my own knee a once-over (if only he'd done so 15 years before, I lamented to myself) and told me that he'd be happy to add me to his patient list if I ever needed him in the future.

In the summer of 2008 Andy Barr left his post at the club, taking on the role of senior physio with the New York Knicks basketball team. Not long afterwards I also bid farewell to the Reebok, having reached the conclusion that, after a medical career that had spanned a decade, it was probably time for a change. Sprinting onto the pitch with a knee that felt like a bag of bolts was becoming more painful by the week. And not only that, 10 years spent rehabilitating footballers on a daily basis, and witnessing them win the war that I'd lost, had finally started to chip away at me.

So, at the ripe old age of 40, and knowing deep down that physio was no longer the right vocation for me, I arrived at a career crossroads. After talking things over with my wife, I decided to take a long-ish break in which I could recharge my batteries, consider my options and chill out with the children. By that time we'd had another addition to the family (my beautiful daughter, Hannah) and I relished the prospect of spending some quality time with my little girl as she approached that endearing walking-and-talking stage.

So Jo went off to work in Manchester and I became Daddy Day Care, taking my toddler to Cale Green Park each day and having a fine time pushing her on swings and guiding her down slides. More often than not, being out in the fresh air would cause Hannah to doze off in her buggy, and whenever this was the case I'd grab myself a coffee and a cake and head for a shady park bench, taking full advantage of this newfound me-time to sit down and gather my thoughts. Moments of solitude had been as rare as hen's teeth, and it felt liberating to be able to lean back and let my mind wander.

I'd often find myself taking a trip down memory lane, analysing my football career, brooding over certain scenarios, and debating whether I could have done anything differently. It was during one such meditation that the realisation hit me that one simple question could have changed the entire course of my life.

It hadn't occurred to me to query a thing when a few weeks after my injury in September 1990, the details of my pending surgery were outlined to me. I remember sitting nervously in a Platt Lane meeting room and being told that a consultant in the north-west, who was pioneering a brand-new procedure, had been tasked with repairing my cruciate ligament.

'Don't worry about a thing, Paul,' I was assured. 'You're safe in our hands.'

Hindsight is a wonderful thing, but it was at this moment that I wished I'd paused for thought, raised a quizzical eyebrow, and spoken up.

Did you get some advice from the physios at Lilleshall?

This perfectly reasonable question might then have prompted the club to pick up the phone and speak to the expert FA physios, whose remit included recommending the best surgeons to football clubs. They'd have pointed them in the direction of the most experienced specialists in the UK who were saving the careers of other players with similar injuries. With this considered advice ringing in their ears, the club might then have weighed up the options and referred me to a consultant best-suited to my specific needs. With any luck the operation would have been a success, and who's to say how my life might have turned out.

But things took a different course that day. Assuming that Manchester City had my best interests at heart, and trusting that my employers had done their homework, I didn't question their judgement or examine my options. As a consequence, that potentially critical phone call to Lilleshall never took place. No second opinion was sought, and no alternative surgeons were considered. My operation failed, my career imploded and my nightmare began.

With this shoulda-woulda-coulda scenario weighing heavily on my mind, I slowly wheeled my slumbering daughter out of the Cale Green Park and headed homewards.

I re-entered the workplace, albeit half-heartedly, when my springtime sabbatical came to an end. Solely to keep the wolf from the door, I flirted with some private physiotherapy work in the summer of 2009, basing myself at a small practice in Alderley Edge, a well-to-do Cheshire village popular with soap stars and footballers. Having spent my working life as a team player, I found my new one-man-band status pretty hard to adjust to, compounded by the fact that my heart was no longer in the job.

Just as I felt my motivation starting to wane, Ian Cheeseman, BBC Radio Manchester's City correspondent, rang me with some cheering news. His bosses, it transpired, had commissioned a new weekly radio show aimed at City fans – *Blue Tuesday* – and he needed to recruit an ex-player as his co-presenter. Having heard me recently being interviewed by 5 Live and talkSPORT (they occasionally asked me on air to chat about City) Ian reckoned that I'd be the ideal candidate. The BBC wouldn't be able to cross my palm with much silver, he explained, but that didn't bother me. The chance to pursue an exciting new career avenue – perhaps one that could eventually unshackle me from physiotherapy – was tempting enough for me, and I bit his hand off at the opportunity.

I hoped this new collaboration with Radio Manchester, would be a little more successful than the last. A few years previously a colleague of Ian's, Jack Dearden, had asked me to join him in the Eastlands press box to act as the match summariser for City's game against Tottenham Hotspur (the regular pundits, Fred Eyre and Nigel Gleghorn, were unavailable). I wasn't on physio duty at Macclesfield that particular Sunday, and so was more than happy to oblige.

'Just one thing, though, Jack,' I said. 'I promised my little lad I'd take him to the Spurs game. Would it be okay if he sits next to me?'

'Sure,' replied Jack, 'as long as he keeps quiet.'

Zac, who was about six years old at the time, was duly read the riot act and I bought him a copy of the *City Magazine* to keep him occupied and filled his pockets with half the contents of a nearby sweet shop.

In spite of the 0–0 scoreline, the match was full of incident. I sat next to Jack with my headphones on and my notebook ready, trying my utmost to speak clearly and concisely as I followed the action. Everything seemed to be going well until a break in play when Zac, forgetting that we were on air, tugged at my sleeve, leant towards me and opened his mouth to speak. I threw him a stern look and swiftly put my finger to my lips, but it was too late.

'Dad, where've you put my Quavers?' he loudly demanded, broadcasting to thousands of listeners across Greater Manchester. I sheepishly unearthed the said snack from my coat pocket and looked over to Jack, whose expression was one of abject horror. The show's producers were none too pleased, either, and – funnily enough – Lake & Son's Punditry Services were never re-hired.

I was determined to redeem myself on *Blue Tuesday*, though, and, together with Ian and the station's Head of Sport, Sarah Collins, I worked really hard to prepare myself for our debut broadcast on 11 August 2009. I was quaking in my boots when the red ON AIR light flashed up at 6 p.m. that Tuesday night, and I'm sure if I ever decided to listen again to that first show I'd probably cringe at my shaky delivery and the liberal sprinkling of ums, ahs and obviouslies.

However, as the weeks passed I gradually got into the swing of things, becoming more confident at the mic and feeling more au fait with the link-ups and running orders. Our regular 'Where Are They Now?' slot became my favourite part of the programme, since it gave me the chance to reconnect with old pals like Steve Redmond and Neil McNab (I hadn't spoken to the latter, who chatted to us from his home in Atlanta, for a decade) as well as more recent fans' favourites such as Shaun Goater and Andy Morrison.

One of the most memorable interviews we broadcast featured Tony Coleman, a former City winger from the 1960s who'd emigrated to Australia after his career had ended. TC's caustic comments about his compatriots (Aussies, he alleged, were 'Neanderthals' who hated Brits and mistreated Aborigines) made headlines the next day. Similarly contro-versial was Rodney Marsh, who came into the studio to talk about his new autobiography and gave us a no-holds-barred account of his rough childhood and extraordinary career.

Sometimes, though, it was the non-football chat that made for the most compelling listening. City hero Uwe Rösler spoke frankly and movingly on air about his successful fight against cancer, and former midfielder Jeff Whitley revealed his long battle with drugs and alcohol. Most memorably, Frank Swift's grand-daughter, Kari Dodson, joined us to pay an eloquent and touching tribute to the former City keeper-cum-journalist, who tragically lost his life in the 1958 Munich air disaster along with 22 others, including eight Manchester United players.

'When City fans chant about Munich they seem to forget that one of their own was on the plane that night,' she said.

I was driving home after a show one night when another Blues' legend, Mike Summerbee, gave me a call on my mobile with the offer of more work (thus proving the adage that you wait ages for a bus, and then two come along at once). As the newly appointed commercial ambassador at Eastlands, he'd been tasked with assembling a team of former players to meet and greet the club's corporate sponsors on match days.

'I've got a few from my era on board, but we could do with some younger blood around the place, Paul, a few lads from the 80s and 90s,' he said. 'And now that you've left Bolton, I was wondering whether you fancied it?'

'I'd love to, Mike . . .' I replied, chuffed to bits at this unexpected development.

Had this conversation taken place in the old days of Maine Road, I'm not sure that I'd have accepted so readily. But times had changed. Not only had City settled in nicely at the new stadium, but in August 2008 the club had been taken over by the Abu Dhabi United Group, becoming the richest club in the world in an instant. The prospect of working at Manchester City Mark II, with its new location, new regime and new horizons, held much more appeal for me than it would have done a decade earlier.

It was a real honour to don my official Manchester City suit each fortnight and work alongside such legends as Colin Bell, Tony Book and Joe Corrigan. Bell, in particular, had been a boyhood idol of mine and, in spite of his iconic status, struck me as an extremely unassuming and modest person who seemed oblivious to the reverence and adulation that followed him around the stadium.

I also discovered how much of a contrast it was to attend a match day as a retired player in the Noughties, as opposed to a sidelined player in the 90s. With my footballing days well behind me, and no longer having to fob people off with my 'back in six weeks' line, I was able to happily chew the fat with sponsors and supporters, actually enjoying the chit-chat that I'd once found so excruciating.

Towards the end of 2009 I had the opportunity to rekindle some more old friendships (and fill some gaping holes in my diary) by offering my physio know-how to some former City players. Keen to catch up on all their news, and happy to sort out their aches and pains, I travelled up to see Paul Moulden in Bolton, Alan Oakes in Northwich, Jason Beckford in Urmston and Ken Barnes in Macclesfield, among others.

Having suffered a stroke, followed by a fall-induced hip fracture, Ken wasn't in the best of health. When we heard he'd taken a turn for the worse, Jason and I went to visit our much-loved youth team mentor in hospital, and were saddened to see him looking so frail. As we were walking out of the ward, none other than the great Bert Trautmann strode in.

'Hello boys,' smiled City's goalkeeping legend who, in contrast, seemed as fit as a fiddle. 'How's the old guy doing?'

'Not so bad,' we said, downplaying things a little, as you do in such circumstances, 'but he'll be chuffed to bits to see you, Bert . . .'

A few weeks later I received an SOS call from Ken's son Peter. His father was leading the physio staff in the out-patients department a merry dance by all accounts, rebuffing their advice and refusing point blank to do his exercises.

'Dad needs someone who'll be a bit firmer with him,' explained Peter, 'and I reckon he might take more notice of you, Lakey. You couldn't go over and see him, could you?'

I was more than willing to help, considering the huge part that Ken had played in my fledgling career at City, and I turned up at his home in Macclesfield the next day. I arrived to find him in a much more confused and cantankerous state than when I'd last seen him. He insisted on calling me Roy (I think he mistook me for Roy Bailey, City's former physio) and when I tried to cajole him into a few gentle leg bends he brandished a crutch and let rip with a barrage of expletives.

'Don't swear at Paul, love, he's only trying to help,' whispered June, his doting wife. But it was water off a duck's back for me; I was well accustomed to his industrial-strength language, and I knew, as did June, that his words were born of frustration, not malice.

Realising it was going to be a hard sell, I decided to change tack by bundling everything into a footballing context.

'Ken, just think of these exercises as pre-season training,' I said brightly. 'Remember what you used to yell at me all those years ago? No pain, no gain, son? The hard work starts on this pitch, right here, right now . . .?'

These analogies seemed to spark him into life, and from then on I tried as much as I could to divert the conversation to football, if only to take his mind off all the pain and discomfort. Despite his physical limitations, when he spoke about the game he was as lucid as ever, his eyes flashing whenever the talk turned to a match, a goal, a player.

'If only you'd seen my old pal Bobby Johnstone in action,' he said to me one morning. 'Now there was a player who had *everything* in his locker, even when he had to play on cow-fields, wearing hobnail boots to kick a bloody big leather football around.'

But Ken's highest praise was reserved for Bert Trautmann. He relished telling me how City's former keeper could command an area and fill a goalmouth like no other, and how his bravery had shone through during that famous 1956 FA Cup Final.

'Bert had enough courage for the whole team put together,'

said Ken. 'You can't tell me that anyone nowadays would play with a broken bloody neck.'

Often the conversation would veer onto the current crop of footballers, Ken shaking his head as he talked about how the comforts and trappings of the modern game had taken the edge off some players, and had suppressed their drive to succeed, even their will to win.

'In spite of all this money, son, I'm not sure if these boys enjoy it like we used to,' he recalled. 'There's a pride in wearing your team's colours, y'see, and I just hope they don't lose that.'

He then paused, looked down at his crutches, and tutted loudly.

'And if you think I'm using these in public, Roy, you can f*** off.'

As his old age and ill-health caught up with him, Ken's life force gradually ebbed, and he sadly passed away in July 2010.

'I can't believe he's gone,' said a devastated Peter when I rang him to offer my condolences to the Barnes family. 'He wasn't just my dad, Lakey, he was my best mate, and I'm going to miss him so much.'

He then asked if I'd be willing to give a eulogy at the funeral service. I agreed to it, desperately hoping that I'd be able to hold my nerve and do Ken justice.

Hundreds of mourners turned up at Manchester Crematorium to pay their respects, a true testament to a wonderful person who'd left us with so many great memories as a player, a coach, a chief scout and a friend. The congregation was like a Who's Who of past football stars, including

City stalwarts like Glyn Pardoe and Gary Owen, as well as Manchester United's Norman Whiteside and Paddy Crerand.

'Ken was a lovely man, a true inspiration, and there will never be anyone quite like him,' is how I ended my tribute. 'He lit up a room, he lit up our lives, and last week a little light over Manchester went out for ever. Rest in peace, Mr Barnes.'

Ken may be gone, but he'll never be forgotten. A football legacy that includes two consecutive FA Cup Final appearances (in 1955 and 1956), and the scoring of three penalties against Everton in 1957, will ensure that he'll live for ever in the hearts and minds of Manchester City fans.

Ken is one of many ex-players whose outstanding achievements have served to secure their place in the club's Hall of Fame, as well as its history books. Neil Young, one of the best forwards to ever pull on a sky blue shirt, will always be remembered for the trusty left foot that scored the winner in the 1969 FA Cup Final. Super-striker Dennis Tueart is still revered for his overhead kick in the 1976 League Cup Final, and Joe Corrigan's long career between the posts is epitomised by his Man of the Match-winning performance at Wembley in 1981. A four-goal ambush of Notts County in 1995 helped to assure Uwe Rösler of his cult hero status, and Georgi Kinkladze seared himself on to the memories of the Maine Road faithful courtesy of that spectacular jinking goal against Southampton in 1996.

Sometimes, though, I wonder how *I* will be remembered by City fans in years to come. Will it be for lifting the FA Youth Cup for the first time in the club's history, or for becoming one of City's youngest ever captains? Will it be for the spectacular volley I scored against Millwall, or for the pinpoint pass that set up David Oldfield's goal against Manchester United? Or will I be remembered, as I suspect, for swallowing my tongue against Leicester in 1989, or for snapping my cruciate against Aston Villa a year later?

I'm almost resigned to the fact that my career will probably be defined by my troubles, not my triumphs, and that my millstones, not my milestones will be remembered. Tellingly, the question I'm most often asked nowadays isn't 'what was it like being in the World Cup squad?', or 'what was it like playing in the 5–1?' but 'how's that knee of yours, Lakey?'

My knee, in answer to that question, is completely knackered. Riddled with osteo-arthritis, and with muscles that are gradually wasting away, it gives me grief every waking hour. I've lived with the pain for nearly two decades now, and the constant, pounding soreness and the sharp, stabbing twinges have become part of my daily life.

On a good day I might not need to take any anti-inflammatory pills and be able to move around relatively freely, performing the occasional impromptu walkabout or bone-creaking stretch to prevent the joint from locking or seizing up. On a bad day, however, my knee throbs and swells and, much to my embarrassment causes me to limp like an old, lame cowboy ('you look more like a war veteran than an ex-player,' said my mate Billy Duffy when he recently witnessed me in the throes of a Bad Knee Day). Just to compound matters, my left leg hasn't been in great shape, either. After years trying to compensate for my right limb, it's recently begun to bow very badly and earlier this year I had yet more surgery to straighten it.

The way things are going, it's looking likely that I'll become one of the youngest ex-professionals to undergo a double knee replacement. I'm trying to stave off the operation for as long as I can, though, since prosthetic knees have a life span of between ten and 15 years – with a maximum of two per lifetime – and I don't really fancy consigning my 70-year-old self to a wheelchair.

It's this physical hardship that has without a doubt been the most difficult thing to handle since my retirement. Hand on heart, I've been able to cope with missing out on all the riches and the accolades that a long stint in football could have brought, and have reconciled myself to a life without the fast cars, flash clothes and fancy houses that a sustained career would have bankrolled.

What I've never come to terms with – and never will, I suspect – is being unable to practise any form of sport. I haven't been able to play a proper game of football since 1994, simply because I can't kick a ball without my knee ballooning to double its size, and I struggle even to jog across the road these days. Most other leisure activities are no-go areas too; years ago I used to love a game of tennis in the sun, or a canal-side run in the drizzle, but there's not a cat in hell's chance of that now. Sometimes I feel physically sick when I see a neighbour jogging past the house glugging a bottle of water, or I spot friends heading off to the local sports club with their racquets slung across their shoulders. Even seeing an old-age pensioner on his way to a game of bowls fills me with envy.

Over the years I've tried to avoid feeling resentful about my predicament, but for someone whose life and career once revolved around activity and fitness, it's been the bitterest pill to swallow. Not a day goes by without me craving the challenge, the achievement and the freedom that sport brings.

Although I generally heed all the medical advice to rest my legs and take it easy, sometimes a devilish little voice in my head will urge me to throw caution to the wind. There have been occasions when I've seen my son's City football in the back garden, thought bollocks to it, and, with breathtaking stupidity, have smashed it as hard as I can into his mini goal net. Then I've turned around in mock celebration, only to see Jo standing at the kitchen window, shaking her head, knowing as well as I do that I'll be regretting my action for days afterwards.

In contrast to my physical woes, however, my emotional health is in great shape. Thanks in no small part to the support of my friends and family, depression hasn't figured in my life for over a decade, and my pill-popping and therapy sessions have hopefully been consigned to history. Whilst I'm much happier in my own skin, and feel much better equipped to deal with life's peaks and troughs, I'm not daft enough to think I'm immune from a relapse. Depression, like 'flu, can quite easily return, and I much prefer to consider my illness as dormant, not departed.

As I've embarked upon my gradual road to recovery, it's been heartening to witness the difference in attitude towards depression in football. Players with emotional issues are now treated with compassion, not cynicism, and there exists a climate of sympathy and understanding in which lads such as Neil Lennon, Robbie Savage and Stan Collymore can openly admit to being sufferers.

Charities such as Time To Change and Kick It Out, which both campaign for an end to mental health discrimination, are doing sterling work to help raise awareness within football and other sports. As a consequence, even the old-school managers seem to be veering away from the 'what's he got to be depressed about?' mindset, and instead fostering an environment in which players with psychological problems can be identified and supported.

Not every athlete with depression is easy to spot, however, and many aren't comfortable with the idea of going public. The tragic death of German goalkeeper Robert Enke, who tried desperately to keep his personal demons under wraps, is a case in point, and should serve as a warning that many are still suffering in silence. Like most football fans, I was both shocked and devastated to hear the news of his suicide in November 2009, only two days after he'd turned out for Hannover FC.

On the anniversary of his death, extracts of Enke's diary

were broadcast on Radio 5 Live. It made painful listening, and his forlorn words haunted me for some time afterwards.

'There's no way it can go on like this,' he'd written at the height of his troubles. 'I feel anxious, and helpless, and I haven't left my hotel room. I'm afraid of people's looks. If only I could live without the fear and the nervousness.'

I hope and pray that my own dark days are behind me, but there are still instances when I see or hear things that wrench me from the present to the past, dredging up sharp memories of unhappier times.

These trigger points often hit me when I least expect them. Take the film *Billy Elliot*, for example. I remember watching it at home one Sunday night with Jo, assuming that this tale of a pirouetting Geordie boy would be a syrupy, sentimental chick-flick, something that I could watch half-heartedly while reading that day's papers. Little did I know how compelling I'd find the film, and how affected I'd be by it.

The final scene, with its spellbinding portrayal of a young, strong athlete at the peak of his career, leaping majestically skywards as his dad watches proudly in the audience, was almost too much for me to bear. Take away the stage, the tights and the ballet shoes, and replace them with a pitch, a kit and some football boots, and it could have been my story, and as the end credits rolled, so did my tears. Never before had I been so moved by a film, its themes of boyhood hope and fatherly support touching the rawest of nerves.

I experienced another vivid flashback a couple of years ago

when, along with my mate Dominic, I went to see Simple Minds play at the MEN Arena. We were actually more bothered about the support act, OMD, although we hadn't quite allowed for the grisly spectacle of two 40-somethings dad-dancing to 'Enola Gay'. Once the duo had exited stage left, probably having given themselves hernias, the main act made their grand appearance. Jim Kerr and the boys, as slick as ever, performed a greatest hits medley which culminated in their most famous track, 'Alive and Kicking'.

However, as the lights dimmed and the keyboard intro started up, I had what I can only describe as a panic attack. It was that particular rock anthem – adopted by Sky Sports as its main theme – that had blared out of the public address system when I'd made my ill-starred comeback against QPR in 1992. As all those unpleasant feelings flooded back, my chest tightened and my heartbeat quickened. I garbled some excuse to Dominic about getting a beer, but instead hurried up the steps and barricaded myself into the nearest toilet, covering my ears until the song ended.

Fortunately, not every blast from the past produces such negative emotions. A much nicer dose of nostalgia came my way a couple of Christmases ago, while rooting in the loft for some decorations. Jo and Hannah had gone shopping, and Edward's attempt at dressing the tree had descended into chaos, the lounge carpet covered in crushed baubles and trampled-on fairy lights. Emergency supplies were needed, so I went upstairs to hunt some down.

As I teetered on a stepladder, guiding out a box of silver

bunting with a mop handle, I dislodged a Tesco carrier bag. Presuming it contained some long-lost Christmas knick-knacks, I loosened the tight knot and was beaten back by the familiar smell of turf and leather. Inside lay a pair of black and white Adidas World Cups, size 11, still caked in mud and with dried grass wound tightly around the studs. The last boots I'd ever worn at Maine Road. The same pair that I'd wrapped in a plastic bag after my testimonial game, and that had lain forgotten in the attic for over a decade.

I balanced these old faithfuls on the palms of my hands, gazing at the knotted laces and the three white stripes, thinking how long it had seemed since I'd last worn them.

They need a bloody good clean, them things . . . I imagined my dad saying. *Go and fetch me a cloth and some Stardrops, son, and I'll give 'em a quick scrub* . . .

Suddenly interrupting my daydream was my son, hollering up the stairs, puzzled as to why I was taking so long.

'I'll be down in a minute, Eddie,' I replied. 'Daddy just needs to tidy something away . . .'

I carefully replaced the boots in the bag, re-tied the knot, and nestled them into a snug corner of the loft. Then, with a box of tinsel under my arm, I headed back downstairs to my giddy, glittery son, with the smell of Maine Road still lingering in the air.

As Edward grew older, it became increasingly apparent to Jo and I that we had a unique child on our hands. By the age of three he was reading fluently and reeling off his times tables, not to mention reciting his alphabet backwards and counting to 50 in French. Our eyebrows would rise higher and higher as we watched him sketch the flags of Europe from memory, or dash off a comprehensive list of Roman numerals. Edward was like a little professor, devouring information and often exposing our knowledge gaps in the process.

'Daddy, what's the name of Saturn's largest moon?' he'd ask me over breakfast, expecting the answer to just trip off my tongue.

'Er, give me a sec to think about that, Eddie,' I'd reply, before sneaking out of the room, Googling on my mobile, and returning to tell him that the answer was, of course, Titan.

The fact that he showed limited interest in other children, shunning the communal activities at toddler group and preferring to play alone, didn't overly concern us; in our eyes he was just a fiercely independent, single-minded little boy. Neither were we hugely worried about his aversion to make-believe games, nor his preoccupation with numbers and letters. Edward was Edward, adored by all for his cute idiosyncrasies.

It was after his first day at school that his teacher took Jo and I aside, gently suggesting to us that as well as the social quirks that we'd already identified, Edward might in fact have more deep-rooted issues. Slightly taken aback by this, we nevertheless heeded her comments and agreed for him to be assessed by a psychologist and a paediatrician. Within weeks the diagnosis was confirmed: Pervasive Developmental Disorder, a mild form of autism.

The tests had shown that, whilst he was exceptionally bright in many areas and presented as a very happy and affectionate child, our son displayed certain personality traits that correlated with PDD. As Edward carefully constructed a Lego spaceship in the play area, the consultant sat us down to discuss his diagnosis in more detail.

He explained that children like Edward often view life in an extremely literal, factual way. As a result, they tend to shy away from imaginary play, seeking solace and comfort in numbers and statistics and developing fixations on very specific subjects, such as outer space or prehistoric animals. Preferring to adhere to strict, orderly routines, they need a great deal of structure in their lives and occasionally react badly to sudden or unexpected change.

Children with similar conditions, according to the consultant, also found it difficult to grasp certain conventions of social behaviour.

'Kids like Edward can be quite self-centred, so communication skills don't always come naturally,' he said. 'Sometimes they have to be taught things that their friends may do instinctively, such as how to show empathy, how to accept defeat, that kind of thing.'

Finally, he outlined how 'sensory processing issues' were commonplace, Edward's hypersensitivity to sudden, loud noises going some way to explain his long-standing phobia of large crowds and booming fireworks.

'There'll be a few challenges ahead, I'm sure,' he admitted, 'but from what I've seen of Edward, there's every chance that he'll do really well in life. He'll just need a bit more of a helping hand, that's all.'

That night, as our son slept soundly in the next room, Jo and I lay in bed, staring at the ceiling and, as our rock 'n' roll lifestyle dictated, listening to Radio 4's Shipping Forecast.

'I know you're worried about Eddie,' I said, sensing my wife's anxiety, 'but don't be, he'll be fine. He's got me and you in his corner, hasn't he?'

I woke up the next morning and walked Edward to school, pointing out the usual cats on doorsteps and funny-shaped clouds.

'Bye bye, Daddy,' he said when we reached the doorway, flashing me a smile and blowing me a kiss.

'See you later, buddy . . .'

My heart melted as I watched him skip into the classroom and make a beeline for his favourite number puzzle. I turned around and headed back home, feeling privileged to have been handed the job of guiding this little gem through life.

Following Edward's diagnosis, we were swamped with advice from every direction, ranging from parent support networks to kids' youth groups. Conscious that he found many team sports a real trial – particularly football – we decided to try to find a suitable substitute to help keep him fit and healthy.

Standing out from the crowd was a charitable organisation called Jump Space, a trampoline club based in the centre of Stockport. By actively welcoming children on the autistic spectrum – as well as their siblings – and by focusing on non-competitive activities, it seemed just the ticket. Bowled over by Jump Space's team of sunny staff, we signed Edward up on the spot, and within weeks he was twisting, turning and tuck-jumping like a natural.

'I'm higher than the moon,' he'd yell, his smile widening and his confidence rising with every bounce.

Hannah soon followed suit in joining the club, and Jo and I found ourselves becoming part of its extended 'family'. We were befriended by lots of dedicated parents, many of whom had inspirational stories about how trampolining had helped their kids both physically and emotionally.

Like most charities, Jump Space was continually strapped for cash. Aware of its potential to make a difference, I decided to pull my finger out and do something practical to help. I became its official patron and, using my contacts in football, set about identifying a variety of different fundraising opportunities. Within a few weeks the Manchester City Supporters' Club had adopted Jump Space as its primary charity, and a City-supporting owner of a local coach firm, Haytons, had donated a free trip to Chester Zoo for the children.

On a roll, I decided to try to set up a meeting with Manchester City's chief executive, Garry Cook, in the hope that he'd be able to help out in some way. Nothing ventured, nothing gained, I suppose. I'd already met him a couple of times before, most notably at the 20th anniversary of the 5–1 derby. I'd helped to organise a player reunion at a supporters' club in the Cheshire village of Poynton, and City's CEO had made a surprise appearance. As he sat chatting to a table of ex-players that included Jason Beckford, Gary Fleming and Steve Redmond, my first impressions were of a very affable, approachable guy. Later that evening, he'd given a rousing speech about Sheikh Mansour's City vision, a far-reaching blueprint which ranged from stadium improvements and squad developments to building legacies and winning trophies.

A fortnight after making contact with his secretary, I found myself sitting opposite Garry in his Eastlands office, waxing lyrical about Jump Space, explaining how so many kids had benefited from all its good work, and how it had been my personal crusade to raise as much cash for the charity as possible. The meeting's outcome exceeded all expectations, with Garry giving the go-ahead for a bucket collection outside the ground before a forthcoming match, something that would be guaranteed to raise sizeable funds.

We walked out of the office building together, chatting about all the goings-on at the City of Manchester Stadium, before Garry switched the conversation to me, asking how things had gone since my time at Bolton Wanderers. I told him about my presenting job on *Blue Tuesday*, and my hospitality duties on a match day, and how much I was enjoying both roles.

'And how's your physiotherapy practice going?' he asked.

'It's all right, thanks,' I said, although my expression probably told a different story.

The next day my phone rang; it was Garry again.

'Just wondering whether you could meet me for coffee next week, Lakey,' he asked, 'only there's something I want to run by you.'

'Our chat the other day got me thinking,' he said, when we met up at Eastlands for a second time. He told me that he'd been really impressed by all the work I was doing for Jump Space, and how my passion and enthusiasm for the charity had shone through during our meeting. He'd also, he admitted, had an inkling that I was no longer motivated by physiotherapy.

He then got to the crux of the matter, informing me that the club was planning to expand the fundraising arm of its City in the Community scheme, and that it was seeking to appoint an ambassador to help spearhead the initiative. They were looking for a former player, preferably someone who had a feel for the club, its fan base and its community; someone who could communicate well, who felt comfortable in the media spotlight, and who had experience of working with charities.

'I think you'd fit the bill perfectly,' he said.

On 19 March 2010, all suited-and-booted, I attended a staff presentation day at Eastlands, a quarterly event that the club regularly hold in order to acknowledge long-serving employees and recent staff arrivals. Mine was the final name on Garry Cook's list of new recruits, all of whom had been greeted with a rousing round of applause.

'And last but not least,' he announced, 'I'd like to introduce Paul Lake, our new Ambassador for City in the Community.'

I stood up and gave a quick nod.

'I've just got two words to say to you, Lakey,' he said with a smile.

'Welcome home.'

Picture Credits

The author and publisher would like to thank the following copyright-holders for permission to reproduce images and lyrics in this book:

Lyrics to *Life Turned Upside Down* reproduced with kind permission of Badly Drawn Boy Music Ltd

Youth team doing the can-can (picture by Magi Haroun)

Paul Lake stretchered off during Manchester City v Bradford City, 1988 (picture by Colorsport)

England under-21 line-up v Albania, 1989 (picture by Colorsport)

Paul Lake, Republic of Ireland B v England B (picture by Colorsport)

Paul Lake swallowing tongue (picture by *Manchester Evening News*)

Maroon City kit. Tottenham Hotspur v Manchester City, 1990 (picture by Colorsport)

Yellow City kit. Arsenal v Manchester City, 1989 (picture by Colorsport)

Paul Lake and Ian Bishop celebrate, 1989 (picture by Getty Images)

Paul Lake and Viv Anderson, Manchester City v Manchester United, 1989 (picture by Colorsport)

Paul Lake, Tony Cascarino and Dwight Yorke (picture by Action Images)

Portrait of Paul Lake (picture by *The Observer*)

Paul Lake at Lilleshall (picture by Rex Features)

Paul Lake rehabilitating in swimming pool, 1994 (picture by *Manchester Evening News*)

Testimonial, guard of honour (picture by PA Sport)

Testimonial, waving (picture by PA Sport)

Last day at Maine Road (picture by PA Sport)

Paul Lake as Macclesfield Town's physiotherapist (picture by Getty Images)

Paul Lake with Ian Brightwell and Tony Book, 2010 (picture by Roland Cooke)

Paul Lake on the cover of match day programme, 2011 (picture by Sharon Latham)

Paul Lake holding FA Cup (picture by Kevin Cummins)

Paul and Joanne Lake sat under Paul's name (picture by Kevin Cummins)

All other images are courtesy of Paul and Joanne Lake's personal collection.

Index